Juvenile Justice in Victorian Scotland

For Daniel and all of my family

Juvenile Justice in Victorian Scotland

Christine Kelly

EDINBURGH
University Press

Edinburgh University Press is one of the leading university presses in the UK. We publish academic books and journals in our selected subject areas across the humanities and social sciences, combining cutting-edge scholarship with high editorial and production values to produce academic works of lasting importance. For more information visit our website: edinburghuniversitypress.com

Edinburgh University Press Ltd
The Tun – Holyrood Road
12 (2f) Jackson's Entry
Edinburgh EH8 8PJ

First published in hardback by Edinburgh University Press 2019

Typeset in 10.5/13pt Sabon by
Manila Typesetting Company

A CIP record for this book is available from the British Library

ISBN 978 1 4744 2734 0 (hardback)
ISBN 978 1 4744 8431 2 (paperback)
ISBN 978 1 4744 2735 7 (webready PDF)
ISBN 978 1 4744 2736 4 (epub)

Contents

Acknowledgements

I would like to express my sincere thanks to the British Academy for the award of a British Academy Postdoctoral Fellowship (2013–16). I am also grateful to the AHRC for its earlier support of my doctoral research.

I acknowledge with great appreciation the superb guidance and support of Lindsay Farmer and Fiona Leverick at the School of Law, University of Glasgow. Special thanks also to Nicola Lacey at LSE for encouraging my work.

WELLINGTON REFORMATORY,
PENICUIK

Wellington Reformatory, Penicuik, 1875 (Courtesy of the National Library of Scotland)

Introduction

In 1851 an article in the popular journal *Household Words* edited by Charles Dickens described a radical experiment in Aberdeen and was full of admiration for a new diversionary approach to juvenile offenders:

> The plan appears to have been strikingly successful; and what magic was there here? Why should the country shudder in a cowardly manner over details of horror when a little money and a little courage will do so much? Aberdeen has done an act of real charity and good sense here, blessed itself and blessed these poor vagrants. The poor must be taught, somehow, if society means to exist.[1]

This described the beginnings of the pre-statutory day industrial schools system in Scotland.[2] In singing the praises of this initiative the writer hoped that it offered a novel way of helping the many impoverished children roaming the city streets of mid-nineteenth-century Britain. The idea of day industrial schools was the brainchild of a remarkable Scottish philanthropist and judge, Sheriff William Watson of Aberdeen. The schools he set up in the 1840s were preventive in aim and welfare-based in approach, designed to rescue the most vulnerable children from a life of crime. Instead of being sent to prison, vagrant, destitute children and juvenile offenders were referred by the courts to the schools, where they received food, education and training in a trade. Dickens's journal was right to be impressed. Watson's well-intentioned system was adopted in other towns and cities in Scotland and England; and it was of great importance in influencing the development of juvenile justice throughout Britain and also internationally.[3]

Unfortunately, the story does not end there. In many ways this book charts the course of a voyage ending in deep disappointment and disillusionment for juvenile justice reformers in Scotland. In an ironic twist, the body of legislation for which the reformers so arduously campaigned, and the changes it brought in its wake, gradually undermined the original ideals of reform as a different, markedly more punitive approach eroded the distinctively welfare-based ethos on which the early Scottish schools were based. The early reformers could not have foreseen that by the closing decades of the nineteenth century diversionary systems for young offenders would have evolved into a mechanism ushering large numbers of children into lengthy detention in a national UK-wide statutory system of certified residential reformatory and industrial schools which were predominantly penal in character. This was a process which entailed criminalisation of children on an immense scale, impacting excessively on Scottish children in particular. And yet, despite the huge disparity between the aspirations of the early reformers and the eventual outcome, there continued to be a residual current of the original humanitarian influence flowing through the Scottish system – one which was to leave its mark.

This makes a fascinating story, of course: tales of self-sacrificing philanthropy, charismatic Scottish reformers, their exultation at the success of their early pioneering efforts and their despair as it all slowly transformed before their eyes. What propelled these reformers into action in the first place was a powerful Victorian phenomenon: pragmatic, religiously inspired philanthropy. This was a primary catalyst for change which reacted to the impact of increasing industrialisation on the children of the urban poor, many of whom had a precarious hold on life. Cities were overcrowded and populations displaced. Children were subjected to relentless exploitation in the labour market, often running away to escape slave-like conditions,[4] and the sight of children wandering about and begging on the streets was commonplace. These children were known as juvenile vagrants[5] and this status granted them instant admission to the realms of criminality: vagrancy was an offence punishable by imprisonment under local Police Acts. Apart from the trauma of imprisonment, the stigma associated with it presented an insurmountable obstacle to finding employment, condemning a child to a life of penury. This was the background which prompted religious philanthropists to press for reform, and in Victorian society philanthropic dynamism was a force to be reckoned with.[6]

The emphasis in this book on mid-nineteenth-century philanthropic action as a prime factor in juvenile justice reform contrasts in some respects with the work of writers such as Garland who see the key period in transformation as the era between 1895 and 1914.[7] Garland has influentially argued that these years involved a move from the uniform discipline of the Victorian penal system to a very different focus on individual reformation and specialised categorisation of offender types. This change in the penal landscape is explained in the context of far-reaching social and political changes in the early twentieth century which formed the basis of the welfare state. In this world of 'penal-welfare',[8] Garland attributes great significance to the impact of new knowledges justifying extended intervention into the lives of offenders.[9] According to Garland, this 'modern penal complex'[10] was also associated with a departure from the concepts of classical jurisprudence and the legal criteria concerned with issues of criminal responsibility. His explanation has a Foucauldian influence,[11] with an emphasis on discovering the 'underlying generative structure' and associated 'political conditions' of penality.[12] However, Garland also challenges Foucault: whereas Garland sees the decades at the turn of the century as the beginning of modern penality,[13] Foucault regards the 'birth' of the prison as the turning point.[14] Martin Wiener has also detected fundamental changes in this period but adopts a more culturally focused approach in his analysis, paying less attention to political factors in the shaping of penal policy.[15] While Bailey cautions against overestimating the influence of new positivist ideas, stressing other factors, including the role of radical humanitarianism in reform processes, very many scholars have, in line with Garland and Wiener, identified similar themes associated with the maelstrom of new ideas, knowledges and political discourse at this time.[16] Mair, Burke and Vanstone point to the role of penal reform groups in pressing for new probation legislation.[17] Hendrick and Bradley both underline the impact of new scientific knowledges; similarly, Logan stresses new ideas in her work on gender, feminism, socialism and policy networks in relation to the constitution of juvenile courts.[18] Behlmer makes the convincing link between the Children Act 1908 and the burgeoning body of child welfare legislation in the Victorian era.[19] Many of these scholars see the Children Act 1908, with its emphasis on child welfare, as creating a new foundation for the future of juvenile justice, while also recognising that it represented a codification of the law relating to children. This book reinforces the continuities with the nineteenth-century history, highlights its significance, and identifies the Children Act 1908 as a staging post to reform well marked out by earlier developments.

Some of the book's principal arguments modify explanations in the existing body of scholarly work on juvenile justice history, conflicting in particular with three specific aspects of Garland's influential argument in *Punishment and Welfare*.[20] The first point concerns the impact of the juvenile court created under the Children Act 1908. It has been influentially argued by Garland in the British context that the juvenile court formed an important part of a changing penal landscape where there was extended scope for intrusion and control over family life.[21] Clarke also recognised the capacity of juvenile courts to intervene in family life, as have other scholars like Mahood.[22] Indeed, this Foucauldian theme runs through studies of the juvenile court in other jurisdictions too, with Donzelot making similar observations in the French context and Lasch's comments on the American situation.[23] However, the book presents evidence that in most respects the juvenile court was conducting business much as usual as far as children were concerned: the grounds of admission to the schools were not greatly extended by the Children Act 1908 and there was great continuity with existing legislation and practice. Although it is recognised that the juvenile court was an important advance, the emphasis here on the significant elements of underlying stability contrasts with Garland's assessment.

Secondly, the book calls for re-evaluation of the significance of the public function of reformatory and industrial schools for criminal and destitute children. This involves recognising their role as an integral part of the criminal justice system. Scholars such as Mahood, Cale and Moore have emphasised the sociological importance of the schools as child-saving institutions rather than stressing their position within the criminal justice system.[24] Similarly, although Garland recognises the influence of the schools in terms of their reformative agenda, he sees them as being marginal to the criminal justice system.[25] Though founded on the 'voluntary principle', they were statutorily certified establishments under Home Office direction, subject to statutory inspection and in receipt of public funding, to which many thousands of children were sent to be detained by order of the courts. As such, they were central to the operation of the criminal justice system. This re-evaluation of the centrality of the schools has significant implications. There is clear evidence that the ethos of the reformatory-industrial schools system in Britain from the mid-1850s was one in which there was a focus on developing individual programmes of reformation adapted to suit the character of individual children.[26] This challenges existing understandings,[27] suggesting that ideas about reformation of individual offenders were widely accepted and put into practice far earlier than Garland and many other scholars allow – in the middle, rather than at the end, of the nineteenth century.

And the third point concerns the influence of scientific discourse,[28] questioning the extent of its genuine impact on perceptions of the young offender. Evidence is presented that the effect of scientific notions on the perception of the young offender was less influential than has been supposed: while there was certainly awareness of new positivist ideas in some quarters, in practice it was pragmatic common sense which ruled the day – there was strong resistance to arguments that the child who offended was in any sense different from other children or predisposed towards criminality for some hitherto unappreciated scientific reason. It is suggested that redirecting the focus onto the longer view allows us to see that certain features of Garland's penal welfarism, like the impact of new scientific knowledges, were not truly apparent until well into the twentieth century. For instance, in Scotland it was not until the 1930s that psychological and psychiatric disciplines began to exert tangible influence, with the professional training of probation officers and the spread of Child Guidance Clinics.[29]

While the interpretation of reform offered here is distinct in several respects, particularly in placing special emphasis on the role of philanthropic activity in the nineteenth century, in general it bolsters explanations in the existing literature. An enduring theme here is that of public intervention in the private sphere. This was one of the defining characteristics of the Victorian era in Britain. As has long been recognised, this pattern of state assumption of legislative control over previously private reform activities encompassed a host of issues related to child welfare and social policy throughout much of the nineteenth century.[30] In line with this, one way in which legislative control was exerted over voluntary initiatives was in the shape of statutory regulation of industrial and reformatory schools. Much of the scholarship on these institutions exemplifies this process, including Radzinowicz and Hood, Shore, Hurt, Godfrey et al. in the wider British context, and Mahood, Ralston, and Barrie and Broomhall in the context of Scotland.[31]

The adoption of voluntary schemes by the state in its centralisation of social organisation was an important strand in development of governance in nineteenth-century Scotland. And indeed this co-opting of local, voluntary, philanthropic activity by the state has been a continuing feature into the twentieth century, as, for example, the history of probation in Scotland in the 1920s and 1930s amply demonstrates.[32] As has been identified by many scholars, the trend from the local towards national forms of regulation was reflected across the field of criminal justice history, from Farmer's analysis of the development of summary procedure, to the work of Barrie and that of Carson and Idzikowska on policing history, as well as Barrie and Broomhall's study of the development of police courts.[33]

In according a central position to the role of voluntary action in providing a primary impetus for reform, my work views matters through a different lens from the scholars who are more persuaded by the disciplinary perspective of Foucault or the social control theories of Donzelot: for instance, Mahood, Littlewood or Cale.[34] My approach has more in common with Rothman's ideas in his account of the gulf between human aspiration and practical outcomes, or conscience and convenience.[35] But this is an immensely complex history. And in many ways my work accepts the validity of Moore's argument that even the later-nineteenth-century industrial schools should be recognised as an important strand of the growing child protection movement.[36] The argument is made here that the predominantly punitive character of the British statutory system of industrial and reformatory schools departed considerably from the welfarist ethos of the original system of Scottish day industrial schools. However, it is important to recognise that no sharp dichotomy exists between welfarist and punitive systems. Cox, Mahood and Donzelot all correctly point out that in practice matters are less clearly defined, with seemingly contrasting approaches combining disciplinary, controlling and protective features.[37] The book will endeavour to explain the multifaceted nature of these institutions for children: a far from uniform network which certainly encompassed relatively benign, child-centred aspects as well as having unquestionably punitive features.

DIFFERING APPROACHES

There is a wealth of historiography on the history of juvenile justice, particularly on the situation in England and Wales,[38] Ireland[39] and the wider international front.[40] Far less attention has been devoted to the Scottish dimension, although there has been a welcome flourishing of interest in the topic recently. Exploring developments in England and Wales is very important for understanding changes in Scotland, and reference is frequently made throughout the book to work with this focus. As well as the work of historians interested in the English reformatory movement,[41] there has been important work from a sociological perspective.[42] Looking further afield to developments on the continent, there has been interesting research on the influence of the Mettray experiment for young offenders in France, showing that this provided a role model for similar establishments in other countries.[43]

One of the most innovative contributions on the situation in England is a new study by Godfrey, Cox, Shore and Alker which examines the life courses of five hundred people who experienced committal to industrial and reformatory schools in the north of England from the 1860s to the 1920s.[44] Making use of new digitisation methods and impressively extensive data sets, and influenced by modern long-term longitudinal studies,[45] they apply refreshingly novel insights to the subject: these include issues of onset and desistance as well as questions of risk prediction and labelling theory. The authors do not underestimate the negative effects of these institutions, such as the incalculable impact of child removal and the often harsh, cruelly oppressive regimes. Despite these elements, the overall conclusions they form are more optimistic than in most accounts: they point to beneficial and protective features like training for employment, work placements and the evidence of affective bonds between staff and children. Many children went on to lead lives free from offending, with steady work, enjoying families of their own, living an ordinary existence as part of working-class communities. The low reoffending rates and employment placements were flagged up in media reports as evidence of the success of the Victorian juvenile justice system. However, the authors were robust in refuting the idea that the Victorian system represented a template for modern practice. The human costs in terms of brutal child removal were too high and the historical and social conditions were completely different, as were the types of behaviour which led children into the Victorian criminal justice and care system. Many questions are raised by this fascinating and unique study. One is the way in which the success or failure of the early juvenile justice system is measured. Most of the schools claimed great success in reducing reoffending, but until now there was little in the way of information about the subsequent life courses of the children sent to these institutions.

A fascinating feature of the study is the attempt to capture the voices of the children themselves through letters sent by former pupils back to their old schools. These reveal cases where bonds of friendship and support were formed, leading to continued links with institutions. Other writers have succeeded in accessing the views of children in a variety of ways. Shore's work on early nineteenth-century England has tried to reach the voices of children through sources such as records of interviews with young offenders incarcerated on the *Euryalus* hulk and other institutions in the 1830s, in addition to trial reports and journalistic reporting of cases.[46] Her aim, to restore humanity to the young offenders of the past, resonates with the work of other scholars. Mahood's wide-ranging sociological study of Scottish child-saving institutions from 1850 to 1940 contains interviews with survivors of early twentieth-century juvenile justice institutions, uncovering the testimony of those who endured the rigours of life in these disciplinary and socially controlled environments.[47] The work of Barrie and Broomhall on Scottish juvenile justice also offers direct testimony from children in the form of children's words reported in journalistic accounts of cases. Cox's work on girls in the juvenile justice system in Britain analyses sources such as letters, case files and personal memoirs in her study highlighting the highly gendered nature of juvenile justice, especially in relation to the sexual policing of girls through institutionalisation in a range of certified schools and rescue homes.[48]

This concern to connect with the authentic voice of the child also appears in the work of Humphries, an economic historian who analyses a number of working-class autobiographies in *Childhood in the British Industrial Revolution*. Humphries argues that these autobiographies demonstrate remarkably high levels of child labour across the whole British economy throughout the industrial revolution.[49] These testimonies afford genuine insight into the place of industry in Victorian childhoods. Though not focusing on juvenile justice, Humphries's analysis is of real relevance in understanding the nature of work undertaken by children in reformatory and industrial schools, some of whom were required to undertake tasks such as brick-making, described by Humphries as 'lucrative but backbreaking' work.[50] No wonder, then, that one inspectorate report castigated brick-making in a Scottish reformatory school as having a 'lowering' effect on the boys forced to do this work.[51]

Sources like these are invaluable. It is not easy to hear the voices of children or their families in many of the sources available to researchers. Their stories are often buried in a plethora of official records, reports and archival documents which inevitably privilege the voices of the powerful in society. The sources relied on in this book do not readily expose the views of children or families: I have drawn on a wide range of primary sources. These include cases of children brought before the courts, both those reported in official law reports and in archival records; legislation and contemporaneous commentary on statutes; print culture like newspapers, and articles in Victorian journals such as the *Reformatory and Refuge Journal*; parliamentary papers; as well as pamphlets, articles and books written by reformers. However, in the midst of these sources it is possible to detect first-hand testimony of the way families were affected by the early juvenile justice and care systems. For instance, the echo of real childhood experience survives in an archival file containing this poignant message written in August 1874 by a thirteen-year-old boy from Edinburgh whose dying, widowed mother petitioned to have him

admitted to an industrial school, the training ship *Mars* at Dundee, under
the pretext that his behaviour was beyond control, a regular ground of
admission under section 14 of the Industrial Schools Act 1866:

> Dear Sir,
> I write this few lines to let you know that I am willing to go to the training
> ship if my mother is willing to let me.[52]

Signed by both mother and son, these few words suggest that this mother
had nowhere else to turn and sought some secure refuge for her son after
her death. This underlines the vulnerability and desperation of many
children committed to such institutions in the Victorian era.

In a late-nineteenth-century case report there is reference to a newspaper account of a dramatic outburst in a police courtroom in Glasgow.
Here, an emotional mother was pleading with the court not to commit
her daughter to the industrial school:

> Mother,-'Oh no, sir, her father is a most respectable man and he will go
> wrong in his mind if you do.'[53]

In this case the High Court rectified an abuse of procedure in Glasgow
police court and suspended an order to send the ten-year-old girl to
Maryhill Industrial School for five years. It is obvious from the mother's
exclamation here that the family regarded the prospect of the industrial
school with horror. These two cases demonstrate the ambiguous and
complex position occupied by these institutions: on the one hand a form
of refuge; on the other, feared penal establishments.

Although at the other end of the scale in terms of social status, there
is also real authenticity in the autobiographical, handwritten diary of
the Scottish reformer Sheriff William Watson, another source examined
here. Despite being less personal, even parliamentary papers and reports
offer the forthright opinions of many of those involved in the early
juvenile justice system: these include managers of institutions, police
officers, reformers, judges, prosecutors, probation officers, clergymen,
representatives from youth organisations, and volunteers and officers
of the Royal Scottish Society for the Prevention of Cruelty to Children
(RSSPCC). Real testimony is present in these sources, across the spectrum of society.

As previously noted, the historiography on the history of criminal
justice in Scotland is considerably less extensive than that on other jurisdictions, although there has been an encouraging growth of interest in
the subject recently. Scholarship in the field includes Farmer's highly
influential history of criminal law and procedure, Barrie and other

scholars on police history, Barrie and Broomhall on police courts, Kilday on women and violent crime, McNeill on probation, and Jackson and Bartie on postwar youth.[54] In their recent work on early juvenile justice in Scotland, Barrie and Broomhall have stressed the importance of looking at how cases were handled in the courts, something I also emphasise. Innovatively, they have explored print culture and journalistic sources to examine cases in the police courts and, while my work concentrates on cases reported in official case reports and archival sources, I have also found newspaper reporting a valuable source.[55]

Further work on Scotland includes the work of Clark on pre-statutory Scottish industrial schools, written from the educationalist's viewpoint.[56] Ralston has written on Scottish reformatory and industrial schools in the period up to 1872, pointing to the philanthropic contribution of the schools, as Moore and others do in the English context.[57] As noted earlier, Godfrey et al. have also recognised the positive and protective elements which existed in the system in England.[58] However, they place equal emphasis on the damaging and disciplinary impact. Taking the long view in assessing the nature of these institutions for children in Scotland over the nineteenth and early twentieth centuries, their predominantly penal character emerges as a defining characteristic. Mahood's work also supports this view.[59] An important caveat here is that, despite this, the Scottish system always contained a kernel of humanitarianism, evidenced particularly in the approach of Scottish courts with their distaste for child imprisonment and their tendency to view the schools as a refuge for otherwise destitute children.[60]

Writing from a sociological rather than a legal standpoint, Mahood and Littlewood have contributed much to understanding of the Scottish child-saving movement. They have highlighted the gendered and sexualised discourse, the middle-class familial ideology and the almost racialised 'othering' of the working class in juvenile justice reform. My work on the details of case law, legislative and institutional change has much more of a legal emphasis, but my research into archival cases has uncovered evidence of the type of working-class complicity and resistance Mahood in particular talks about. However, it could also be argued that Mahood and Littlewood overestimate the coercive and controlling nature of child-savers.[61] My research on early twentieth-century probation reform suggests that many probation officers adopted an empathetic approach which helped young people turn their lives around.[62] For instance, Edinburgh probation officers in the 1920s were a disparate group of people. Some adopted a disciplinary and authoritarian attitude. But others were inspiring and genuinely engaged with their probationers.

McNeill has emphasised the potential of probation for promoting desistance, and this was clearly demonstrated in the case of some Edinburgh probation officers well able to relate to probationers.[63]

OVERVIEW OF THE BOOK

As is appropriate for a legal/institutional history, this book is grounded in close attention to changes in the law, particularly focusing on the period from the mid-nineteenth century until the early twentieth century. The focus of the book is its examination of the legal factors which underpinned the criminalisation of children in Scotland – in case law, archival case studies, and procedural and legislative change. Case studies are analysed throughout the book, including cases in the new juvenile courts. Very importantly, they demonstrate the way the changes in the legislation were applied in practice. As Barrie and Broomhall recognise, examining legislative change does not by itself offer a complete picture.[64] Looking at the practice of the courts exposes how the system really operated on the ground in a way that simply charting legislative developments cannot. The case law shows that often the way courts dealt with cases in practice did not accord with strict legislative requirements.[65] So, examining the approach taken by courts is essential to understanding the impact of legislative change.

The first chapter places the book in its historical, theoretical and cultural setting, exploring the background against which juvenile justice reform occurred in Scotland and placing this in the wider context of exchange between reformers on the international front. The aim here is to explain the way in which children evolved as a distinctive group in terms of criminalisation, providing a fuller understanding of the legal processes of reform analysed in the book. The second chapter analyses the growing pressure for reform in the mid-century, examining the pioneering diversionary systems for young offenders and the pressure for legislation. As throughout the book, this analysis is set in the legal context with examination of relevant case law, legislative and procedural factors. The third chapter moves on to examine the period 1860–84, looking at the impact of the developing statutory system and its central features. Again, underpinning the whole analysis is examination of cases illustrating the way the system was applied in practice. It demonstrates the unforeseen consequences of this legislative and centralising process: in essence, the distinctiveness of the Scottish day industrial school system was sacrificed, its original welfarist principles undermined as it became aligned to the British system regulating certified residential industrial and reformatory schools of a penal character. The chapter also covers efforts to restore the original elements of the project and the calls for reappraisal, culminating in Watson's final, poignant public appearance when he passionately denounced the statutory system. The fourth chapter places the focus on the period 1884–1910, analysing the situation in Scotland at the turn of the century; by this time the statutory system had evolved into a net-widening diversionary mechanism under which thousands of children were detained in institutions of a penal character. An important aim of this chapter is to assess the impact of the Children Act 1908 and the introduction of the juvenile court, which means looking beyond this timeframe to the 1920s and 1930s. Crucially, this chapter provides a detailed analysis of archival case studies revealing the way children were dealt with by the courts, including the High Court of Justiciary. The final chapter brings together the main themes discussed in the book and discusses its key insights. It will look at the legacy of reform, commenting on some of the connections between the nineteenth-century history explored in the book and later developments in twentieth-century Scotland, including some observations on the links between the earlier history and the seminal Kilbrandon Report in 1964.[66]

The account is set against a background of widespread changes in criminal administration in Scotland, such as the development of policing, the extension of summary jurisdiction,[67] the impact of new criminal prohibitions designed to create order in the expanding urban communities and the development of probation.[68] Analysing the different components which worked together to criminalise children means looking at how they were policed, how they were subjected to criminal procedure, how they were affected by changes in legislation and how they were affected by sentencing decisions. Looking at the way in which all these elements operated together makes it possible to build up a picture of the way children were criminalised in Scotland.

Fortunately, the main Scottish reformer Sheriff William Watson was a keen writer of pamphlets and articles recording his thoughts on the criminal justice system as it related to children and these offer a wonderful insight into the important legal issues of his time. One of the most exciting aspects of his writing is that it indicates that some of the important concerns which troubled lawyers in the mid-nineteenth century continue to fuel debates on criminalisation today: issues such as over-criminalisation, what counts as harm, and justifications for the creation of criminal offences and imposition of punishment.[69] Watson strongly believed that criminal law should have a moral foundation (which for him meant common-sense ideas of morality) and he was therefore perplexed by new criminal prohibitions which seemed to undermine the moral basis of criminal law. So there is much here that is of interest to contemporary scholars of criminalisation.[70]

This goes some way to explaining why the historical perspective on the criminalisation of children is so vital. It adds insight in showing that the way things developed is not necessarily as people think: for example, it reveals that a welfare-based approach to juvenile offenders was flourishing in Scotland in the 1840s, more than a century before the landmark Kilbrandon Report which paved the way for the introduction of the children's hearings system in Scotland.[71] And what are often thought of as new issues may and do in fact turn out to have a long historical pedigree – as well as over-criminalisation,[72] this applies to transatlantic criminal justice policy transfer,[73] the inappropriateness of transjurisdictional youth justice policy convergence within the UK[74] and other themes and preoccupations which were as contentious in Victorian times as they are today.

1

The Young Offender

INTRODUCTION

> The concept of the young offender, with all that it implies for penal policy, is a Victorian creation. Until well into the nineteenth century there were no differentiations accorded to age in the method of bringing offenders to trial, in the form of trial itself, in the punishments that could be imposed, nor, generally, in the way in which they were enforced.[1]

This observation by Radzinowicz and Hood identifies the Victorian era as the period in which the concept of the young offender emerged. This conceptualisation was translated in practical terms into legal and institutional change. At the beginning of the nineteenth century, children were barely distinguished from other offenders in the criminal justice process. Although a lack of capacity in infants under seven was recognised, most children were subject to the same procedures as adult offenders.[2] They were incarcerated along with adult prisoners and were subject to the same types of punishment. Yet by the end of the century the notion of the young offender as belonging to a distinct category in terms of criminalisation was sufficiently well established to allow for the creation of a court specially designated for the young, the juvenile court, and it was accepted that young offenders would be dealt with in separate institutions, the industrial and reformatory schools, rather than prison. How did this recognition of the special status of young offenders emerge in the course of the nineteenth century?

The main issue here is how the change in attitude occurred which for the first time saw children being significantly distinguished from adults in the processes of criminal justice. The purpose of this analysis is to provide a foundation for the following chapters on how children were criminalised within the nineteenth-century Scottish criminal justice system (although little is actually said about Scotland in this chapter, for reasons which will be explained shortly). With this in mind, the chapter seeks to uncover the understandings of childhood which informed approaches to the young offender, considers how they changed over time, and how this was reflected in the institutional and legal changes which occurred over the course of the nineteenth century. The chapter begins with a discussion of the reasons for studying historical criminalisation of children, setting out a framework for understanding criminalisation. In the following section the contrasting background to juvenile justice reform in Scotland and England is explored, focusing on why Scotland was different from England. Importantly, this chapter then examines childhood in the nineteenth century, beginning with changing conceptions of childhood and the position of children within different institutional settings, with a view, ultimately, to forming an assessment of what all these changes meant for criminalisation. The final substantive section concentrates on the child in the criminal justice system. As will become evident, the story being told is far from straightforward and there are competing, contradictory elements and ambivalent attitudes in evidence: as scholars such as Hendrick have pointed out, there was an inherent conflict entailed in the dual perception of the young offender as a vulnerable child in need of protection on the one hand and yet in some senses as presenting a threat on the other, a theme highlighted in this chapter.[3] In approaching these contradictions this chapter adapts the theory of the civilising process advanced by Norbert Elias.[4] In discussing children generally the age category being referred to here is those under sixteen, although when talking of historical conceptions of childhood it is the culturally contingent idea of the child rather than a particular age category which is being discussed.

THE HISTORICAL CRIMINALISATION OF CHILDREN

There is a widespread perception nowadays that children have been exposed to a particularly virulent strain of criminalisation[5] exacerbated by a moral panic about the levels of offending by young people.[6] Public concern about youth misconduct has been the subject of much debate in recent years, most notably following riots in London and other English cities in August 2011,[7] when questions were raised about allegedly excessive sentences imposed by the courts on riot offenders.[8]

However, moral panics about the behaviour of young people are far from being without precedent. In fact, they are a perennial feature of intergenerational relations, as was adeptly demonstrated by Pearson in his fascinating historical survey about perceptions of juvenile criminality.[9] This raises the question of whether the current headline-grabbing preoccupation with the criminalisation of the young truly is a justified commentary on an entirely new degree of criminalisation or whether it is more accurately to be seen as a case of *plus ca change, plus c'est la même chose*. To determine which is the more appropriate description it is necessary to uncover how children were criminalised historically, and the nineteenth century is a good place to start looking, not least because it was during the course of the nineteenth century that children first came to be seen as raising distinct issues in relation to criminalisation.

More broadly, the main reason for considering criminalisation is to expose to the clear light of day the process by which individuals are brought within the ambit of the criminal justice system, a process which can have profound and deeply undesirable consequences for the lives of those subjected to it, not least of which are potential loss of liberty and extreme social stigma. In contemporary terms the issue of criminalisation has troubled many commentators, who have pointed in particular to the worrying proliferation of criminal offences in the statute books in recent years sometimes seemingly as a matter of political expediency, or even sometimes for symbolic effect, and with little regard for their impact on the overall coherence of the criminal law.[10] This highlights the need to investigate criminalisation and that means studying criminalisation in the past as well as the present. When commentators talk of 'over-criminalisation', is this describing a completely new phenomenon or are there parallels in the past; and how do the processes involved in criminalisation change?[11] For example, how do the actions of the agencies involved in criminal justice, like the police, impact on criminalisation and how does this vary under changing circumstances? The answer to these questions can only be given by examining criminalisation in historical terms.

Turning now to the reasons for concentrating on how children were criminalised in nineteenth-century Scotland, one of the primary reasons for the Scottish focus is that there has been comparatively little research on the history of specifically juvenile justice in the Scottish context. As discussed in the introductory chapter, the scholarship which exists on this topic generally tends to focus on the situation in England, and the existing historiography on Scotland is far less extensive, although there has been a welcome flourishing of interest in the subject recently. However, in highlighting the position in Scotland the present study is not intended to be an appeal to parochialism. It aims to recognise the unique features of the definitive legal institutions of Scotland and their history but to do so within the wider context of the UK and beyond. In the present day, Scotland differs from England in having a separate structure of juvenile justice, the children's hearing system, based on the Kilbrandon philosophy of decriminalisation of children, a child welfare-based approach aimed at destigmatisation and non-distinction between children who offend and those in need of care, regarding both as victims of external social circumstances.[12] Ironically, since the advent of the Scottish Parliament, which might have been expected to have the effect of enhancing the unique child-centred quality of the Scottish approach to juvenile justice, some commentators have noted an unwelcome infiltration of more punitive attitudes, which they interpret as a threatened erosion of the principles upon which the children's hearings system was based.[13]

The point being underlined here is that Scotland has a rich tradition of its own in terms of law,[14] education, religious development and culture, all of which have shaped its attitude towards young offenders. The distinct route by which the Scottish system of juvenile justice has arrived at the forum of the children's hearings system needs to be mapped out. However, part of that journey was shared to some extent by young offenders throughout the rest of the UK. Throughout the nineteenth century and for most of the twentieth, until the appearance of the Scottish Parliament in 1999, the Westminster Parliament legislated for the whole of the UK, although of course there were Scottish statutes. Many of the statutory provisions which affected the position of children within the system of criminal justice were much the same north and south of the border. In spite of the many differences between the jurisdictions, they did share a broad British and European cultural heritage which will be referred to in the course of looking at the development of ideas of childhood in the nineteenth century. Against this background it is very important to study the work which has already been done in tracking changes which occurred in England which are, of course, of great significance for understanding developments in Scotland. That body of work is therefore the starting point in this examination of the emergence of children as a distinct group in relation to criminalisation.

This raises the question of how we can assess the way in which children were criminalised. In other words, what sort of framework or markers can be used to evaluate criminalisation as applied to this group? This interpretation approaches criminalisation in a different way from those who focus on criminalisation as being about criminalising *something* (a practice or activity) rather than criminalising *someone*.[15] This investigation is very definitely about the criminalising of a category of people, which means examining how they were subjected to criminal process and potential punishment. However, the two ideas are not mutually exclusive: an integral part of looking at how this category of people, children, was criminalised is examining the kinds of conduct – in other words, the *things* – children were involved in which were prohibited by the criminal law.

According to Lacey's helpful interpretation, criminalisation is a concept which could be said to cover just about every aspect of the criminal justice system, including 'almost every theoretically interesting question about criminal law, criminal responsibility, criminal justice and punishment'.[16]

Taking this to include criminal legislation, the political motivations behind such legislation, practices of policing, prosecution, criminal law in books, judicial practices, criminal procedure, sentencing, punishment and the operation of the penal system, it is seen as incorporating formal criminalisation such as legislation and judicial decisions and substantive or operational criminalisation. Discussing criminalisation in its formal mode of criminal legislation backed up by the threat of state punishment, Ashworth and Horder describe the types of justification called for to legitimise this exercise of state power, noting that justification is supplied in terms of democratic principles and 'sufficient reasons'[17] provided by reference to notions of wrongdoing, harm and culpability. Like Lacey, they point out that, while formal criminalisation may be the starting point, the impact of this legislative action is felt in the way it is enforced in practice by agencies within the criminal justice system, with sometimes unexpected results. Analysing the interplay between political factors and criminalisation, they state that 'the frontiers of criminal liability are not given but are historically and politically contingent'.[18] This observation should be qualified by adding that the shape of the criminal law is also culturally contingent, which means that the the way in which it is applied and subject to change is certainly influenced by prevailing societal mores, the product of myriad influences, including, as will be discussed later, literary, religious, educational and scientific ideas. This exercise in following the trajectory of criminalisation in relation to children throughout the course of the nineteenth century will illustrate how the course and application of the criminal law is strongly and inevitably, even if somewhat imperceptibly, influenced by cultural changes and alterations in societal attitude.

Clearly, tracking the course of criminalisation involves looking at formal criminalisation in the sense of legislation as well as judicial decisions and also looking at the practical outcomes in terms of substantive practices. This entails studying the impact of practices of policing, prosecution, procedure and punishment as actually applied to children. By examining changes in such areas of practical criminalisation it is possible to trace systematically the route by which children came to be seen as raising distinct issues with respect to criminalisation. How children were policed is closely linked to the issue of which crimes were prosecuted and the numbers of children entering the criminal justice system. Once they were ushered into the system, children were subject to legal procedure and it is important to consider the effects of this: for example, how did the use of summary procedure or the introduction of the juvenile court affect the prosecution of juveniles? How were they affected by legislative changes: for example, the body of legislation governing admission to reformatory and industrial schools or the many new criminal prohibitions created to try to maintain order in growing cities? The matter of punishment is central too, and the most evocative issue of all. The effect of not distinguishing child from adult offenders in terms of the imposition and enforcement of punishment meant that children could be subjected to the whole spectrum of whipping, imprisonment in adult prisons (where they were prey to abuse), transportation and even, in some cases, execution.[19] It was not until the Children Act 1908 that penal servitude and judicial execution of juveniles were expressly prohibited. Throughout the course of the nineteenth century and the opening years of the twentieth century, changes took place which reflected the growing recognition of the distinctness of children in the realm of punishment, especially the development of separate institutions for juvenile offenders. This broad approach to criminalisation raises a multitude of questions. All of these matters need to be addressed to provide as full and rich an account as possible, and that account has to look beyond the treatment of perceived criminality of children to the question of how the changing attitudes towards children and the increasing awareness of their vulnerability led to changes in the realm of adult criminalisation too, with the creation of offences designed to offer protection to children.

It is essential to have some strategy with which to begin to analyse these developments. To help in understanding the position of children in the criminal justice system in the nineteenth century it is necessary to uncover the cultural factors underpinning the changing constructions of childhood, to look at the role of children in society, how they were perceived, how changing ideas affected the motives and actions of those who were instrumental in pressing for change, how this mapped on to legal and institutional changes at a conceptual level, and how this change in attitude emerged in practice. This is not to suggest that there was necessarily a simplistic and straightforward causal connection between all these elements which inexorably led to the changes that occurred. The strategy being proposed here takes account of the vicissitudes involved in the analysis, aims to probe into and illuminate the interplay and exchanges between all of these factors, and emphasises the critical importance of recognising the role of alterations in cultural attitude in the development of the criminal law as applied to children. But before analysing childhood in the nineteenth century, the next section discusses the background to the process of reform in Scotland and England.

REFORM MOVEMENTS IN SCOTLAND AND ENGLAND

This section considers why the background to reform of juvenile justice in the nineteenth century was different in Scotland from that in England. It concludes with a discussion of how my interpretation of the pattern of reform relates to that offered by others.

It is very important to recognise that although the initial impetus for reform of juvenile justice in both Scotland and England arose primarily out of a shared philanthropic aspiration to improve the position of children caught up in the criminal justice system, the two jurisdictions approached the problem from different angles. Whereas the main focus of Scottish reformers was on preventive[20] action provided by the welfare-based day industrial school, that in England was on reformation of the confirmed offender in the disciplined reformatory environment. This was a key difference of approach, one which had profound consequences for the development of the system in Scotland.

There were other very significant differences between the Scottish and English reform movements. While the Scottish pre-statutory system appealed to philanthropic support from local communities, the English reformatory movement set out to recruit the support of the rich and powerful. Under the pre-statutory system, reformers in Scotland relied on the support of local communities to fund day industrial schools by voluntary subscriptions. The extent to which the schools involved a community effort was shown in Aberdeen, where the Child's Asylum Committee which regulated admission to the schools was made up of representatives from a range of local organisations.[21]

English reformers, on the other hand, sought out people of influence to advance their cause. One of the most effective in enlisting support from powerful patrons was Mary Carpenter (1807–77), the most prominent reformer of juvenile justice in mid-nineteenth-century England.

This deeply religious, earnest daughter of a Unitarian minister, Lant Carpenter, was the eldest of six children. Her earliest years were spent in Exeter but in 1817 the family moved to Bristol, where she developed an interest in improving the lives of destitute and delinquent children. Socially well connected, she was a prime mover in the English reformatory movement, acquiring a reputation as an international expert on juvenile offending.[22] In spite of her modest and unworldly demeanour, she had a coterie of aristocratic friends. One of these was Lady Byron, who provided funds for the first reformatory for girls, Red Lodge in Bristol, housed in an impressive Elizabethan mansion.[23] In the campaign for legislation, Carpenter enlisted the help of the wealthy Tory MP, Viscount Adderley, later Lord Norton. A fellow evangelical, he proved an invaluable ally, drafting the Bill for the Youthful Offenders Act 1854[24] on the advice of Carpenter, among others.[25] The reformatory movement succeeded in appealing to other members of the landed gentry too,[26] some of whom were keen to establish reformatories on their country estates. This provided landowners with a useful source of free agricultural labour but meant harsh discipline and arduous work for the reformatory boys.[27] So the reformatory movement in England can be seen as encompassing a broad range of interests. At one end of the scale was the idealistic, religious philanthropy of Mary Carpenter preaching the child's need for love in the idyllic surroundings of Red Lodge; at the other were the aristocrats exploiting the labour of reformatory boys. And, ultimately, it was those who advocated the efficacy of the disciplinary approach who ruled the day, even though they were strongly opposed by the likes of Mary Carpenter and Matthew Davenport Hill, both adamant that the retributive idea of prior imprisonment as a condition of reformatory admission should be resisted.[28]

In Scotland the basis of the pre-statutory reform movement was different: it was far more egalitarian, inclusive and humane, appealing to a sense of civic responsibility and local cohesiveness for support. It stressed the importance of the child as part of the family unit and of maintaining the integrity of family bonds, and endeavoured to raise the social conditions and moral outlook of whole families, not only children. In many ways the movement can be seen as a dynamic missionary effort, an attempt to improve the lot of the poorest and most excluded. The literature of reform is infused with this sense of mission, the purpose of which was to evangelise the most degraded members of society in mid-nineteenth-century Scotland. This is a recurrent theme in the writings of Sheriff William Watson and also in those of his prominent fellow reformer, the Edinburgh minister, Rev. Thomas Guthrie.

In Scotland the prime movers in the campaign for change were often judges, especially Sheriffs, and other members of the legal profession. In England one of the most important reformers, Carpenter's fellow Unitarian, Matthew Davenport Hill, was also a judge.[29] His important influence as Recorder of Birmingham and pioneer of an early form of probation is discussed further in the next chapter. Similarly, King has shown the reforming capacity of judges in the Old Bailey in the first three decades of the nineteenth century in devising a diversionary sentencing policy sending young offenders for reformatory training.[30] But the influence of the judiciary was even more marked in Scotland. North of the border it was the Sheriffs who led the way, notably William Watson in Aberdeen and Sir Archibald Alison in Glasgow. Sheriff Hugh Barclay of Perth was also active in the reform movement, writing a book on juvenile delinquency[31] and helping to draft the first Scottish legislation on industrial schools.

In the early nineteenth century the recognisably modern role of Sheriff was relatively new. The administrative and legal arrangements put in place following the Jacobite rebellion of 1745 were designed to garner previously feudal jurisdictions into the control of the Crown through the medium of a hierarchy of Sheriff and Justiciary Courts.[32] Central to the operation of this system was the part played by local Sheriffs who were legally qualified judges with authority to oversee the lower courts. Sheriffs were required to reside in their Sheriffdoms for a minimum of four months every year and supervised the now professionalised administration of justice where crimes were prosecuted by public prosecutors. With Sheriffs and the Lord Advocate now at the heart of legal and also political power, there was a real opportunity for those of a reforming mind to use their pre-eminent position to effect change within their local jurisdiction and to influence change on a wider front. It was within this context that innovators such as William Watson and Archibald Alison were able to operate so effectively in a way that would not be possible for Sheriffs nowadays.

The important point here is that the Scottish reform movement contrasted with that in England in many respects: despite the fact that the initial pressure for reform in both countries was energised by evangelical, religious inspiration, they approached matters in very different ways. With the benefit of hindsight it is possible to see the momentous significance of the decision by Scottish reformers to join forces with English reformers in the quest for legislation. It proved to be the turning point for the Scottish pre-statutory system, although this was not evident at the time. Insidiously, by stealth, over the course of little more than a decade, the development of the statutory system resulted in a body of legislation which, together with other centralising factors, sought to force the Scottish system into an English mould. This completely undermined the holistic, welfare-based nature of the original Scottish system.

The interpretation offered in this book emphasises the centrality of religious philanthropy as a vehicle for penal change in the area of juvenile justice. It was the role of reformers resisting the effects of industrialisation on the children of the urban poor which was the primary catalyst for reform. In advancing this argument the book stresses the dynamic influence of human motivation. This challenges influential, Foucauldian-inspired accounts such as Garland's, which see penal policy as 'determined by unacknowledged, deep structures of power.'[33] Although my argument stresses the importance of philanthropic motivation, it also recognises the yawning chasm between humanitarian aspiration, reflected in the good intentions of the reformers, and the final dismal outcome of their reforms in practice. This approach strikes a chord with David Rothman's analysis of American criminal justice history,[34] particularly his observations on reform schools for delinquents, which highlights a similar divergence between the original aims of reform and the operational pragmatism of those implementing the changes. His explanation of the shortfall between idealism and practical reality in nineteenth-century America shows parallels with the account given in this book. Another account which is highly relevant to this book is Susan Margarey's analysis.[35] She argues that a combination of changes in legislation and the policing of the young acted together to criminalise children in early nineteenth-century England. This is discussed more fully later in this and the next chapter, where it is argued that this is also what happened in Scotland in the same period.

CHILDHOOD IN THE NINETEENTH CENTURY

This section focuses on what it meant to be a child in the nineteenth century. It examines changing conceptions of childhood and how these were reflected culturally and on a practical level in different institutional contexts. To help understand ideas of childhood, the section draws on the insights of the French scholar, Philippe Aries, and also those of the German sociologist, Norbert Elias. As becomes evident in later chapters, their abstract ideas can be linked in some important respects to the development of diversionary systems for young offenders in Scotland. The section introduces the idea of childhood as a social construction, before considering the work of Aries and Elias. It then looks at how the idea of the child was reflected in the cultural contexts of literature and religion, and eventually in practice in the workplace, home and school.

Changing ideas about childhood

The essential point to register here is that childhood is a social construction, as scholars such as Hendrick ably demonstrate.[36] The way in which children have been perceived, the way in which they have been treated and the status accorded to them has undergone considerable changes throughout the course of history. The role of children in society has, of course, had implications for the way in which they were regarded within the systems of criminal justice, and it is this relationship between changing cultural perception and changing institutional application in the realm of criminal justice and all the steps between attitudinal and actual change which is fascinating to trace.

In today's world it is taken for granted that children are vulnerable, in need of protection and care – a special case, to whom special rules apply. Recent years have seen an international focus on children's rights with the advent of The United Nations Convention on the Rights of the Child. This came into force in 1990 and has been almost universally ratified, though in many countries it remains very much an aspirational ideal. The Convention declares certain standards which it regards as essential, asserting, for instance, under Article 12, that the child has a right to be consulted in matters affecting his or her welfare in accordance with the maturity of the child.[37] There is also much emphasis in current domestic family law legislation on the needs of the child being a prime consideration, and the importance of the voice of the child being listened to. Section 11(7) of the Children (Scotland) Act 1995 provides that in proceedings concerning parental rights the welfare of the child is to be regarded as paramount. Similarly, under section 2(1) of the Act it is made clear that parents possess rights in respect of their children in order to be able to discharge their parental responsibilities. There is enormous value placed on respecting the special position of children nowadays and it goes without saying that childhood is, at least in the western world, seen as a time free from the responsibilities of adulthood, a time of nurturing, learning and play. This view of children and childhood as a special category to whom special rules apply is reflected in criminal justice terms in the Scottish context in the choice of forum for young offenders under the age of sixteen: the child welfare-oriented setting of the children's hearings system is based on the holistic principle of non-discrimination between children referred on offending grounds and those referred because they are in need of care and protection.[38]

While modern ideas about childhood might seem self-evident, immutable and fixed, studies of the history of childhood indicate that ideas about the role of children are malleable and contingent. They have changed considerably over time throughout western society. What it means to be a child today is something different from what it meant to be a child in the nineteenth century. In order to be treated differently, children had first to be recognised as different from adults in some significant way that merited a different kind of treatment. The ramifications of this proposition for the treatment of children in the criminal justice system form the practical subject matter of the study of criminalisation in relation to children.

One of the most influential commentaries on the history of childhood in western society is the work of Aries, which creates a very helpful bridge between childhood studies and criminalisation, as is discussed next.

Aries and Elias

The field of childhood studies has great significance for understanding the emergence of children as a distinct group in relation to criminalisation. One particularly exciting connection is the link between *Centuries of Childhood* by Aries and *The Civilising Process*[39] by Elias, whose work has been widely applied to the relationship between violence and civilisation, and the history of punishment.[40]

Both Aries and Elias are concerned with the picture being painted on the broad historical canvas, considering long-term historical trends and identifying changes taking place over centuries. Aries studies developing ideas of childhood which were by the nineteenth century becoming widely accepted: his main concern is to establish how the change in perception occurred which saw the idea of the role of the child move from one of relative insignificance on the margins of collective life to the modern position, evident by the nineteenth century, occupying the pivotal position around which the world of the private family revolved.[41]

Investigating the timespan from the Middle Ages to the present within French society, Aries states that 'there was no place for childhood in the medieval world'[42] and that the idea did not emerge until the seventeenth century. He defines the concept of childhood as being 'awareness of the particular nature of childhood, that particular nature which distinguishes the child from the adult, even the young adult'.[43]

Aries contends that the idea of childhood developed as a consequence of increasing differentiation of children from adults, which is exactly what Elias argues happens in the course of the civilising process. Aries makes use of sources such as medieval art, children's dress and games to develop his argument. He shows that in medieval art there was no realistic depiction of children's bodies and they were presented as miniature adults, while from the seventeenth century there was a naturalistic representation of children and an interest in creating portraits of individual children. Similarly, in the area of dress it was not until the seventeenth century that children were dressed in special clothing for children. The same trend is evident in his analysis of children's games and pastimes. He demonstrates the change from medieval times, when many games which had been played by adults and children in all classes of society were abandoned by upper-class adults and became the province solely of the children of the upper classes, as well as both adults and children in other sections of society. Aries argues that in the medieval world children were assimilated into the adult world as soon as they were no longer infants, about the age of seven, as was demonstrated by the notable absence of constraints on making inappropriate references in front of children or attempting to protect their innocence. He contends that the main reason for the change in the seventeenth century was the increasing focus on education of children, which marked out childhood as a period of learning and preparation for adulthood. Children were no longer to be thrust out into the adult world from their cradles. This concern with education effectively, he argues, created childhood. However, Aries does not see education as necessarily a wholly benign development: in a passage reminiscent of Foucault, he sees it as a sinister move from a world where the child experienced relative freedom to one characterised by 'an increasingly severe disciplinary system' epitomised by the eighteenth and nineteenth centuries in the oppressive, punitive, 'total claustration of the boarding school'.[44]

The point in examining childhood for Aries is to uncover the origin of the modern idea of the private world of the family with the child at its centre. He is preoccupied with the modern centrality of the idea of the family and is seeking to show how the change occurred from the idea of the child as being peripheral and marginal to society, simply part of a collective whole, to becoming the focus of the private family unit behind the 'wall of private life'.[45] This emphasis on the creation of the private domain and its relationship with societal relations is a concern shared with Elias.

On a practical level it is possible to see elements of Aries's ideas reflected in developments in nineteenth-century juvenile justice reform.

Firstly, in the disciplinary nature of reformatory education there are echoes of Aries's ideas on the relationship between residential education and discipline. Secondly, in the development of the pre-statutory system in Scotland in the 1840s and early 1850s it is possible to see parallels between Aries's idea of the central position of the child, as the focus of family life, and the ideas of the Scottish reformers, especially William Watson. One of Watson's main concerns was with protecting the integrity of the family unit and the child's position within it. He saw the role of the child as pivotal: by educating the vagrant or offending child, instilling him with Christian values and elevating him to the ranks of respectability through honest industry, Watson hoped to create an example for the rest of the child's family to follow.[46]

Elias

Centuries of Childhood has been described as 'an extended gloss on Elias's perception'.[47] The empirical methodological approach adopted by Aries in his use of sources is similar to that employed by Elias. In his work, Elias examines the history of manners from the Middle Ages by analysing books on etiquette and instruction, and a range of other sources from literature, music and art. He illustrates how acceptable standards of behaviour and social mores change over time in accordance with what he terms a civilising process. For the purposes of the present discussion there are two particularly useful elements to be drawn from the interpretation Elias offers. The first is his demonstration of how in the course of the civilising process children are increasingly differentiated from adults – the theme echoed by Aries. The second contribution is his view on the nature of changing social sensibility, which can be understood as societal reaction reflecting emotional responses. Both of these aspects have direct bearing on the debate about the differentiation of children from adults in the nineteenth-century criminal justice system. Elias argues:

> The distance in behaviour and the whole psychological structure between children and adults increases in the course of the civilising process.[48]

Adeptly using extracts from books of manners, Elias is able to show how in earlier times certain instructions are intended to teach adults proper behaviour in a range of matters such as table manners, spitting and the subject of bodily functions. However, in later editions the text assumes that adults have, over the course of time, adopted the recommended mode of conduct and therefore aims at instructing only children on these points of behaviour. He also uses his sources to demonstrate how, over time, the manners adopted by the social elites are gradually acquired by other sectors of society. Elias is convincing in highlighting the growing divergence between adults and children with the passage of time. Commenting on the eighteenth-century habits with regard to nose-blowing, he notes that 'only children are allowed, at least in the middle classes, to behave as adults did in the Middle Ages'.[49]

Elias is, of course, addressing changes which occur over a very long period and, as is the case with Aries, the growing 'distance in behaviour' he identifies as emerging between adults and children is a divide which by the nineteenth century is becoming accepted as the norm. Elias's explanation has obvious relevance for shedding light upon the change in attitude occurring in the course of the nineteenth century, which saw children becoming more fully differentiated from adults in the processes of criminal justice. Was the growing recognition of the distinctness of children in criminal justice a reflection of the Eliasian idea of the civilising process? This is a compelling argument.

Certainly, the second aspect of the Elias argument, which is concerned with the psychological dimension, is extremely interesting. As Garland points out in his discussion of Elias in *Punishment and Modern Society*, the empirical basis of Elias's work is just the starting point for an analysis of the relationship between changing 'psychical structures' and 'changing structures of social interaction'.[50] Elias develops his theme by discussing the transformation in societal structure through the ages, from the aggressive knightly warrior societies to the more peaceful courtly societies of the sixteenth and seventeenth centuries, where the exercise of violence is vested in a central authority, and on to the market societies in the eighteenth and nineteenth centuries. He argues that as social relations generally became less aggressive there was an accompanying emphasis on the importance of refinement and cultural distinction among the social elites which, over time, through the civilising process, was disseminated to other levels of society. The main hallmark of this concentration on cultural refinement was the necessity for self-restraint and discipline in a kind of Freudian internalisation of social mores, described by Elias as 'the psychical process of civilisation'.[51] A central feature of this process is identified by Elias as an increasing sensibility to aspects of life considered unpleasant, distasteful and an affront to polite society. This, the argument goes, accounted for the removal to the private domain of scenes regarded as unsightly. It was no longer considered acceptable to present dinner guests with a whole animal to be carved at the table, and the carving had to take place behind the scenes. Elias notes that the unpleasantness and violence did not disappear; it was simply moved away from centre stage.

Garland regards this analysis as having enormous relevance for the history of penal change. He interprets the general thrust of Elias's argument as having great explanatory potential for changes in 'punitive manners'[52] over the period discussed by Elias. He identifies parallels in Elias's account with the move behind the scenes of the punishment of offenders. Garland applies Elias's theory to the history of punishment to argue that his account could be read as explaining that as the sight of human suffering became an affront to sensibilities there was a gradual change of arena for punishment from the public displays of punishment to punishment behind the walls of prisons.[53] As sensitivities increased, so did the distaste for the infliction of violence on offenders, and eventually the more brutal sanctions were replaced by the less offensive, less visible option of the prison. Garland qualifies his interpretation by noting that acceptance of this revised version depends on whether Elias's psychic theory on heightened conscience and sensibilities and concomitant privatisation is thought to be credible. He also notes that Elias's cultural explanation of civilisation is inextricably linked with other factors such as societal and structural organisation, which means that the civilising process has nothing determined about it. It is in fact a delicate edifice easily fractured by major alterations in societal structure and the pressure of revolutionary changes.

Apart from its application to the history of punishment, Elias's theory has also proved a fertile source for developing ideas about long-term patterns of violent crime within society, with Eliasian concepts of 'relative pacification of ever broader groups of people' in the course of the civilising process being used to account for an overall decline in, for example, homicidal violence.[54] Similarly, his ideas about the significance of societal structure have been used to advance the notion of *violence-au-vol*, based on the idea that feudal society, with its emphasis on aggression as an integral element of satisfying codes of honour, was linked with high levels of violent crime, whereas the progression to bourgeois materialist industrial society was associated with a high level of property crime.[55] Elias's insights have fuelled debates on these matters in recent years, ever since his work was 'discovered' when it re-emerged in English translation in the 1970s, decades after it first appeared in German.[56] However, his writings have not gone uncriticised. Much of the criticism questions whether it is valid to formulate matters in terms of a 'process' and highlights the counter-trends which seem to undermine his argument, whether the modern 'permissive society' which might seem to flout notions of civilised behaviour, or the existence of 'stateless civilisations' which exhibit civilised types of behaviour despite not conforming to the societal structures described by Elias. His work has also been criticised for an over-emphasis on aggression which pays insufficient attention to harm inflicted in other ways.[57] Critics have also pointed to events in modern history which entail deeply disturbing reversals of civilisation, such as genocidal atrocity.[58] However, others suggest that Elias's work complements writing such as Bauman's on the Holocaust, deepening understanding of such 'regressions to barbarism'.[59] As John Pratt argues, 'it is evident that the qualities of the civilising process itself are no guarantee of a civilised end product (and that Elias's work is not based on some teleological notion of human and societal betterment, as has been a regular line of criticism)'.[60]

Accepting Elias's account, in spite of its complexities, helps to explain the growing recognition of the distinct position of children in the nineteenth century, which was critical in the emergence of children as a special group in relation to criminalisation. It also helps to explain the heightened sensitivity to the suffering of children of the impoverished classes. This manifested itself in a number of ways, from the increasing public disquiet about the exploitation of children in the labour market to the newly perceived unacceptability of incarcerating children in adult prisons. It also appeared in the increased sensitisation to the vulnerability of children which precipitated the development of their differential treatment in the processes of criminal justice. The cultural explanation is appealing because it offers an answer to the question of why there was for the first time such a general awakening of the public conscience.[61] Increasing public sensitivity responded not only to children but also to others suffering oppression, most notably those subjected to slavery. Indeed, historians draw parallels between the anti-slavery campaign and the pressure to liberate children from the chains of toil in the factories.[62] Elias's cultural account of civilisation is very plausible[63] and the significance of this for the changing position of children in the nineteenth-century criminal justice system and for the argument that the course of criminal law is culturally contingent is clear.

The idea of a civilising process is certainly appealing and sits comfortably with notions about the advancement of humanitarianism, which undoubtedly was a potent element in nineteenth-century reform of the criminal justice system, particularly in relation to children. As Martin Wiener notes, the Whiggish idea of the slow but steady triumph of humanitarianism in relation to criminal justice policy has had many influential adherents over the years.[64]

However, the story is more complicated than that, and reading Elias can assist in understanding the complexities. Elias's theory can account for the civilising, humanitarian trend, and can also provide insight into less savoury currents flowing in another direction. Some commentators have recently expanded on the concept of 'decivilising processes'. For example, Dunning and Mennell contend that 'what is likely to happen is that civilising and decivilising processes [will] occur simultaneously in particular societies, and not simply in the same or different societies at different points in time', an idea adopted and expanded on by John Pratt in discussing the contemporary debate about 'a punitive turn' in criminal justice policy.[65] This is an idea which can be applied in the context of considering the processes of criminalisation as applied to children in the nineteenth century to explain the existence of progressive, enlightened narratives vying with contradictory forces pulling in a more reactionary direction. At the same time that there was a heightened sensibility towards the special position and vulnerability of children which emphasised, for example, the unacceptability of children being imprisoned along with adults, there were less benign influences in operation which regarded the children of the poor as a potential threat to social stability to be tackled by oppressive criminal justice practices. For instance, as will be discussed later, it has been argued that there is evidence that methods of policing and prosecution as applied to children acted to bring increasing numbers of children within the ambit of the criminal justice system.[66] There has been evidence of this in the English context, and it will be demonstrated in later chapters that this is what happened in Scotland too. Acknowledging these competing civilising and decivilising narratives or trends is important in trying to understand how children were criminalised within the nineteenth-century criminal justice system.

There are other ways in which Elias's work helps elucidate matters. In many respects the goal of the pre-statutory day industrial school movement was to elevate the children in their care to the ranks of respectability. This involved the transmission of values deemed necessary for the respectable citizen, such as religious adherence, diligent work and cleanliness. By adopting the manners and lifestyle of the respectable orders of society, children could shake off the stigma of vagrancy and criminality and be reincarnated as valued members of society. This was definitely a civilising exercise. But, while the civilising effect was an integral part of Watson's mission, this was not simply about superficial aspects of respectability. Though great emphasis was placed on matters such as a tidy appearance, this was not the main point. The primary goal was to impart moral, religious values. For example, Watson quoted with approval an observation from an Edinburgh minister on the benefits of day industrial schools:

> Mothers have been shamed into attention to their children by having them sent back without breakfast because of the dirtiness of their persons or clothes. I think I might go farther and safely assert that not merely a civilising but a moral influence has emanated from the children to their parents. Hymns and psalms and Bible lessons and healthy reading preparatory for next day's school work are rarely altogether unprofitable.[67]

This suggests that concern with outward matters such as appearance was an ancillary aspect of the ultimate aim of moral transformation.

As noted earlier, the work of Elias has often been applied in analysing the relationship between violence and civilisation, and has been used to account for an overall decline in homicidal violence in the course of the civilising process. It is extremely interesting to see, then, that most of the cases of children from the nineteenth century discussed in this book do not involve violent conduct. They are generally concerned with minor thefts, vagrancy or low-level disorder. This contrasts with the contemporary situation. where there is much concern about violent offending by young people. This suggests that the emphasis has shifted over time, with the focus now on more aggressive conduct.[68] This theme will be discussed more fully in chapter five of the book.

Next, what might be described as progressive trends influencing criminalisation in relation to children will be discussed – the influence of literary notions of childhood and the impact of religious views of childhood – all of which lined up squarely behind the civilising, humanitarian narrative in portraying the child as innocent, vulnerable and in need of protection.

Cultural influences in literature

In trying to uncover the sources of cultural change in *The Civilising Process*, Elias looked to written sources, including literary texts. For most historians of childhood, literary and philosophical writings are an important indicator of changes in attitude towards children. As Hendrick notes, there is a widely held belief among scholars that the late seventeenth and eighteenth centuries heralded a new, more sensitive, approach towards childhood,[69] and the writings of John Locke and Rousseau have been regarded as particularly influential.

Published in 1693, Locke's *Some Thoughts Concerning Education* advanced some novel ideas about children. Predominantly secular in tone, which in itself marked a departure from the religiously inspired approach common at the time, Locke's work stressed the individuality of each child and the importance of upbringing in shaping the child, who was represented as a *tabula rasa* or blank slate with regard to ideas but not personal qualities.[70] This more child-centred approach found a disciple in Rousseau, the author of the enormously popular *Émile*, which appeared in 1762. Rousseau emphasised the natural goodness of children – a view which challenged ideas about the child as tainted by original sin and therefore requiring reformation and redemption. He advocated that children should be raised 'in the ways of nature',[71] which meant practical changes such as maternal breastfeeding instead of wet-nursing and no swaddling, and also allowing the child to discover the natural world by experience. The most groundbreaking philosophical insight that Rousseau had was that it was vital to recognise that the child had to be valued and recognised as a child and not just as a small adult.[72] Along with this recognition came the idea that the child should be allowed to revel in the ephemeral happiness of childhood, a transient time which was to be enjoyed while it lasted.[73] These notions of childhood made an impact, at least among the social elite, where, Cunningham notes, there is evidence that Rousseau's ideas on child-rearing were followed, particularly the advice about maternal breastfeeding and swaddling.[74]

While Rousseau's ideas of childhood emanated from an elite literary and philosophical source which was the province of the upper echelons of society, they helped foster a more widespread cultural shift – an Eliasian type of dissemination of cultural values – in the new perception of children as individual, unique and different from adults in a special way that would eventually see them, for the first time, regarded as meriting differential treatment from adults in the criminal justice system.

The new perception of children promoted by Rousseau was embellished by the portrait of the child figure in the literary flourishes of the Romantic poets Blake, Coleridge and Wordsworth, writing in the late eighteenth and early nineteenth centuries, whose works combined forces to represent a highly sentimentalised version of childhood, a version that was to become very familiar to the readers of the great works of Victorian literature into the mid-nineteenth century. Blake's vision was of childhood as a perpetual source of innocence, which ideally should sustain an adult throughout his life, while the view associated with Wordsworth, and the one which is generally thought of as embodying Romanticism, was of childhood as a golden, fleeting time of life which was to be treasured before it disappeared for ever with the onset of adult life. Wordsworth's idealised vision of childhood is encapsulated in lines from his *Ode on Intimations of Immortality from Recollections of Early childhood* written in 1807:

> . . . trailing clouds of glory do we come
> From God who is our home:
> Heaven lies about us in our infancy[75]

Here was the ultimate sanctification of Childhood, and an ideal which had immense impact throughout the nineteenth century. Its influence can be seen decades later in the sentimentalised portrayal of the child figure in major works of literature of the mid-nineteenth century such as *Oliver Twist* and *David Copperfield* by Charles Dickens or the depiction of Eppie in *Silas Marner* by George Eliot. Similarly, George Eliot's portrayal of the idyllic childhood of Maggie and Tom Tulliver in *Mill on the Floss* has been described as epitomising 'Wordsworth's world of innate childhood pleasures'.[76] But the major significance of the Romantic vision went well beyond its effect on literature. The Romantics may have been members of a literary elite addressing a select element in society, but they were part of a transformation in ways of thinking about the role of children in society. They contributed to a new cultural milieu which took root in the nineteenth century, one which began to regard children as vulnerable and in need of protection. Their influence was palpable in the passionate pleas of the factory reformers seeking to protect children from the brutalising effects of the workplace. Cunningham argues that the legacy of Romanticism added an emotional depth to the humanitarian campaigns of the reformers, and notes that one such reformer writing a survey of factory conditions in 1836 included a quotation from Wordsworth's *Intimations of Immortality*.[77] As Hendrick points out, this emotive quality associated with Romanticism can also be seen in protest in the 1830s against the exploitative use of small children as chimney sweeps.[78]

The plight of children used as chimney sweeps had been highlighted long before this time by the writings of Jonas Hanway in 1785 in *An Earnest Appeal for Mercy for the Children of the Poor*, and their cause had been taken up in verse by Blake in *Songs of Innocence* in 1789. Robert Pattison, writing on the child figure in English literature and the legacy of the Romantics, argues that the notable humanitarian campaigner, Lord Shaftesbury, who is credited with being the driving force behind the 1875 legislation which finally, after years of campaigning, banned the practice of using children as chimney sweeps, had in effect been motivated by sentiments inspired by Blake's Romantic vision.[79] The Romantic vision of childhood was a central feature of the idea that children should not only be protected from the brutalising effects of work, but that there was no place for work at all in childhood, a central idea in paving the way for compulsory schooling.[80] This was part of a major cultural shift.

The Romantic conceptualisation of childhood made its presence felt in the language used by those campaigning for reform of juvenile justice, who often appealed to a powerful combination of evangelical ideals and Romantic notions of childhood – such as the importance of restoring child offenders to a condition where they received protection. Hendrick stresses this important interaction between Romantic and evangelical ideas of childhood in his analysis, and it was well exemplified by the reformatory campaigner Matthew Davenport Hill when he commented in 1855:

> The latter [the delinquent] is a little stunted man already – he knows much and a great deal too much of what is called life – he can take care of his own immediate interests . . . He has consequently much to unlearn – he has to be turned again into a child.[81]

The effect of the Romantic idealisation of childhood is hard to over-state. The appeal to sentimentalism was an intrinsic element of Victorian culture. It became embedded in its literature and ways of thinking about children, and it became a potent weapon in the hands of reformers seeking to improve the lives of children in the nineteenth century.[82]

The impact of religion and international influences

The ideas of Rousseau and the Romantics were of enormous importance in the conceptualisation of childhood. Religious ideas about the nature of childhood were also highly influential in the nineteenth century.[83] In most discussions concerning theology there are widely varying interpretations, and this is all too evident in the contradictory religious views on the nature of children. Some commentators point to the evangelical revival of the nineteenth century as being associated with an emphasis on the child as tarnished with original sin, a fallen creature in need of training, discipline and redemption, a view espoused by the evangelical founder of the Sunday School Movement in the early nineteenth century, Hannah More. In direct opposition to the Romantic concept of the innate goodness of children, she insisted that it was a 'fundamental error' to regard children as 'innocent beings whose little weaknesses, may, perhaps want some correction, rather than as beings who bring into the world a corrupt nature and evil dispositions, which it should be the great end of education to rectify'.[84] Within the evangelical tradition there is evidence of contradictory opinions on this crucial question. For instance, the evangelical reformatory campaigner, Mary Carpenter, had no time for the idea of ingrained evil.[85] Certainly the notion of the child as a fallen creature was not universal within nineteenth-century Christianity. Cunningham states that 'Christians happily accepted' the Romantic vision, and he quotes the future Cardinal Newman in the 1830s as saying, with Wordsworthian fervour, that he believed that the child was a blessed creature who had come 'out of the hands of God with all the lessons and thoughts of heaven freshly marked upon him'.[86]

Whatever their position was on the question of original sin, religiously motivated philanthropists of the nineteenth century, who were mainly from the evangelical tradition, were united in their desire to rescue children, whether from the miseries of child labour or the degradation and dangers of destitution, abandonment and criminality. It is evident from much of the rhetoric of the evangelical reformers that many of them adhered to a vision of childhood which combined elements of the ideas of Rousseau, the Romantics and Christian theology. Mary Carpenter, for example, was indebted to Rousseau's ideas when she expressed her belief that 'a child should be treated as a child'.[87] In an attitude similar to her fellow evangelist and reformatory campaigner, Matthew Davenport Hill, she espoused the Romantic concept that the ideal childhood was one where the child was protected, when she talked of the need to restore the child who had offended to 'the true position of childhood'.[88] She added, 'He must be brought to a sense of dependence' where he is 'guided by wisdom and love; he must, in short, be placed in a *family*'.[89] This vision highlights the centrality of the Victorian emphasis on the sentimentalised domestic ideal of the family, which was so highly valued by evangelicals. Mary Carpenter summarised her aspiration as being to achieve 'true reformatory action with the young',[90] with the aim of effecting 'true and powerful action on the soul of the child, by those who have assumed the holy duties of a parent'.[91] This statement of her Christian mission is very clearly imbued with the legacy of Rousseau and the Romantics.

Mary Carpenter's evangelical view of the child offender as a soul in need of salvation did not attach blame to the child, seeing the child as a victim of social circumstances or as lacking in moral guidance. Her view of children was a reflection of her Christian belief in forgiveness and redemption. Rejecting the conventional approach to the punishment of child offenders, she advocated a period of corrective training which sought to rehabilitate the offender through, firstly, recognising the inherent dignity of children as 'coheirs' of 'an eternal existence'[92] and, secondly, the realisation that 'love must be the ruling sentiment',[93] because for children 'it is an absolute necessity of their nature, and when it is denied them they become no longer children'.[94]

Formidably single-minded, Mary Carpenter was to become the most significant figure in the English reformatory movement. Her religious zeal was the driving force behind her philanthropic dynamism, something she had in common with William Watson. Indeed, her writing shows that she was greatly inspired by Watson's success in establishing the Scottish pre-statutory system.[95] Where she diverged from him was in her concentration on the child's need for reformation. Far more pragmatic, Watson's view was that children's offences were usually 'trifling' matters.[96] As previously noted, the fundamental goal of reform for Watson and his supporters was prevention rather than reformation,[97] a major difference of approach which had significant implications for developments in Scotland.

In spite of the differences between jurisdictions, religious philanthropists eagerly exchanged new ideas about juvenile justice reform. As well as being strongly influenced by developments in Scotland, Carpenter looked to international developments for inspiration. As a Unitarian, she had close links with religious groups in New England and was aware of new initiatives being tested there.[98] But the experiment which has been credited as exerting more influence than any other over the English reformatory movement was Mettray near Tours in France,[99] and there is evidence that this was also a development of which Scottish reformers were aware.[100] Mettray was founded in 1840 by Frederic Auguste Demetz, who himself had been on a fact-finding mission to Quaker- and Methodist-run institutions for young offenders in the US four years previously,[101] so it is clear that there were channels of influence flowing in many directions.

In stressing the importance of establishments based on a family type of structure in her proposals for dealing with children who had offended, Mary Carpenter was seeking to emulate the success of Mettray and similarly run institutions elsewhere in mainland Europe, such as the Rauhe Haus near Hamburg. These were agricultural colonies run along family lines by religiously motivated philanthropists. These schools flourished in France, Germany, Belgium and the Netherlands, a European phenomenon fostered by a cross-border network of philanthropy which focused on ideas for responding to problem children.[102]

In allying herself with the regime at Mettray, Mary Carpenter was forging links with a wholly new concept of dealing with young offenders.

In *Discipline and Punish*, Foucault is unequivocal about the importance of Mettray:

> it is the disciplinary form at its most extreme, the model in which are concentrated all the coercive technologies of behaviour. In it were to be found 'cloister, prison, school, regiment'.[103]

The institution at Mettray was based on a highly disciplined and regulated model where the inmates were divided into family-type groups structured in a hierarchical manner. Inmates were subjected to a regime of close inspection, education and agricultural work, and motivated by a system of rewards and punishments and rigid order, where the most minor offences were disciplined as a means of preventing more serious misconduct. The main form of punishment imposed was isolation in the inmate's cell, where the defining motto of the institution was written on the wall: 'God sees you.'[104] This was designed to encourage moral introspection and examination of conscience, a confessional approach and a powerful inducement to reform. Foucault saw Mettray as the precursor of the disciplinary technologies of the future.

Visits to Mettray by English philanthropists, including Matthew Davenport Hill, convinced them of the merits of the regime, which claimed a spectacularly high rate of success in reforming its inmates.[105] In 1849 the Philanthropic Society established an institution modelled on Mettray on a farm at Red Hill, Surrey; young offenders were sent to Red Hill when they had received a pardon from the courts, as a condition of which they were detained in the reformatory instead of being sent to prison.[106] The success claimed for the venture motivated the philanthropists to campaign for legislation to set up reformatories on a formal basis. This reflected a pattern occurring elsewhere in Europe as philanthropists in other countries pressed for legislation, as a result of which state-subsidised institutions for children were created.[107] According to Radzinowicz and Hood, the English reformatory legislation 'was a significant recognition that philanthropic initiative needed the backing of the criminal law'.[108] But for the Scottish reformers the backing of the criminal law came with a hefty price tag. In the next chapter we shall see that Scottish philanthropists seeking to set up the pre-statutory system of day industrial schools on a more secure footing campaigned for legislative action alongside those involved in the English reformatory movement. This was to have unforeseen consequences for the Scottish system, where the welfare-based ethos was very far removed from that of Mettray's disciplinary ideal: they could not have known that under the constraints imposed by a national framework of legislation, Scotland would soon have a Mettray of its own only a stone's throw from the Scottish capital. As will be discussed further in chapter three, Wellington Reformatory Farm School near Edinburgh was in many ways the Scottish incarnation of Mettray. The Inspector of reformatory and industrial schools, Sydney Turner, noted the resemblance to Red Hill in Surrey, where he had been instrumental in creating the English adaptation of Mettray.[109] Like Red Hill, Wellington's architecture was based on a number of pavilion-type buildings each designed to house a small number of boys in family-style units.

One of the most interesting aspects of this analysis of the religious view of childhood is that it has been possible to identify and isolate some of the essential components which fused together to create a definitive stage in the recognition of children as distinct from adults in the processes of criminal justice, the development of the reformatory system. Studying extracts from the writings of the evangelical philanthropists to uncover the constructions of childhood to which they adhered has revealed a cluster of cultural assumptions. The reformers did not limit themselves to one narrow religious construction of childhood; unconsciously or otherwise, they subsumed ideas from Rousseau, the Romantics and the Bible, as well as predominant cultural notions like the Victorian domestic ideal of childhood as part of the bourgeois family. Their visions of childhood attached themselves to the epitome of Foucauldian coercive technology, and, with missionary zeal, English reformers sought to transplant a version of this new disciplinary ideal to native soil.[110] Of course, it has to be said that Foucault's interpretation is not one that the evangelical reformers themselves would ever have remotely recognised as having any merit, guided as they were by their unwavering, well-intentioned certainty in the power of their particularly active and muscular form of Christianity.[111] And it could well be the case that Foucault's argument overstated the coercive nature of Mettray.[112] But the important point to be emphasised here is that the formalisation of diversionary practices in legislation marked a critical turning point in the culture of criminal justice as applied to children. Despite the many problems that the legislative framework was to create for Scottish children in particular, on one level this was at least a positive acknowledgement of the wisdom of Rousseau's insight, enshrined parliamentarily, that a child was a child.

Evangelicals, juvenile justice reform and social control

So far this account has concentrated on a cultural perspective of events. Of course, it has to be conceded that the perspective offered by Aries and Elias can be criticised for a cultural focus which pays insufficient attention to economic determinants and the demands of the expanding capitalist economy. From the Marxist viewpoint, seemingly benign, humanitarian, civilising advances promoting the welfare of children can be seen as masking a strategy of social control which, according to this understanding, provided universal education for the masses simply to produce docile and malleable citizens well imbued with a disciplinary work ethic which would further the needs of the growing economy.[113] Similar arguments about an insidious agenda of extending social control aimed at preserving social order and maintaining the dominant power of the ruling class have been made about the early nineteenth-century humanitarian efforts to reform the criminal justice system.[114]

However, in a study of evangelicals and their influence on penal reform in the early nineteenth century, Richard Follett points out that there was nothing covert about the aims of the humanitarian reformers.[115] Follett examines the role of the parliamentary evangelicals active in penal reform, particularly those associated with Wilberforce – known as 'the Saints' – whose very active brand of optimistic faith led them to press for changes in the criminal justice system. He describes the role of Thomas Buxton, who was inspired to campaign for penal reform after witnessing the plight of children incarcerated in Newgate Prison, some of whom were imprisoned for capital offences. As will be seen later, Buxton did much to highlight the problems of street children in pioneering a criminological investigation into juvenile criminality. Follett argues that these humanitarian, evangelical reformers were quite open about wishing to preserve the existing social hierarchy. They saw nothing wrong in that; they did not set out to overthrow what they regarded as the natural order in which they assumed a comfortable position themselves: they simply wished to make things better, and they did.[116]

While not acceding to the Radzinowicz view of the steady progress of humanitarian reform and taking note of the counterarguments, Follett is struck by the potency, efficacy and genuine altruistic motivation of these parliamentary evangelical reformers. He cautions against the structuralist temptation to succumb to the 'politicisation of all relationships in society' and notes a revisiting of the social control debate by Michael Ignatieff in the light of the recognition that accounts too directed towards seeing penal reforms as the reproduction of power relations were missing an essential human component.[117] The point here is that while humanitarian reformers may, from an objective standpoint and with the benefit of Marxist insights, not have been entirely selfless, in that they could be regarded as having contributed to the reproduction of power relations by supporting the existing social order and to that extent endeavoured to keep everyone in their rightful place, that is certainly not how they would have seen it. As far as they were concerned, they were simply seeking, as Buxton put it, 'to assist in checking and diminishing crime and its consequent misery'.[118]

Ideas put into practice

The civilising, humanitarian narrative, with its emphasis on the need to protect the vulnerable, innocent child, was a key element in underpinning the idea that the brutalising effects of work were incompatible with the new vision of childhood, and that children should be liberated from the burdens of the wage-earning. This represented a major change in perception. At the end of the eighteenth century and well into the nineteenth century, there had been a cultural expectation that the children of the poor would help contribute to the family income. Indeed, children were a significant element of the workforce, and the rapidly expanding economy made full use of cheap child labour. The historian E. P. Thompson states that 'there was a drastic increase in the intensity of exploitation of child labour between 1780 and 1840'.[119] Humphries too attests to the high levels of child labour throughout the British industrial revolution.[120]

Children were employed from an early age in a variety of different areas such as mines, factories, domestic cottage industries and as chimney sweeps. They worked hard for long hours, often in dangerous conditions. The pillow lace industry employed children as young as three or four to handle bobbins. During the course of the nineteenth century a number of commissions were set up to investigate the employment of children, and gradually statutory restrictions were introduced. For example, under The Factory Act of 1819 no child under the age of nine was to be employed in cotton mills, and The Factory Act of 1833 extended the restrictions to other types of factories and imposed a requirement of a minimum of two hours schooling a day for children aged nine to thirteen. By the time of The Factory Act of 1878 the minimum age of employment was raised to fourteen. The changes did not meet with universal approval. They met with resentment not just from employers but from some parents too, who saw nothing wrong with the existing practices and were anxious not to lose the income provided by the labour of their offspring. The cultural resistance to change was also bolstered by reluctance to interfere with the presumption that parents could determine for themselves how their children would be brought up. However, the growing recognition of the need for the statutory protection of children in the area of employment did reflect a gradual sensitising of public opinion to the rights of children, accompanied by increasing awareness of their special vulnerability.

Hand in hand with the new statutory protection of children in the workplace came the development of the principle of education as a universal and compulsory requirement for all children. The introduction of mass compulsory education with the Education Acts of the 1870s set the seal on the new vision of childhood.[121] From then on, the legal requirement to attend school imposed a new daily discipline and order on childhood, creating a wholly new idea of a 'national', regulated childhood for all which, at least conceptually, was envisaged as encompassing children throughout all of society, regardless of location or class.[122] This new conception of a dependent childhood which eschewed the concept of the child as wage earner was fostered by the Romantic vision.

However, this vision of universal full-time education was compromised for many children, especially in the textile-manufacturing areas, by a practice known as the half-time system, which continued to operate after the Education Acts of the 1870s. This led to some children entering half-time employment after the age of ten. They attended school for half the day and worked in mills for the other half, which was exhausting for the children concerned: as Brian Simon argues, 'on any human grounds the system was indefensible', and, as Simon shows, it was a cause taken up by the growing socialist movement.[123] Clearly the new education system had its shortcomings. Idealised visions certainly did not translate into a new utopia for children, and, as both Aries and Foucault emphasise, the regime of the school opened the way for a whole new world of disciplinary initiatives governing children's lives. Thus, the undoubted progression represented by education had its inevitable downside – the civilising aspect and the less wholesome, arguably decivilising, aspect. Nevertheless, the advent of mass compulsory education was one aspect of a seismic change of attitude which had its counterpart across the whole of children's lives, including how they were perceived within the criminal justice system.

And in the secluded domain of the home, according to Aries in his discussion of the changing ideas about childhood over the centuries, the child had become by the nineteenth century and up to the present time, the focus of the private world of the family.[124] The child had become clearly distinguished sartorially in terms of separate dress for children, and in terms of educational provision, with entry into the adult world now deferred until the proper period of education had been completed. There were now children's games and pastimes, and a whole new literature specially catering for children.[125] The child was now a child.

This was a recognisably modern notion of childhood, and it was sanctified by the bourgeois Victorian idealisation of the family. However, the idealisation did not reflect the reality of life for many children, especially the children of the urban poor, who were the children most likely to come to the attention of the criminal justice system.

THE CONCEPT OF THE YOUNG OFFENDER

As has become evident, the new, more modern ideas of childhood were critical in forming the idea of the child as distinct from adults. Progressive, humanitarian trends emanating from the worlds of literature, evangelical action and politics combined forces to protect the vulnerable and innocent child in the workplace, and redefine the school as the proper locus for childhood. However, in this section it will be shown that at the same time as the civilising narrative was beginning to see the need in the criminal justice system for separate institutions for young offenders, decivilising impulses were operating perversely in another direction to mobilise the might of criminal justice agencies to deal oppressively with children of the urban poor, who were perceived as young offenders posing a real threat to social order.

The growing cultural awareness of the distinctness of children generally, and in the criminal justice system in particular, was inextricably linked to the development of the concept of the young offender. With the institution of the reformatory system came official recognition that the young offender was a separate category of 'criminal', and that a different type of treatment was therefore called for. But what exactly was a young offender in nineteenth-century terms, and how did the young offender come to be recognised as a different sort of criminal? This raises the question of what was perceived as offending behaviour by children. It also raises some terminological issues about how offending children were referred to. The term *juvenile delinquent* was in use throughout the nineteenth century. Its use can be seen in the name of the early nineteenth-century Society for Investigating the Causes of the Alarming Increase of Juvenile Delinquency in the Metropolis and was used in the society's Report of 1816 into juvenile delinquency.[126] It was also used by Mary Carpenter in her treatise of 1853, *Juvenile Delinquents – their Conditions and Treatment*. Although the description was in common use throughout the nineteenth century, scholars point to the term having developed a different connotation by the late nineteenth and early twentieth centuries, a meaning which had more in common with some contemporary interpretations of delinquency.[127]

For instance, Hendrick argues that before the 1880s juvenile delinquency was a concept that was understood to apply exclusively to children of the impoverished classes, but new ideas about the psychology of adolescence towards the end of the century heralded a change in ideas about delinquency, which came to be seen as being related to age and psychology rather than purely associated with economic and social factors.[128]

In this analysis, the less censorious term *young offender* has been used to describe the children convicted of criminal activity in the nineteenth century. This term is more appropriate than describing such children as juvenile delinquents, not just because this avoids any terminological confusion related to period, but because closer analysis of the kind of conduct that was considered 'criminal' activity by children reveals that the use of a term denoting censure is far from warranted: in the main the children regarded as criminals were destitute, abandoned street children whose 'crimes' represented a survival strategy.

How did young offenders come to be regarded as an identifiable group? Growing awareness of young offenders as an identifiable and particularly troublesome social problem was evident from the second decade of the nineteenth century. Peter King argues that changing social and economic factors in this period of intense industrialisation led to large numbers of children being forced to live on the streets. Linked to this was a new 'desire to discipline rather than ignore juvenile offenders', marking a departure from traditional diversionary practices with regard to offending children.[129] King states that this was related to changes in criminal justice administration, meaning that fewer capital sentences were carried out. The moves 'towards indicting young offenders and then having them tried summarily . . . were both reacting to, and fuelling a new set of discourses'.[130]

This reactionary response to young offenders occurred at a time of intense sensitivity to the dangers posed by urban unrest in the aftermath of the French Revolution. In a classic example of competing narratives, this perception of the young offender as a threat was countered by humanitarian philanthropy, which sought to help the vulnerable children of the streets and understand what was causing them to offend. Motivated by the same brand of 'active', muscular religious passion as those instrumental in the reformatory campaign, evangelical philanthropists carried out the first systematic attempt to analyse the cause of juvenile crime. In 1816, the Society for Investigating the Causes of the Alarming Increase of Juvenile Delinquency in the Metropolis, including Thomas Buxton, brother-in-law of prison reformer Elizabeth Fry, and the Quaker Peter Bedford, known as the 'Spitalfields Philanthropist', conducted an innovative questionnaire-based inquiry into the extent and causes of juvenile criminality in London.[131] When this pioneering criminological study was completed, one of Bedford's friends wrote that the findings 'were truly awful to contemplate'.[132] The Report spoke volumes about the problems faced by destitute and desperate children.[133] Typical life stories of young offenders indicated that the problem of juvenile criminality was associated with profound social problems of deprivation, abandonment and neglect, which showed that 'commission of crime' was an integral part of a terrible struggle for survival for many children. The Report concluded that the most important causes of delinquency were parental neglect, lack of education, unemployment, gambling, irreverence, the inadequacy of policing – essentially corruption – and the severity of the criminal law.[134] The effect of the Report was to provide inspiration for humanitarian attempts to set up voluntary institutions aimed at the reformation, and not simply the punishment, of juvenile offenders, and also to encourage efforts to bring about legal change. This new focus on the 'problem' and causes of youthful offending and the appearance of new discourses about the subject, referred to by King, brought recognition of young offenders as belonging to a distinct group, which was a necessary precursor to the differentiation of children from adults in the criminal justice system.

Contributions by other scholars discuss the continuing development of the recognition of the young offender as a specific category throughout the first half of the nineteenth century.[135] For instance, May notes the importance of statistics about purported rises in juvenile crime and the impact of a number of unofficial investigations into the causes of juvenile crime in the 1830s and 1840s. These factors highlighted the awareness of the young offender as a distinct group. May's findings on the burgeoning literature on juvenile crime were reflected in the Scottish context too, with much pamphlet literature on the topic. May comments that middle-class investigators like lawyers and ministers who conducted the inquiries into the conditions of juvenile crime were shocked by their discoveries which 'violated their images of childhood'.[136] The evidence was mounting that a new cultural configuration was taking place in which constructions of the child as innocent and vulnerable were disturbingly at odds with the reality of life for impoverished street children.

Juvenile delinquency

In 'The Invention of Juvenile Delinquency in Early Nineteenth Century England',[137] Susan Margarey presents an argument that can be interpreted as illustrating a clear example of the decivilising impact of criminal justice practices in criminalising children. She argues that the 'problem' of the young offender was constructed in the early nineteenth century by a combination of changes in legislation and the policing of the young, which acted together to criminalise children.[138] She cites as important instances of legislative change two measures introduced during Peel's reforming era as part of a scheme to modernise the criminal justice system. The Vagrancy Act of 1824 created the offence of being 'a suspected person or reputed thief'[139] and designated as 'rogues and vagabonds'[140] those found betting in the street. Susan Margarey points out that this may have been directed at particular problems caused by identifiable groups causing a nuisance such as 'Bouncers and Besters',[141] but the effect it had in practice was to extend the boundaries of what was recognised as criminal conduct to include innocent games of marbles or pitch and toss played by children in the street for small amounts of money, or even just buttons.[142] The Malicious Trespass Act of 1827 also operated to criminalise children: the Act amended existing legislation so as to remove the harsh penalty of possible transportation for entering an orchard or garden and stealing produce like trees and plants, but it also made it an offence to damage fruit growing in a garden or orchard. This meant that children picking apples from a tree overhanging a garden wall were criminalised.[143] In these early nineteenth-century examples the criminalisation of children turned out to be almost an incidental feature of the legislation. The statutory provisions were not concerned with children in particular, but their implementation by the agencies of criminal justice impacted heavily on children in criminalising behaviour by them which was perceived to be a nuisance.

Margarey also notes the effect of the introduction of the 'new police'[144] on the increase in the number of children being arrested, arguing that both Metropolitan Police Acts targeted working-class leisure activities, especially those of children playing on the streets.[145] She comments that the methods adopted by the police also acted to the disadvantage of children: there is evidence that policing of children was carried out particularly vigorously because police presenting cases in court could incur costs if there was no conviction and they were more likely to succeed against children. Margarey's argument suggests that the concept of the young offender was effectively created by the unintended consequences of legislative action, which were then compounded by the practices of the new police. As will be seen in the next chapter, Margarey's interpretation has striking parallels with developments taking place in Scotland in the same period: the combination of the development of urban policing, the expansion of summary procedure and the impact of new criminal prohibitions on children's activities on the streets all operated together to criminalise Scottish children in a blend of factors which strongly resonated with the situation in metropolitan London described by Margarey.

While Margarey's argument is convincingly borne out by similar Scottish developments, other scholars like Shore and Cox are more cautious about the idea of the 'invention' or 're-invention' of delinquency in specific periods, pointing out that such ideas are problematic because similar types of troublesome conduct and regulatory reactions were equally evident in the seventeenth century as well as the nineteenth.[146] Nonetheless, Shore agrees in *Artful Dodgers* that the early nineteenth century has been recognised as a 'watershed' in its focus on delinquency because of the coalescence of seminal changes in society across politics and the economy.[147]

Developments in Scotland also resonate with King's research on the role of diversionary practices in London. As noted earlier, his work on the London Refuge for the Destitute reveals that in the first three decades of the nineteenth century, judges at the Old Bailey were engaged in diversionary sentencing policies where judgement was respited and young offenders were sent instead to the reformatory institution, the Refuge for the Destitute.[148] He demonstrates how the Refuge changed over time from an establishment dealing with both destitute and criminal cases to one focusing on young offenders. Fascinatingly, he argues that the reformatory's transition to a prison-like institution was precarious in legal terms, existing on the margins of legality, because it had no legal authority to detain inmates against their will. Despite this, of the three reformatory institutions in operation in England at that time, the Refuge was the only one which succeeded in procuring state funding; the other two, the Philanthropic and a small asylum at Stretton on Dunsmore, depended on philanthropic funding. The part played by the judiciary here in devising new diversionary methods has significant parallels with the role of Scottish judges in seeking alternatives to imprisonment for young offenders. As Shore and Cox have emphasised, the quest to find new ways to respond to problematic youth was a familiar theme in many jurisdictions.[149] In the French context, for example, Nilan's analysis of children's trials in the French legal journal *La Gazette des Tribunaux*, 1830–40, uncovers many of the same issues and responses to juvenile offending as in 1840s Aberdeen: these included juvenile vagrancy, parental indifference, similar explanations for the causes of crime, and philanthropic and judicial reaction.[150] So developments in Scotland did not occur in isolation.

By the latter part of the nineteenth century, it is commonly argued, the idea of the young offender altered with the advancement of yet another conceptualisation of childhood – the scientific construction which was born with the advent of new psychological understandings of the nature of adolescence.[151] Gillis talks of the 'discovery' and 'invention' of adolescence as this stage of life became subject to closer scrutiny, with this developmental phase being regarded as causally linked to misconduct.[152] However, it is important to point out that, while it is true that new scientific ideas about young offenders were widely circulated, there was also considerable resistance to certain strands of new scientific thought about the causes of juvenile criminality, as will be discussed in chapter four. But despite this, the late nineteenth-century scientific focus on the child was certainly influential. This concentration on childhood was accentuated by the introduction of mass compulsory schooling. Education for all made childhood a matter of regulation and discipline for all. Childhood was investigated as never before. Hendrick notes that the medical profession, along with social scientists and voluntary workers, seized on the school population as an object of study; he argues that by the 1890s '"the child" had been discovered', a discovery which encompassed both physical and psychological understandings.[153] This scientific dimension offered a new level of awareness, a new perspective on notions of childhood; this complemented the already recognisably modern concept of childhood described by Aries, which had emerged in the course of the civilising process. This had been invested with a new emotional intensity by a powerful blend of cultural influences, including literature and religion. All in all there was no longer any room for doubt that 'a child was a child', and it was only a matter of time before this undisputed recognition became embodied in criminal justice terms in the shape of a court designated specially for the young, the juvenile court.[154]

CONCLUSION

The question posed initially was how the fuller recognition of the special status of young offenders emerged in the course of the nineteenth century. By the end of the century, children were dealt with in separate institutions, the reformatory and industrial schools, and the new juvenile court had been established. As has become apparent, the new modern ideas of childhood were seminal. They created the image of the child as a distinct being, different from adults and not just a smaller version of adults: the child was innocent, vulnerable and in need of protection. This image was fostered by a new cultural configuration across the fields of literature, religion and political action inspired by civilising, human-itarian impulses, which culminated in a new awakening of the public conscience. There was a heightened sensitivity to the special position of children, which emphasised the wrongness of children being imprisoned with adults. It stressed the need to expedite their passage through the criminal justice process. In line with the new appreciation of the child's vulnerability and impressionability there were moves to extend the use of summary procedure for young offenders in order to process their cases quickly and avoid periods of remand where they were likely to be con-taminated by contact with adult prisoners.[155] On the other hand, there were more *regressive* impulses (to borrow Elias's terminology),[156] which viewed children of the streets as a threat to social stability which had to be dealt with by means of oppressive criminal justice practices, thus effectively criminalising large numbers of children. This tension between differing perspectives is evident throughout the nineteenth century.

A significant conclusion to be drawn from this chapter is the impor-tance of a framework for analysing criminalisation of children. There were certain key elements consistently operating in criminalisation, including the role played by criminal justice actors such as the police or the judiciary. This point is underlined by Lacey's, Ashworth's and Horder's recognition that while formal legislation may be the first stage, the practical impact of formal criminalisation is felt in its enforcement by criminal justice agencies. How children were policed is one of the key elements in studying criminalisation. It was the way in which legislative change was implemented by vigorous policing practices, which led to large numbers of children being ushered into the criminal justice process in early nineteenth-century London and also in Scotland, as will be seen in the next chapter.[157] This was at a time, as today, when there was a 'moral panic' about juvenile crime.[158] A similar pattern of over-enthusiastic policing in response to public concern about offending has also been detected in the closing decades of the nineteenth century, when it has been argued there was more robust policing of boisterous behaviour on the streets, and a move away from dealing informally with minor mis-conduct to prosecution.[159] And this is a pattern which has contemporary parallels too.[160] Many issues in present-day juvenile justice have well-established historical antecedents.

Analysing the part played by the judiciary is vital too. This involves considering not only the traditional role of judges in sentencing and the imposition of punishment; it also entails examining their activities on a political level in bringing about change in ways of dealing with young offenders. Policing and judicial activity have to be considered in

conjunction with other crucial issues, such as how children were subjected to criminal procedure. Another key factor to examine is how they
were affected by changes in legislation, particularly the legislation on
industrial and reformatory schools, or the new criminal prohibitions
designed to maintain order in expanding towns and cities. These are
key elements in the criminalisation of children in nineteenth-century
Scotland.

2

Pressure for Reform

INTRODUCTION

The aim of this chapter is to examine the criminalisation of children in Scotland in the period 1840–60. In the course of these decades there were some remarkable developments in approaches to juvenile offending which were to have far-reaching consequences for children throughout the remainder of the nineteenth century. If one year out of these twenty were to be selected as the most significant, the one which in many senses marked a watershed, it would be 1854. This was the year that saw the introduction of two important statutes which represented the foundation of a whole body of legislation governing certified reformatory and industrial schools in Scotland.[1] This was the statutory framework defining the parliamentary response to 'criminal and destitute children'.[2] For ease of analysis, this discussion will adopt the terms 'pre-statutory system' to refer to the years prior to 1854, before the introduction of the legislation, and 'statutory system' to refer to the post-legislative situation in 1854 and thereafter. The chapter explores the various strands of the pre-statutory system. It then tracks developments through to the early stages of the statutory system.

New approaches to juvenile crime occurred in the wider context of seminal changes taking place in the administration of justice in Scotland, such as the development of policing and the expanding use of summary process in the courts. These changes were accompanied by a major increase in the criminalisation of children. There is evidence that with the introduction of regular urban police in Scottish cities there was more vigorous policing, which brought more children within the ambit of the criminal justice system, and that the availability of summary processes then accelerated children's progress through the system, drawing them deeper into the criminal justice net.[3] These issues are discussed in the first substantive section of this chapter, which looks at the background to reform in Scotland in the 1840s.

Still in the pre-statutory period, the chapter considers the effect of new schemes adopted in Scottish cities to try a fresh approach to the problems posed by juvenile crime, looking in particular at the systems operating in the 1840s in Glasgow, Aberdeen and Edinburgh. These systems emerged as a result of local, philanthropically inspired initiatives, the most notable example of which was a scheme of industrial schools set up by Sheriff William Watson in Aberdeen. His vision was particularly influential in inspiring reform initiatives throughout Scotland, and indeed across the whole of the UK, but other Scottish cities had their own unique ways of responding to the pressures of coping with the problems posed by nineteenth-century urban youth.

By the early 1850s there was a growing demand for legislative action to put industrial schools on a statutory footing and to empower magistrates to have the legal authority to compel children to attend industrial schools under court order. This campaign for legislation occurred within the context of an impetus for reform on the issue of juvenile offenders gathering momentum south of the border, and against a wider backdrop of parallel developments occurring in other jurisdictions.[4] Next the chapter examines the impetus for reform which ushered in the statutory system. It considers the role of the Scottish reformers William Watson, Alexander Thomson and Thomas Guthrie and their interaction with reformers in England such as Mary Carpenter; and it looks at the emergence of the legislation. The final section of the chapter examines the early years of the statutory system. This incorporates a case study of a test case under the new legislation, the first High Court case in Scotland under the Reformatory Schools Scotland Act of 1854, with a discussion of its significance.

Much of the history of criminalisation of children in nineteenth-century Scotland is a story of diversionary tactics, of new methods deflecting children to some degree from the arena of criminal justice processes applied to adults. For example, in Glasgow in the 1840s a system of pre-trial diversion for juveniles was developed in which a child charged with an offence could opt to become an inmate of a House of Refuge rather than proceed to trial. The same period also saw Scottish magistrates sending children appearing before them directly to the emerging network of industrial schools instead of to prison. In some cases, magistrates simply dismissed children appearing before the courts on a first offence to the care of parents or guardians with a caution. For many magistrates there was a growing feeling of dissatisfaction with the use of imprisonment in dealing with juvenile offenders. Not only did it expose children to adverse influences, it was also a hopeless deterrent, and a spell in prison branded a child for life, making it difficult to secure future employment. Many magistrates were also well aware of the absurdity of imprisoning young children for minor offences like begging or trivial theft when they were utterly destitute and the commission of these offences was their only means of survival.

As fuller recognition of the special status and vulnerability of young offenders emerged in the course of the century, diversionary methods were used to create systems consistent with the new awareness of the special position of children. There were moves to extend the use of summary procedure for young offenders in order to process their cases quickly and avoid periods of remand where they were likely to be contaminated by contact with adult prisoners. This was a reflection of the new appreciation of the child's vulnerability and impressionability. As argued in the previous chapter, this heightened sensitivity to the plight of children incarcerated along with adults was inspired to a large extent by civilising, humanitarian impulses, all part of a new awakening of the public conscience. This fostered the recognition of the special position of children in the criminal justice process as well as other areas of life, highlighting their vulnerability to the excesses of exploitation in the labour market and also the need to introduce measures to protect them from the relentless demands of economic expansion.

Unfortunately, this diversionary route in the sphere of criminal justice led to an unexpected destination. Diversion may have seemed to be a benign, civilising, child-friendly approach but it had unintended, arguably decivilising, consequences which saw more and more children drawn into the criminal justice net. This is what happened with the development of summary procedure. This is also what ultimately happened with the creation of the statutory system certifying separate establishments for young offenders and those regarded as in danger of becoming offenders, as large numbers of children came to be detained in reformatory and industrial schools, institutions which were penal in nature.[5] In many ways this can be seen as a tale of good intentions turning out badly. The architects of reform were motivated by the highest of humanitarian principles, and there was without doubt much to admire in the Scottish pre-statutory system they developed. William Watson in particular laboured tirelessly to improve the position of the most disadvantaged children, those destitute and vagrant who were most likely to find themselves before the courts. Sadly, to a large degree the statutory system which evolved from 1854 onwards departed significantly from the ideals of the reformers, creating a framework which was often oppressive for the children it was designed to help.[6] The change in the character of the system did not happen overnight. It was not even fully evident by 1860, the end point of the present chapter, for reasons which will be discussed. However, as subsequent chapters will reveal, over the course of time there was a marked change in ethos.

Much of the chapter concerns responses to minor offences committed by children. In general, most of the crime committed by children was of a fairly trivial nature, often petty thefts. Of course, there were also instances of more serious offending by children. The first part of the chapter refers to some cases in the 1840s involving more grave offences coming before the High Court of Justiciary, for which the penalty of transportation was imposed. By the early 1850s, transportation had more or less been abandoned as a punishment,[7] and even in the most serious cases judicial execution of juveniles was not in practice carried out.[8] However, imprisonment of children was commonplace and continued to be used as a punishment throughout the century. When certified reformatory schools for convicted juvenile offenders were introduced, the legislation required that admission be preceded by a minimum period of prior imprisonment, initially of fourteen days (although this was not the case for industrial schools, as will be explained later). The legislation empowered judges to send convicted children to the reformatories, but sentences solely involving imprisonment remained an option for judges and continued to be used, as did other forms of punishment such as whipping or the imposition of fines.

In most cases, children who came to the attention of the criminal justice system did so because of minor misconduct. Following the introduction of the statutory system, many of these children found themselves detained in institutions. But, although it is true that nearly all of the children in reformatories were there for fairly minor matters, it would be a mistake to assume that the statutory reformatory system was reserved only for minor offenders. In Scotland there were cases where children who had committed theft by housebreaking, regarded as a serious crime, were sentenced to five years in a reformatory.[9] (Five years was the standard period of committal to reformatories, even for trivial thefts.[10]) And in England in 1861, two young children found guilty of manslaughter were sentenced to a month's imprisonment followed by five years in a reformatory school. This was the case of two eight-year-olds, Peter Barratt and James Bradley, when a two-year-old boy, George Burgess, was killed.[11]

Much of the material in the later section of the chapter on the statutory system involves a discussion of the initial pieces of legislation relating to reformatory and industrial schools in Scotland. The existing literature on this topic concentrates on the general historical or sociological perspective[12] but does not address the legal dimension. As noted earlier, the welcome exception is recent work by Barrie and Broomhall on police courts in nineteenth-century Scotland, which does explore court practices.[13]

I have attempted in this book to examine the full details of legislative provisions and their interpretation by the courts, demonstrating the way changes in legislation were applied in practice to children. This has presented many challenges. This is complicated by the fact that one of the first major pieces of legislation introduced in Scotland in 1854 applied only to Scotland,[14] while the other 1854 Act applied across the UK,[15] meaning that in Scotland both Acts applied but in England only one of the Acts applied. There were teething problems with the setting up of the statutory system, and later amending legislation applying across the UK was introduced,[16] followed by an Act applying to England only.[17] All this is immensely complex to map out, absorb and then explain. It is further complicated by the fact that although some of the legislation applied across the UK, there were considerable differences in the pre-statutory situation in Scotland and England. Scotland had a pre-existing network of well-established day industrial feeding schools, which was not the case in England, yet a national inspectorate was set up to oversee both Scotland and England, resulting in pressure to fit the operations in both countries into the same mould. In essence, Scotland and England were approaching the problem from different starting positions and this caused considerable confusion, which was reflected in a legislative morass.

THE PRE-STATUTORY SYSTEM: THE SCOTTISH SYSTEM IN THE 1840s

According to one historian, 'life in Scotland in the 1840s was competitive, unprotected, brutal and, for many, vile'.[18] Faced with the problems associated with rapid industrialisation and population growth, Scottish cities were an inhospitable and dangerous environment for the children of the urban poor. New building required for industrial development had displaced many families, forcing them to move from areas formerly lived in by the poor to already overcrowded areas where conditions were often appalling. A contemporary source commented on the situation in the alleys of Glasgow in 1848:

> In every variety of form, – misery, crime, disease and filth exist here. In the houses, – dirt, damp, and decay reign triumphant.[19]

Apart from the squalor and disease, the writer also recorded the plight of many children who were orphaned, abandoned or driven from homes where they were unwanted. Such children were forced by poverty to beg or steal to survive. The situation in Edinburgh was similar. Testifying to a whole range of social problems facing the poor, Thomas Guthrie said that many children were encouraged to steal by their parents and that the sight of children begging on the streets was common.[20] Vagrancy was an immense problem both in cities and in rural areas. Giving evidence to a parliamentary committee on the subject of Criminal and Destitute Children, Guthrie described the transient population of juvenile vagrants as 'the waifs' who in his view formed the basis of the 'large mass of criminals'.[21] Sheriff Watson in Aberdeen also had much to say on the subject of juvenile vagrancy, which he too saw as the avenue to a life of crime.[22] With problems of this magnitude it is not surprising that many children came to the attention of the courts.

We can gain a very good impression of how the courts dealt with juvenile offenders by examining evidence provided to the 1847 *Select Committee of the House of Lords to inquire into the execution of the criminal law especially respecting juvenile offenders and transportation*.[23] This is a very significant source of information containing evidence from a number of Scottish judges, including the two most senior Senators of the College of Justice, the Lord Justice General, Lord Boyle, the Lord Justice Clerk, Lord Hope, several other High Court judges and a Sheriff from Perth, with details of their perception of the criminal justice system as applied to young offenders. The initial part of the chapter draws on this Report as one important source for examining the position of children within the criminal justice system in Scotland in the 1840s. The accounts provided by the judges are particularly interesting in their references to the new system in operation in Glasgow, which is described in more detail later in the chapter, but their references to the Glasgow initiative were set within the context of more general responses to questions posed about the effectiveness of the Scottish courts in dealing with young offenders.

Answering a question about instances of 'boys of fifteen and under' appearing before the High Court either in Edinburgh or on circuit, the judges said that these cases usually concerned children who had repeatedly appeared before the inferior courts and had a long record of previous convictions.[24] They indicated that cases before the High Court involving first offences were rare, only occurring where the young person had been acting with older people or where the offence was of an 'aggravated nature'.[25] The Lord Justice Clerk explained the significance of the role of the public prosecutor in Scotland in deciding the appropriate forum for trial.

> Juvenile offenders are seldom brought before the High Court for a first offence, very rarely indeed. The system of a Public Prosecutor secures the appropriate selection of the proper tribunal. Hence, except in some rare cases where the Lord Advocate or his Deputes have had sufficient ground for such a decision the juvenile offenders are all tried in the first instance *summarily*, either in a Police Court or before the Sheriff, without juries, the greatest length of imprisonment being sixty days, and then are directed to be tried on after offences before the Sheriff and a jury when longer imprisonments are pronounced.[26]

In those cases where young offenders were convicted before the High Court, he explained that they were normally sentenced to long periods of imprisonment, noting that transportation was reserved for 'a very bad case'.[27] He argued that the system of imprisonment had 'wholly failed' to 'reclaim' young offenders:

> The *short* imprisonment to which such offenders are subjected on summary convictions in police courts or before the Sheriffs generally produce no other effect than to *render them utterly indifferent to that punishment*, especially as the separate system in many places cannot be acted upon in regard to them.[28] We have seen cases of lads of sixteen or seventeen who from the age of ten or twelve or upwards have been six, eight or ten times convicted, sometimes tried before the Sheriff and a jury, and sentenced to long imprisonments in which the separate system was acted upon; but returning *undeterred and unreformed*. But I ascribe the failure as to boys very much as to the evils of association with bad companions during the short imprisonments to which they are at first subjected, and to the impossibility of making any impression on them during, say, forty or sixty days.[29] (All emphasis in original text).

He recommended a programme of prison expansion in the larger cities to enable the separate system of detention to be fully implemented so that young offenders would be detained in individual cells, thereby removing them from contamination and giving them the opportunity to take advantage of 'admirable instruction, strict discipline and useful labour'.[30] He praised the Governor of Aberdeen gaol for having effected the separate system in his prison even for short sentences.

Reviewing the changes which had occurred during his career, which had included spells as an Advocate Depute and as Solicitor General, he alluded to a very significant statute also discussed by some of the other judges, an Act introduced by Lord Advocate Sir William Rae in 1828.[31] This Act allowed Sheriffs to try summarily, subject to review by the High Court, any cases which the public prosecutor did not consider suitable for the High Court. He attributed to this statute a decrease in the numbers of boys and girls appearing before the High Court. However, he complained about young offenders being 'tried too often in that summary form', resulting in them becoming hardened by repeated short prison sentences and ending up as 'incorrigible' by the time they came to be sentenced to long periods of imprisonment.[32] He also noted that since 1830 the numbers of young offenders under the age of fifteen had greatly increased throughout the country, even becoming common in small towns which were never before troubled by juvenile crime.

This perception of rising levels of juvenile crime is indicative of the less than salutary impact of a measure which, in theory, should have ameliorated the position of children in the criminal justice system. The use of summary jurisdiction for young offenders was intended to deal swiftly with their cases, thus eliminating the contaminating effect of spending long periods in prison awaiting trial. However, here we see that while children were processed more quickly, the effect was like that of a revolving door, where they were repeatedly being given short prison sentences, acquiring a long record of previous convictions, and then appearing in a higher court under solemn procedure to be given long sentences or sometimes even transported to a convict colony. The extension of summary procedure churned young offenders through at a faster rate, producing seasoned child convicts more efficiently than ever before. It is likely too that under summary procedure there was more readiness to prosecute trivial matters: while the scarcity of records means that it is difficult to substantiate this proposition with statistical evidence, the likelihood of a trend in this direction is supported by research carried out on parallel developments in England. The work of Peter King in relation to summary procedure in early nineteenth-century England demonstrates that the availability of a quicker form of process was associated with increased willingness to prosecute minor offences.[33] Clive Emsley makes a similar point with regard to a perceived increase in criminal statistics for convictions in some English courts after legislation widening the use of summary processes there. He argues: 'This seems best understood not as an increase in crime *per se*, but as an increase in prosecutions before summary courts which were greatly facilitated by the legislation.'[34]

In Scotland there is clear evidence to show that children appeared before the courts much more frequently than before. This created the illusion of an increase in juvenile crime. For example, the 1843 Report by the Governor of Aberdeen prison discussed the causes of an increase in commitments of boys under the age of twelve and was unequivocal about the impact of the extensive use of summary procedure:

> Many causes may be assigned for this increase of juvenile delinquency . . . but I fear there is another cause operating gradually, surely, in extending the evil and that is the repeatedly trying of young persons for offences before the inferior courts, where the magistrates cannot sentence to a longer imprisonment than 60 days.[35]

However, the judiciary were strongly convinced of the advantages of summary procedure and presented it as a model to be emulated in less well-developed jurisdictions, by which they meant England. Like the Lord Justice Clerk, the other Scottish judges were able to answer a general question posed on the role of summary procedure for juveniles by responding that it was a well-established aspect of practice in Scotland. Clearly of the opinion that Scottish criminal procedure was far in advance of English practice in this respect, Lord Cockburn commented that he could barely comprehend a legal system without this essential feature.[36]

The Scottish judges were keen to promote the virtues of Scots Law and this was not the only example of barbed comments being made at the expense of the English. For instance, on the question of the type of labour carried out by prisoners, the Lord Justice Clerk pointedly commented that in Scottish prisons there was no time for the notion of '*hard* labour': on the contrary, only '*useful* labour' was permitted in Scottish prisons.[37] This rather scathing attitude towards the English system seems to have been current in Scottish legal circles.[38] In his writings, the Sheriff of Lanark, Archibald, was also keen to convey the superior nature of Scottish legal administration.[39] As Farmer notes, Scottish lawyers were concerned to underline differentiation from English law especially in criminal law, a key area of Scottish national identity after the 1707 Treaty of Union.[40]

The Select Committee also asked if it was advisable to give powers to dismiss cases 'with or without whipping'. In response to this, most of the Scottish judges cautioned against the dangers of whipping.[41] Lord Cockburn remarked that it could be accompanied by 'undetected cruelty' or could have the effect of 'making the culprit a greater blackguard than he was'.[42] On a similar note, the Lord Justice Clerk remarked that whipping was not practised or recommended in Scotland.[43]

The evidence of Scottish judges on the usefulness of summary procedure was extremely influential in the extension of summary procedure
south of the border later the same year under the 1847 *Act for the more
speedy Trial and Punishment of Juvenile Offenders*.[44] Some commentators have argued that this Act and the later amendments of it were
instrumental in the creation of a massive rise in the number of prosecutions of young people in England, to the extent that there appeared to be
a 'youth crime wave'.[45] Arguably this theory on the impact of summary
jurisdiction could be applied to parallel developments in Scotland from
1828 onwards, as the widespread use of summary procedure ushered
large numbers of children quickly through the courts and subjected them
to the conveyor belt of repeated short-term sentences of imprisonment.
As has been noted, the Lord Justice Clerk complained of the 'greatly
increased' numbers of juvenile offenders since 1830, which was shortly
after the introduction of summary procedure under Sir William Rae's
Act in 1828. Unfortunately he did not supply statistics to support this
assertion, but this perception of a growth in juvenile offending appears
to have been widespread.[46]

We can gain a clear impression of the extent of concern about the
impact of summary process on young offenders from reading the letter
written by William Brebner, Governor of the Glasgow Bridewell, to the
Lord Provost of Glasgow in 1829, advocating the setting up of an institution for young offenders, a House of Refuge, in which he complained
about the pattern of repeated convictions (some for a tenth offence),
for which children were committed for short periods, typically of fourteen, twenty, thirty or sixty days.[47] As will be discussed, the efforts to
establish a House of Refuge were successful. One of its main architects
was the distinguished lawyer, historian and writer on criminal law, the
Sheriff of Lanark, Archibald Alison.[48] Not long after Sir William Rae's
Act, Alison wrote in 1832 in his important text *Principles and Practice
of the Criminal Law of Scotland* about a 'vast increase in juvenile delinquency'.[49] The establishment of summary procedure played a crucial
role in the formation of this perception.

NEW INITIATIVES

In this section, three new diversionary initiatives operating in Scottish
cities – Glasgow, Aberdeen and Edinburgh – in the 1840s will be discussed.

The trend towards diversion in dealing with juvenile offenders was
one which was recognised by the 1847 Select Committee: one of the questions posed to judicial witnesses was whether they had ever 'dismissed

the younger prisoners, on conviction to the care of their parents, guardians or masters on their undertaking for their good management'.[50] English witnesses gave evidence on new methods being tried south of the border. For example, Matthew Davenport Hill, who was prominent in the reformatory movement, spoke of his experience of using diversionary methods in his position as a judge in Birmingham, where he was a Recorder. He described an experiment he had been involved in which he considered very successful. This scheme was a pioneering form of probation,[51] in which young offenders were released immediately after sentence to the care of a 'respectable' person, either a relative or, more usually, the young person's employer. The person assuming responsibility had his name entered in a register and guaranteed to supervise the young offender. A crucial part of the system was the continued involvement of the police, who would carry out unannounced spot checks on the progress of the child. Asked what would happen if a child under supervision reoffended, Davenport Hill said he felt he had to impose a very severe sentence in these cases, so he always imposed a sentence of transportation in cases of relapse. He said this system had been ongoing for six years in Birmingham, since 1841.[52]

Scottish witnesses also spoke of diversionary methods being tried out. For example, an Edinburgh magistrate, James Ogilvie Mack, stated that in dealing with the 'very young' first offender in minor cases of theft, 'if the value of the goods stolen is trifling' his practice was to 'dismiss him with an admonition'. On the question of whether he ever dismissed children to the care of parents and guardians with a caution, he replied:

> Yes; I ask them if they will take the children back, and I find generally the Masters are inclined to be lenient to the boys.
> And thereby you avoid for those young persons the contamination of a gaol?
> Yes; I hold it to be almost ruin to send them to gaol.[53]

The Glasgow system: the House of Refuge

In responding to the same question on releasing children to the care of relatives or employers, many of the Scottish High Court judges referred in their evidence to the new system being operated in Glasgow. As previously noted, the Glasgow system was an innovative development, the origins of which can be traced to William Brebner's letter to the city's Provost in 1829.[54] Brebner argued that the cycle of young offenders being repeatedly admitted to the Bridewell prison for petty offences could be broken if there were a House of Refuge for young offenders to go to after release from prison, so that they could acquire some useful skills and be helped to find a position, instead of being released back onto the streets to fall into the clutches of criminal associates.[55] The appendix to the letter contained statements by others supporting the plea for a refuge, one of which recorded that on a recent visit to the prison the writer observed thirty-four children serving sentences of imprisonment 'for short terms mostly for petty thefts some of them very interesting and might become useful and valuable members of society if a proper place of refuge was provided . . . where they would be taken care of, be well educated and taught a regular trade'.[56]

A House of Refuge for boys was set up in 1838, supported initially by voluntary contributions, followed by a House of Refuge for girls in 1840,[57] which was created by building an extension to the existing Magdalene Asylum for prostitutes. The whole scheme was put on a more secure foundation in 1841 by a local Act of Parliament setting up a Board of Commissioners headed by the Sheriff of Lanark, Archibald Alison, to oversee the system; local residents were charged one penny in a pound on all rents over a certain value to raise funds to support these institutions for 'repressing juvenile delinquency in the City of Glasgow'.[58] Accounts of the operation of the institutions were given in collections of annual Reports produced by the managers.[59] The 1841 Act set out conditions for admission to the Houses of Refuge. Section 19 provided for voluntary admission on the basis of a request made in the presence of a judicial officer such as a magistrate; and under section 20, children under the age of twelve being brought for trial could 'with the concurrence of the Board previous to conviction' ask to be admitted and the judge could discharge proceedings on condition that the child became an inmate for a specified period.[60]

In general, the judges spoke approvingly of the Glasgow initiative. Although the Lord Justice Clerk described the system as being in his view ill-advised,[61] the other judges who mentioned it were enthusiastic, one describing it as an excellent innovation and referring to two cases in which he had applied the system. Lord Mackenzie said:

> There is a local Act for repressing juvenile delinquency in the City of Glasgow (4th and 5th Victoriae, c.36)[62] under which Lord Medwyn and I, on the West Circuit at Glasgow, 3rd October 1846, instead of Trial, sent upon their own prayer to the House of Refuge there three boys, one of them for three years, two others for five years. The like had been done by Lords Moncrieff and Cockburn, 26th September 1845.[63]

Similarly, Lord Moncrieff responded to the question as to whether he had ever 'dismissed the younger prisoners, on conviction to the care of their parents, guardians or masters on their undertaking for their good management' by saying:

> If the public prosecutor insist for judgment we can scarcely dispense with it. In some instances of very young offenders, of which I have a note, the Advocate Depute has declined to move for sentence, and then the prisoner has been discharged, and committed to his parents or guardians. But it is to be observed that in a great proportion of such cases the child has either *no* parents or parents of such depraved characters that no good can be expected to him from them. In *several* cases noted by me in 1843 and 1845, the court, sitting at Glasgow, did, in virtue of a statute, with the consent of the prosecutor and the prisoner by his counsel, and with the concurrence of one of the directors of the institution, instead of making any conviction or sentence, pronounce an Order for his reception into the Glasgow House of Refuge, which we know to be an excellent and successful institution.[64]

The 1845 case of *HMA* v. *Mary Ann O'Brien, Agnes Wallace and Janet McNaught* referred to by Lord Mackenzie illustrated this system in operation.[65] It concerned three young girls charged with breaking into a house at Sauchiehall Street owned by a bookkeeper, Andrew Carrick, and stealing various items of jewellery belonging to his wife, a gold mounted item set with pearls and a pair of gold earrings, as well as a gold breast pin, a large knife and a razor owned by Carrick. One of the girls, Mary Ann O'Brien, had a previous conviction for theft. All three girls pled not guilty. The Report records that proof was led and that once the Advocate Depute had closed his proof 'by reading the declaration of the pannels, and having restricted the pains of the law to an arbitrary punishment', Agnes and Janet 'by their counsel and with the concurrence of the Board of Commissioners, severally prayed, in respect of their youth to be admitted inmates into the House of Refuge for females in the City of Glasgow, instead of abiding the issue of their trial'. Under the Act of 1841, the proceedings were discharged against Agnes and Janet on condition that Agnes became an inmate of the House of refuge for three years and that Janet became an inmate for five years. Mary Ann was less fortunate. Lord Cockburn summed up the evidence and the jury found her guilty as libelled. She was sentenced to transportation for a period of ten years.

In the Select Committee Report, Lord Moncrieff was the judge who had most to say in praise of the House of Refuge, referring to its capacity for reforming young offenders. Discussing a decline in numbers of young offenders under the age of fifteen appearing before him on his High Court circuits in different regions in recent years, he noted that in part this was due to Sheriffs giving long sentences to previous offenders, meaning that they were beyond fifteen when they came to appear before the High Court for further offences. However, he commented that he believed the principal reason for the decline in numbers appearing before the High Court in Glasgow was the existence of the House of Refuge, 'which drew a great many of those liberated from the Bridewell'.[66]

In the operation of this Glasgow system there was a clear articulation of formalised diversion. The system was based on a legislative foundation, a local Act of Parliament. It was for the most part endorsed by the judiciary at the highest level. It was seen as an excellent development with reformatory potential. However, it could only proceed with the concurrence of the prosecutor. As Lord Moncrieff pointed out, if the prosecutor moved for sentence, the judges were compelled to deliver it.[67] There is a sense here that some judges would have opted in more cases for alternatives to traditional punishment if they had the freedom to do so. This feeling of being hamstrung by judicial process occurs in other writings about the views of judges of the period. For instance, discussing the development of the system in Aberdeen, Alexander Thomson talked about the magistrates often feeling despondent about having to deal with young children appearing before them, and this being the motivation for their support for the experiment being tried in Aberdeen. He talked about cases which caused judges 'extreme pain', where mere 'infants were brought up on criminal charges – the charges against them were incontestably proved – and yet, in a moral sense they could scarcely be held *guilty*' (emphasis in original text).[68] In the development of new diversionary initiatives, judges, especially Sheriffs, had a prominent role to play. In Glasgow, Sheriff Archibald Alison was at the forefront of the moves to establish the Houses of Refuge. In Aberdeen, Sheriff William Watson was at the helm; and in the pressure to establish similar institutions in Edinburgh, the names of many Sheriffs appeared in the campaign literature.[69]

The Houses of Refuge were Glasgow's unique contribution to the pre-statutory system: this was the only scheme backed by local legislation and it was the only one of the new developments to deal solely with children already being processed by the criminal justice system. It was also unique in being a residential institution. In this respect and also because it dealt only with young offenders, it was like the reformatories to be set up under the later statutory system. However, in addition to the Houses of Refuge, Glasgow also employed another strategy in approaching children in trouble: like other Scottish towns, Glasgow also developed pre-statutory industrial schools in the 1840s, which were run

along the lines of William Watson's schools in Aberdeen. As will be discussed next, these schools were primarily preventive in ethos, and were
designed to stop vulnerable children becoming criminal, but they also
embraced children who had already offended.

The Aberdeen system: the Industrial School

Of all the Scottish cities, the one which led the way along the road to
diversion was Aberdeen. Powered by the visionary religious zeal of
Sheriff William Watson (1796–1887), the experiment establishing industrial schools came to be lauded throughout Britain as a completely novel
and successful enterprise. It was viewed by reformers as a model to be
adopted in other cities. The most eminent reformer of juvenile justice in
Victorian Scotland, Watson was one of eight children born to a pros-
perous farming family in Lanarkshire.[70] He was sent to Edinburgh at
the age of twelve to be educated at the Edinburgh Academy, and then
studied law at Edinburgh University before embarking on a legal career.
Appointed as Sheriff Substitute of Aberdeen in 1829 he was, from the
outset, highly active in civic affairs and philanthropic efforts, especially
in addressing the plight of neglected and delinquent children.

When Mary Carpenter gave her evidence to the 1852 Select Committee
on Criminal and Destitute Juveniles, she had all the facts and figures
about the success of the Aberdeen scheme at her fingertips, to show
what could be done to transform the lives and prospects of vagrant and
destitute children either on the path to or actively engaged in crime.[71]
Similarly, English reformer Matthew Davenport Hill accorded Watson's
achievements the greatest accolade by elevating him to the same status as
Demetz, the famous founder of the celebrated French establishment for
young offenders at Mettray, with the words, 'a Demetz or a Watson, like
the poet, *nascitur, non fit*'.[72] Notable visitors impressed by the schools
included the author William Thackeray, said to have been moved to
tears by the rescue of destitute children.[73] Lord Cockburn too paid a visit
to the schools while on circuit in Aberdeen. In 1845 *Chambers Journal*
praised the schools in a widely disseminated article.[74] Even a contributor to Charles Dickens's journal *Household Words* expressed ardent
admiration.[75]

Watson's co-reformer, Alexander Thomson of Banchory, a wealthy
Aberdeen philanthropist, magistrate and prison board chairman, suggested that the success of Watson's vision could be accounted for by
a unique combination of factors.[76] Thomson claimed that while many
other schemes had been tried elsewhere which had some of the features

of the industrial school, none had possessed all of the ingredients needed for the plan to work.[77] Watson himself defined the industrial school model in Aberdeen in the following way:

> It is the place where children assemble at 7 o clock in the morning, get break-fast, dinner and supper, three hours instruction in reading, writing, arithmetic and geography and are employed five hours in useful industry, each returning to his own home at night.[78]

This described the key elements of the daily routine of the schools which Watson set up, with the goal of rescuing vagrant and destitute children from a life of crime. Both children who were victims of neglect and destitution and those convicted of petty offences were admissible to the schools.[79] The aim was to provide the children with moral, spiritual and physical sustenance, turning them into useful citizens who would be able to earn their own living. The industrial training was considered to be vital both in training the children to become industrious workers and in inducing self-esteem as well as that most essential of Victorian virtues, respectability.[80] Providing children with respectable credentials was essential to enable them to gain employment later on. Watson stressed this point in his writings, commenting that children who had been in prison were tainted by this for life and found it difficult to find work. He argued that industrial school training was a passport to social acceptance

Watson's school
Courtesy of Aberdeen City Libraries

and good citizenship.[81] Children were employed in tasks that could be put to good effect in later life, such as tailoring and shoemaking, as well as other activities such as making salmon nets for the fishermen of Aberdeen and 'picking hair for upholsterers'.[82]

Watson was most concerned that the children should not see themselves as the objects of charity. He wanted them to feel that they had earned the food they received by dint of their honest labour. Other essential ingredients were the values of godliness and cleanliness. Children would receive scriptural instruction, and church attendance on Sunday was expected. The importance of being turned out looking as clean and tidy as resources would permit was highly stressed.[83] Watson's vision was fired by the idea that improving the outlook of the children and raising their hopes, expectations and values would have a highly beneficial effect on their whole families. He strongly advocated supporting the family unit and totally disapproved of later developments under the statutory system which saw children being forcibly separated from their parents.[84]

In his judicial role, Watson had been much troubled by the 'cruel' and 'absurd' plight of young children appearing before the local courts, many of whom were aged only eight to eleven years of age but who were repeatedly being imprisoned for minor offences such as begging, breach of the peace or trivial thefts. He found this especially disturbing because 'it is known that unless by begging or stealing ninety nine in a hundred have no way of subsisting'.[85] Watson attributed the increasing numbers of children coming before the courts to a number of factors. One of these has been discussed at some length in the earlier section of the chapter: the effect of repeatedly trying juvenile offenders in inferior courts and repeatedly imposing short sentences, which created an ever-escalating momentum in the volume of juvenile offenders.[86]

The other cause he discussed was the criminalising effect of a local Police Act of 1829. This Act sanctioned the formation of a regular police force in the town of Aberdeen. It also created a number of new minor offences designed to regulate urban life and control behaviour in public spaces. This Act was a local response to the perceived need for order and civic improvement in Aberdeen, which was a centre of growing population.[87] Watson was concerned about the creation of new offences under this legislation and the way it impacted on the poor, especially the children of the poor. His writing on this subject resonates with work done in England by Susan Margarey on the criminalising effect on the young of offences created in London under the Metropolitan Police Acts of the same era.[88] As noted in the previous chapter, Margarey attributes

much of the blame for the 'invention of delinquency' to the combined
effect of criminalising legislation and summary processes. Arguably this
was a potent combination of factors in the criminalisation of children in
Scotland too.

Watson stated that the new offences under the local Police Act of 1829
were of a kind 'hitherto unnoticed'. In his view, more vigorous policing
by 'the greatly increased number of policemen' appointed under the Act
contributed to many 'men, women and children' being brought before
the courts for breach of these new prohibitions: they were then sentenced by burgh magistrates to short periods of imprisonment, filling the
prisons with offenders of all ages.[89] He noted that the impact of this was
to 'taint the character without reforming the morals', making it difficult
to secure employment.[90] Amplifying on the types of offences he found
objectionable, Watson commented:

> We call those acts injurious which are wilfully injurious to person or property.
> Flying a kite, throwing a snowball or sliding on the ice for which children by
> local police acts or provisional orders may be sent to prison, though abun-
> dantly annoying, can hardly be called crimes, and children rarely commit
> assault unless in fair schoolboy fight when a blue eye or bleeding nose is not
> reckoned of great account. The crime they are guilty of is theft, and of thefts
> by far the greater number are committed by juveniles either on their own
> account or on behalf of adults.[91]

Here Watson was indicating that in his view a crime like theft committed by children might be worthy of censure; but it was unjustifiable to
punish children for trivial offences created by police acts or provisional
orders. The extension of the criminal law in this way was a topic with
which Watson was much preoccupied. In his work entitled *Pauperism,
vagrancy, crime and industrial education in Aberdeenshire 1840–75*, he
stated:

> If it were thought desirable to pauperise and demoralise the poor, and
> increase the number of delinquents, no way would be more effectual than
> multiplying local Police Acts and Provisional Orders, raising harmless acts to
> penal offences punishable by fine and imprisonment.[92]

While it may be stretching the point to suggest that Watson's views
indicate that he would have agreed with Margarey's perspective on the
invention of delinquency, his choice of the words here is certainly consistent with the idea that to some extent a consequence of the creation
of such offences was the manufacturing of an 'increase in the number of
delinquents'. In a passage which resonates strongly with contemporary

concerns about the proliferation of criminal offences, he strongly criticised the creation of a stream of seemingly arbitrary offences. In addition to the provisions prohibiting kite-flying, snowball-throwing and
making or using a slide, he also referred to a ban on throwing orange
peel on the pavement. All of these offences related to activities normally
carried on by children as a matter of course as they played outdoors.
Under this legislation the offences carried a penalty of a fine of a few
shillings or a few days' imprisonment. He noted the unfairness of these
activities being 'magnified into crimes', commenting that often the poor
and 'ignorant' were not aware that these offences existed until they
were hauled up in front of a magistrate.[93] He contrasted these offences
with crimes like stealing, wife-beating or assault, arguing that people
generally had an innate awareness of the wrongfulness of these actions
and were aware that they were crimes, unlike the offences created by
the Police Acts and Provisional Orders which he deemed 'an immense
annoyance'.[94] This injustice was compounded in Watson's view by the
inconsistencies in sentencing in the justice of the peace and police courts,
which he attributed to the judges in these courts not having any legal
training.[95] This meant that offenders could face considerable penalties
for infringing these new prohibitions.

Watson's concerns about the plight of poor children impelled him
to action, and by 1841 he was ready to launch his scheme to attempt
to allay the problems faced by the vagrant and destitute children on
the streets of Aberdeen. He recorded that economic circumstances were
particularly difficult for the poor in the early 1840s: in 1840 the city
police had reported that 280 children were known to them who had no
means of subsistence other than begging or stealing, and the Governor
of the prison had noted that the yearly total of children admitted to
prison had been seventy-seven.[96] Watson was determined to improve
matters for the poorest of poor children. Unable to afford the small
fee for attendance at the local parish schools, most of these children
were also likely to be refused admittance on the grounds of their ragged
appearance.[97] In the mid-nineteenth century, educational provision was
variable, as the traditional Scottish parish schools came under strain
to cope with the demands of expanding urban centres.[98] Considerable
numbers of children received no education. The Second Report of the
Argyll Commission on Elementary Education in Scotland reported in
1867 that there were over 5,000 schools providing elementary education
with 400,000 pupils in attendance, but there were still 90,000 children
not attending any school.[99] Some of the gaps in provision were filled
by religious schools or private institutions funded by subscription.[100]

And it was within this context of unmet need that Watson introduced the concept of the industrial school.

The scheme was initiated against the background of a range of important changes occurring during the period 1840–5, including the establishment of a prison board, a rural police force and poor law boards.[101] Set up on a shoestring and entirely supported by voluntary contributions from local people, the school for boys was started on 1 October 1841 in a schoolroom obtained 'gratis in the loft of an old house in Chronicle Lane with 5 boys brought in by police'.[102] This was followed by one for girls in 1843. Despite the attraction of free food, it proved difficult to retain the attendance of pupils on a voluntary basis. Writings by Alexander Thomson reveal that this difficulty was overcome by an ingenious arrangement, the Child's Asylum, which he described as a 'channel of admission' to the schools.[103] This key component of the experiment bolstered up the weaknesses in the voluntary aspect of the enterprise considerably. The crux of this development was a committee set up to evaluate children's needs in a police-backed, community-based local crime-prevention and welfare-based initiative in which assessments of the needs of individual children were carried out by representatives of local organisations, to all intents and purposes a remarkably innovative and progressive approach.

Explaining this development, Alexander Thomson recorded that in May 1845 it was decided to use an existing local Act aimed at preventing vagrancy to extend the project, in an attempt to reach those children who were still begging on the streets and had not so far been enticed to attend the school with the offer of free food.[104] Under the authority of this Act and at the direction of magistrates,[105] the police rounded up all children found begging on the streets of Aberdeen on 19 May 1845 – seventy-five in all – and brought them to a soup kitchen, which was to be the premises for a new school.[106] Watson vividly recounted the first day's travails at the school and the difficulties in maintaining order with the 'wild, unruly' new recruits.[107] First, the reluctant new arrivals were bathed and fed, but as the day wore on he felt it was 'the longest some of us had known'.[108] Then parents turned up demanding the return of the children and were briskly told to come back to the school in the evening to collect them after supper. The children were warned that they were under no compulsion to return to the school, but under no circumstances would further instances of begging be tolerated by the police. Despite the trials of the day, Watson felt his 'victory complete' when next morning there was a queue of children waiting for admission.[109]

The police were so enthusiastic about the plan that they undertook to pay the teachers' salaries for the new school for a trial period.[110]

But although most of the children returned voluntarily to the school after the initial swoop, it proved difficult to secure the continued attendance of all the children in the absence of official powers of compulsion.

To tackle this issue, in December 1846 the Child's Asylum was set up. This comprised two rooms adjoining the House of Refuge, providing temporary accommodation for children picked up by the police for begging or delinquent conduct, and also a venue where their circumstances could be assessed by a Committee convened on a daily basis.[111] The role of the Committee was to determine the appropriate course of action for each individual child. In most cases, children would be considered admissible to the schools. There was, however, a concern to ensure that the charitable enterprise was not being abused and that only deserving cases were admitted. In some cases it was found on investigation into the circumstances of the children that their parents were deemed to have sufficient means to support the children properly but simply ignored their responsibilities. In these cases the children were not in the first instance admissible to the schools, which were regarded as being reserved for the genuinely destitute. Instead, parents were summoned and advised to discharge their duty. However, where a parent persisted in failing to care for the child and the child was again found on the streets, the welfare of the child was deemed more important than the abuse of charity and the child was admitted to one of the schools.[112]

The essence of the system was that police brought any children either found in a destitute condition on the streets or involved in some criminal conduct to the Child's Asylum, where the Committee carried out an ad hoc appraisal. The Committee reserved the right to refer any matter involving serious misconduct to the procurator fiscal. Having decided that a child was to be admitted to one of the schools, the Committee was still faced with the problem of ensuring attendance. Although there was no legal compulsion on any child to attend the industrial school, it was made clear to children that failure to attend could result in their case being referred to the fiscal, whether on the grounds of vagrancy or any other conduct which constituted an offence. In summary, this approach was a form of local community initiative which evaluated children's needs and supported them with continued supervision in the shape of industrial school attendance backed up by the possible threat of criminal justice action being initiated.

Reviewing this system in 1851, Thomson said that after the first two years of successful operation of the scheme the numbers of children being referred by the police declined as there were fewer vagrant children, but the Committee still continued to meet weekly to inquire into any police-referred cases and also cases of destitute children on whose behalf parents applied for admission to the industrial schools. He noted that the Committee was made up of three representatives from each of the following: the town council, the commissioners of police, the parochial board of St Nicholas, the parochial board of Old Machar, the House of Refuge and the joint management committee of the industrial schools, many of whom were magistrates.[113]

The approach taken by Watson was enterprising, pioneering and in many respects quite audacious. In fact, some of his tactics were even of doubtful legality. There was a substantial question mark surrounding his use of the old Police Act to round up candidates for his schools. In his autobiography, Watson recorded that he overcame the initial misgivings of the magistrates about the legality of the proposed procedure. He boldly answered the magistrates' question, 'Can we legally do that?'[114] with the confident assertion:

> Yes, there is a warrant under an Act of Parliament to apprehend beggars and I will take the responsibility of putting it into force.[115]

When giving evidence to the 1852 Select Committee, Thomson was candid in his admission that he had been asked many times about the dubious legality of this practice. He had no doubt that the steps taken in 1845 by magistrates directing the police to gather up children found on the streets were incompetent in terms of the statute they purported to derive their authority from, but in his view this did not seem to matter as it was an effective strategy. The possible illegality was overlooked by the magistrates, many of whom were in fact members of the committee of management of the industrial schools. Discussing the strategy, Thomson said:

> It is an Act for the town of Aberdeen; orders were given to the police to lay hold at once of every little begging boy and girl in the town, and upon a certain day they were all seized; they were carried to a place which had been prepared for them as a school, I may say, forcibly established; 75 were captured.
>
> Was this done by the authority of the magistrates? Why, it would be difficult to say, because the question has often been put to me whether I had any doubt about the legality of the proceedings. I have not the slightest doubt that the proceeding was highly illegal, but at the same time it was highly expedient, and it has done a great deal of good; but several of the magistrates of the town gave their consent and concurrence, and, in fact, were managers of the school.[116]

Clearly Watson's position as a local Sheriff, his influence with the local judiciary and the involvement of magistrates in the administering of the

schools were sufficient to overcome any qualms about strict legal nice-
ties, allowing a generous discretion to be exercised in favour of Watson's
scheme.

Watson claimed great success for his venture, crediting it with virtually eliminating juvenile vagrancy in Aberdeen.[117] The figures spoke
for themselves, particularly after the process was tightened up after the
introduction of the Child's Asylum and its local community Committee.
Describing himself as 'The Apostle of the industrial school' with a
'mission to plant one in every large town', Watson sought to spread
the gospel of his ideas by becoming involved in advising other towns
and cities about the value of the system.[118] He spoke at public meetings, and his expertise was called upon in practical matters. Thomson
recorded the introduction of industrial schools in other Scottish towns
in the course of the 1840s.[119] Dundee was first to adopt the idea of
the industrial school. Thomson related the success of the initiative there
to the 1852 Select Committee, saying that following the introduction
of the schools in Dundee the levels of recorded juvenile offending had
fallen from 212 in 1846 to seventy-five in 1850.[120] Other towns followed Watson's lead, including Glasgow, Greenock, Inverness, Falkirk,
Rothesay, Ayr, Stranraer and Dumfries.[121] Edinburgh too had adopted
the idea of industrial schools in 1847, but it had proved a tough nut to
crack.[122] It was not won over to the concept until Rev. Thomas Guthrie
(1803–73) instigated a campaign of persuasion with his successful pub-
lication, *A Plea for Ragged Schools or Prevention Better than Cure*.[123]

The Edinburgh system: the Ragged School

Guthrie used his position and powers of rhetoric cultivated as a minister
to put forth a very persuasive and successful argument for the desperate
need for such schools in Edinburgh. The son of a Brechin merchant and
banker, Guthrie was one of thirteen children. Educated at Edinburgh
University, he was ordained to the ministry of the Church of Scotland
but, following the ecclesiastical Disruption of 1843, he became a prominent figure in the Free Church of Scotland.[124]

Guthrie's campaign achieved its objective with the first school, the
Edinburgh Original Ragged School, being established in 1847. He made
his appeal primarily on grounds of compassion and humanity, but also
argued on a pragmatic level, pointing to the ultimate cost-effectiveness
and economic benefits to society if criminal careers could be nipped in
the bud. He marshalled evidence provided by supporters of his cause,
such as the Governor of Edinburgh prison, who testified to the large

number of young children being detained in prison.[125] There was also evidence from Guthrie himself and others testifying to the deplorable levels of destitution among the young in Edinburgh. Most compellingly, there was evidence from Aberdeen: detailed notes on the practice of the industrial schools and the proclamation of a 'marked diminution in the numbers of juvenile delinquents'.[126]

Sheriff Watson himself proudly remarked in a letter of support that begging among children had been virtually eliminated in Aberdeen. Pointing to this success, Guthrie insisted that the provision of food was an essential element in the scheme. Otherwise, he said, children could not be expected to attend for long. Guthrie continued his appeal for compassion with the argument that children found guilty in the courts of petty theft acted out of sheer necessity, often at the instigation of their parents:

> in the case of these unhappy children who are suffering from the crimes of their parents and neglect of society, with what truth might this verdict be returned, proven, but not guilty?[127]

This plea resonates strongly with the indignation of Mary Carpenter when she gave evidence in 1852 to the House of Commons Select Committee appointed to inquire into Criminal and Destitute Children.[128] Commenting on what she saw as the complete uselessness of prison as a method for dealing with children in trouble, she delivered her vehemently held opinion that

> we ought in the first place to consider the position of these children in regard to society. I consider society owes retribution to them, just as much as they owe it to society or in fact more . . . If society leaves them knowingly in the state of utter degradation in which they are, I think it absolutely owes them reparation, far more than they can be said to owe reparation to it.[129]

Guthrie's evidence to the 1852–3 Select Committee indicates that by 1852 over 600 Edinburgh children aged between six and fourteen attended the four industrial schools set up in the city in 1847.[130] Unlike Watson, Guthrie was happy to adopt the term 'ragged school' to describe his version of the industrial school. Many of the schools set up on the industrial model in other towns were also named 'ragged' schools. Watson disapproved of this description: he was always concerned to maintain the dignity of the children he set out to help and considered this term demeaning, pointing out that the children in his schools soon had their rags replaced by more respectable clothing.[131] In most other respects, Guthrie adhered to the system adopted by the

Aberdeen schools. As in Aberdeen, children were educated in both secular and scriptural matters, provided with meals and given industrial
training. In Edinburgh, children were taught trades such as tailoring,
shoemaking and carpentry, which would allow them to gain appren-
ticeships; younger children were occupied with 'teasing hair for cabi-
net makers'.[132] Training was gender-specific, with girls being trained in
sewing, knitting and laundry, skills which would be useful in domestic
service, for which many were destined.[133] The typical school day began
at seven in the morning and ran until seven in the evening.[134] Guthrie
shared Watson's views on the importance of the principle of day attendance in maintaining the family bond, with children returning home to
their families at the end of the school day. However, while Aberdeen
strictly adhered to this policy, Guthrie's school did provide dormitory
accommodation for children whose circumstances were considered to
merit it.[135]

Like Watson, Guthrie was convinced of the effectiveness of the
schools in reducing juvenile begging and also juvenile crime. He declared
that the schools had 'almost cleared Edinburgh of juvenile mendicants',
a huge achievement in a city which had so many children begging on
the streets before the introduction of the schools.[136] He was also able to
provide the Committee with statistics from the governors of a number of
prisons in towns where industrial schools had been set up giving 'a very
satisfactory Report' on the decline in juvenile admissions to prisons.[137]

However, on closer questioning by the Select Committee it became
evident that the relationship between the falling prison admissions of
juveniles and the existence of the schools was not necessarily an indication that less juvenile crime had occurred, but rather that the response to
it was different. Asked if Edinburgh had a local Police Act like Aberdeen
which was used to direct children to the schools, Guthrie replied that
unfortunately it did not, but that nonetheless the magistrates had
adopted the practice of sending children appearing before them for petty
offences straight to the schools rather than impose another punishment
such as imprisonment, a fine or whipping. It was suggested that perhaps
this meant that the fall in prison numbers did not then mean that less
juvenile crime had occurred but rather that children were being sent to
the schools instead of prison. Guthrie replied that since the founding
of the school in 1847, about 200 children had been sent by the magistrates, and out of the '200 children 150 would have led criminal lives but
for our ragged school', so the school was effectively acting to diminish
future crime.[138] In his view there were two factors in operation: a real
diminution in crime attributable to an improvement in the children's

conduct, for which the schools could take the credit, as well as the diversionary practices of magistrates, which also accounted for a reduction in the prison numbers:

> our ragged schools are the places to which our magistrates (I do not know that they have any law for it) now send our juvenile delinquents who have been guilty of some petty crime instead of prison.[139]

On the question of whether magistrates adopted this policy in other towns too, Guthrie replied that they did in Aberdeen and to some extent in Dundee, and though he was unable to comment on the practice elsewhere, he regarded this strategy as very important and one which should be adopted generally.[140] In his opinion the system of 'ragged' schools was at its most efficient in Edinburgh and Aberdeen, although there was a desperate need for more schools in Edinburgh and most other towns. This was a need which could only be met by the state subsidies which would accompany legislative recognition of the schools. To this end there had been an organised effort by managers of industrial schools throughout Scotland to co-operate on proposals for a draft Bill which had been drawn up by Sheriff Barclay of Perth[141] with the assistance of a number of Edinburgh advocates.[142] The Bill sought to place the existing schools on a statutory footing, supplementing voluntary subscriptions with state funding, and to give magistrates the legally unequivocal power to send children to industrial schools.[143] Attendance for children sent under court order would become compulsory. However, it is clear from Guthrie's responses that he did not envisage that compulsory attendance would necessarily mean that children would be separated from their parents: he argued that the question of whether children under court order would have to be accommodated at the schools would be at the discretion of the school managers. The committee members doubted that this was a practicable option. Under the legislation which eventually came into being, detention of children under court order was a central feature.[144]

An overview of the pre-statutory schools

By the early 1850s most large Scottish towns had industrial feeding schools based on the Aberdeen model. There was some local variation. Some were named industrial schools, others described themselves as ragged schools. The schools were primarily day schools but some provided lodging for those who had no home, while others arranged for homeless children to be accommodated with local families. The purpose of the schools was to rescue children from a life of destitution and crime. The schools were supported by voluntary subscriptions and their managers were anxious to prevent charity being abused. For this reason, stringent measures were adopted to vet those applying for voluntary admission to the schools to ensure that they were deserving cases in genuine need. The admissions procedure was designed to weed out those who had parents with sufficient means to support them and who could afford to pay for them to attend the ordinary schools where a small fee was required; and also to filter out those with a valid claim on parish funds under the poor law. The children of paupers were entitled to parish relief and could attend pauper schools in the charity workhouses, instead of being a drain on the scarce resources of the industrial schools.[145] As Guthrie explained:

> We take up all those that have no claim on any parish, what we call in Scotland 'the waifs', the wandering part of the population that float here and there and either have no claim on any parish or refuse to take parish relief when it is offered in the shape of admission to the workhouse . . . These are the children with whom our school is principally filled: and I believe it is from this class that the large mass of the criminals of the country spring.[146]

As well as those applying for voluntary admission to the industrial schools, children were admitted who had appeared before magistrates and were sent by the court. In these cases the magistrates sometimes availed themselves of local legislation to authorise the child's direction to the school; in other instances there appears to have been no pretext of a legislative basis for sending the children to the schools, but the magistrates did it anyway.[147] One of the main reasons for the pressure for legislation was to clarify this issue and give magistrates incontestable statutory powers to order children to attend industrial schools.[148]

As has been discussed, individual cities made their own contributions in developing new responses to juvenile mendicancy and crime. Glasgow's unique contribution was the setting up of the Houses of Refuge under local acts of parliament. These differed from the industrial schools in that the Houses of Refuge were residential establishments solely for children already caught up in the criminal justice process: either they were convicted children who applied for admission on release from the Glasgow prison, or they were children appearing before a court who with the concurrence of the prosecutor applied for admission to one of the Houses rather than proceed to trial. For this reason they can properly be regarded as the first purely reformatory institutions in Scotland. On the other hand, the industrial schools were mainly preventive in philosophy, designed either to rescue destitute children before they descended into crime or to prevent them from falling further into criminal habits if they had already succumbed to temptation. Although Glasgow was the first to develop a reformatory institution, it joined other Scottish towns in also developing industrial schools run along the lines of the Aberdeen schools.

Of course, Aberdeen's contribution was seminal. Although it provided the model for schools in other towns, it probably remained unique in some respects, particularly in having in place its well-developed community-based arrangement, the Child's Asylum Committee. The particular circumstances prevailing in Aberdeen, the size of the city, Watson's charisma and powers of persuasion, and perhaps a developed sense of civic responsibility and accountability, all combined to make such a system work there. In other towns there were certainly committees regulating the admission process to the schools. In relation to Edinburgh, for example, Guthrie spoke about the committees of the schools having an extensive application form for applicants to complete. This formed the basis on which the committees decided on a child's eligibility. It included questions about family circumstances, length of residence in Scotland and details of previous convictions. However, it is not clear whether these committees of Edinburgh industrial schools were representative of a broad range of local organisations, as was the case in Aberdeen, or whether they exercised the same range of functions.

LEGISLATIVE DEVELOPMENTS

The extent of the success claimed for the Aberdeen system in largely removing the problem of juvenile vagrancy from the streets of the city seems to have hinged on the supportive/coercive nature of the Child's Asylum Committee system in dealing with recalcitrant backsliders. Watson appears to have recognised a higher degree of compulsion beginning to take root in his scheme when he spoke about the forceful measures adopted on 19 May 1845 to gather up all the vagrant children on the streets as being like a 'pressing invitation to dinner and to spend the day'.[149]

By the early 1850s strenuous efforts were being made to make the invitation one that could not be refused. Pressure was mounting for the introduction of legislation to put the industrial schools on a statutory footing and to empower magistrates to have the legal authority to compel children to attend industrial schools under court order. As the statements made by Guthrie in his evidence to the 1852–3 Select

Committee reveal, the managers of the schools were active in promoting a push for legislative action. Those prominent in the campaign like Guthrie and Thomson argued that state support was required to secure the future of the schools, which until then had been funded purely by voluntary subscriptions, by no means a guaranteed source of income and certainly not sufficient to meet the demand for expansion.[150] Guthrie's evidence revealed the strong feeling of resentment towards those parents regarded as profligate and dissolute who persisted in squandering their earnings on drink rather than support their families, forcing their children to beg on the streets. There was considered to be a real need to be able to compel such children to attend industrial schools where they would be fed and educated, and also to have the legal power to recover the costs of child support from the parents.[151] The sentiment which often recurred in the discussions on this topic was that the state should act 'in loco parentis': the state should effectively take the place of the parent to meet the child's need where the parent refused to accept his responsibilities and then force the parent to pay for child support.[152]

Interaction with English campaigners

The pressure for legislative intervention was part of a wider initiative taking place across the UK. On 10 December 1851, a Conference met at Birmingham to discuss proposals to campaign for legislation on 'preventive and reformatory schools'. Appearing on the list of those connected with the Conference were the names of a number of Scots, including William Watson, Alexander Thomson and Thomas Guthrie.[153] Also involved were the seasoned English reformatory campaigners Mary Carpenter and Matthew Davenport Hill.

The final resolution of the Conference bore all the hallmarks of Mary Carpenter's vision.[154] As Himmelfarb observed, Mary Carpenter was cast in the contradictory mould of many Victorian philanthropists, both religious and utilitarian, with a Benthamite love of classification. This was reflected in the idea of separate schools for separate classes.[155] The resolution called for legislation to introduce a state system composed of three types of schools: ragged, industrial and reformatory. The ragged schools were to be free day schools for the most deprived children; the industrial schools were to be based completely on Watson's model of day feeding schools, where vagrant and begging children would be sent under court order to be educated and do industrial work;[156] the third class of schools were the reformatories to which children who had been convicted would be sent in order to be reformed. A committee formed by the Conference presented a draft of the proposed legislation to the Home Secretary, Viscount Palmerston, who promised a Parliamentary Committee of Inquiry which took evidence from the reformers, including, as has been discussed, the Scottish reformers Thomson and Guthrie.[157]

Carpenter's design was not to be implemented in full. The first element to which her scheme referred, the English ragged schools, were not typical in Scotland, which of course had a well-established network of industrial schools (confusingly also sometimes called ragged schools) to cater for the most destitute. These English ragged schools were considered unfit to receive government aid, as they did not meet required minimum educational standards. For this reason there was to be no legislation or state funding for the English variety of ragged schools.[158] However, the other two aspects of her plan fared better, and in the course of the 1850s Mary Carpenter had the satisfaction of seeing legislation brought into force on the subject of industrial and reformatory schools. By 1857 both Scotland and England had a statutory framework in place governing these schools.

Carpenter's system of classification appeared to present a rational well thought-out design. She laid particular emphasis on distinguishing between the categories of children who would be eligible for admission to industrial schools and reformatory schools. She stipulated that the industrial schools were to be reserved for the 'perishing' classes, children who were in danger by virtue of their circumstances of becoming criminal; reformatory schools, on the other hand, were to reform the 'dangerous' classes, children who had already been convicted of crime. However, as she was probably well aware, there were certain illogicalities in her approach. For example, when questioned before the 1852 Select Committee about the non-criminal ('perishing', as she put it, or pre-criminal) status of the category of children to be admitted to industrial schools, she had to concede that vagrancy was indeed a criminal offence under the Police Acts: therefore the children destined for industrial schools were in the category of children who were subject to conviction too.[159] In effect, the children eligible to be admitted to industrial schools and also reformatory schools could all be seen as having already fallen into crime. Though this clearly undermined what she saw as the preventive pretensions of the industrial school, she was reluctant to admit it and dodged the question. This classificatory confusion in her scheme also led to considerable disquiet when the proposed legislation for industrial schools in England was being considered in Parliament in 1857, with many MPs not being able to see why the Bill was said by its proponents to be non-penal.[160] The Scottish approach exemplified by Watson was much more pragmatic, less concerned with classification and the separation of children into the different categories which so preoccupied Mary Carpenter.[161] This was to become apparent in the approach adopted by the first Act dealing with industrial schools in Scotland.

The Scottish legislation: Dunlop's Act

The Scottish campaigners saw their efforts bear fruit with The Reformatory Schools (Scotland) Act 1854 (Dunlop's Act), which applied only to Scotland and was later to become known as the Scottish Industrial Schools Act.[162] This was an Act relating to destitute children who had not been charged with any offence. Section one empowered a sheriff or magistrate to send vagrant children who appeared to be under fourteen to 'any reformatory school, industrial school or other similar institution within Scotland' (unless security was found for their good behaviour), whether established by Parochial Board or association of individuals sanctioned by the Secretary of State for the purposes of the Act. The children were not to be detained beyond fifteen without consent, and due regard was to be given to the religious belief of the child or parents. The reason for this provision was that there had been considerable controversy in the parliamentary debates on the legislation about the lack of special educational provision for Roman Catholic children in the existing pre-statutory Scottish industrial schools.[163] The influx of impoverished Irish immigrants referred to by Guthrie had resulted in many destitute Irish Catholic children being admitted to industrial schools which adhered to Protestant doctrine. Guthrie's school came in for particular criticism for proselytising, that is, attempting to convert Catholic children to Protestantism. There were strong objections to this on behalf of the Catholic community and this provision ensured that separate provision would be made for Catholic children.

The definition of a vagrant given in the statute was where a child was found begging and 'wandering' with no home or 'settled place of abode or proper guardianship', and with 'no lawful or visible means of subsistence'. In these circumstances the Act stated that 'though not charged with any actual offence', the child 'shall be brought by any constable or police officer before any sheriff or magistrate'. There were ancillary offences within the statute: section two provided that where a child had wilfully left the school, a procedure under summary complaint initiated by an officer of the school could result in the young person being punished by whipping or by imprisonment for up to twenty days before being returned to the school;

section three provided for imposition of a penalty of up to five pounds for wilfully withdrawing a child from the school, failing payment of which imprisonment of up to sixty days; section four dealt with the question of expenses of supporting the child while in the school.[164] According to this section, the school was entitled to recover the cost of upkeep from parents or anyone else responsible for his support. Failure by the parent to pay the required amount could result in prosecution.

Essentially this Act related to the group of children whom Mary Carpenter would have described as the 'perishing' classes – vulnerable, destitute children found in a 'vagrant' condition who were thought by virtue of their circumstances to be in danger of becoming criminal. The reference to children not being charged with 'any actual offence' meant that the children covered by this piece of legislation were non-criminal.[165] Even though vagrancy was an offence under the Police Acts, children coming under this Act were not charged with vagrancy: in effect, this was a measure decriminalising juvenile vagrancy. The main objectives of the Scottish campaigners, to empower magistrates to have the legal authority to compel children in need to attend an industrial school under court order, and to force parents who had the means to do so to pay for their child's support in the schools, were now enshrined in this piece of legislation. The Act was a specifically Scottish measure designed to cater for the Scottish situation where there was an existing network of pre-statutory schools which sought extra powers to compel attendance. Under the pre-statutory system the schools had adhered to the principle of day attendance except in cases of extreme need, but under the new statutory system children being sent to industrial schools under court order had to reside at the schools. As Ralston notes, Lord Advocate Moncrieff considered that 'mere' day attendance was insufficient to fulfil the intention of the statute.[166] In practice, however, in the initial years of the statutory system many children still continued to attend the schools on a voluntary basis and these children were day pupils.[167]

The UK legislation: The Youthful Offenders Act 1854 (17 & 18 Vict., c.86)

This Act applied throughout the UK. For England this Act heralded the setting up of a network of certified reformatory schools with state funding. In Scotland, Dunlop's Act remained in force, operating alongside this new Act. While Dunlop's Act dealt with vagrant and destitute children who had not been charged with an offence, The Youthful Offenders Act was aimed at children who had been convicted. It empowered courts to send 'any person under the age of sixteen years' convicted of an offence to a reformatory school. Detention in the reformatory was to be preceded by a minimum period of imprisonment of fourteen days. Children were to remain in the reformatory school for a 'period not less than two years and not exceeding five years'.[168] The cost of maintaining the children was to be partly recovered from parents where possible up to the value of five shillings per week, with the Treasury making up the remainder of the cost.[169] Like Dunlop's Act, this statute created a number of offences: for example, parents were subject to penalties if they failed to pay maintenance and could be fined or imprisoned; and under section four, children who absconded or were regarded as guilty of 'refractory conduct' could be imprisoned 'with or without hard labour' for up to three months.

The emergence of this statute was by no means simple and straightforward. The debate surrounding the legislation revealed widely differing approaches, even among those campaigning for reform. Mary Carpenter argued against the 'vindictive principle of punishment' in dealing with children, but she had an uphill struggle trying to convince others of this, even those who would have identified as her supporters and co-reformers. She was totally opposed to children being imprisoned, and, according to Jo Manton, Mary Carpenter's biographer, she was distraught that this initial legislation on reformatory schools imposed the condition that children had to serve at least fourteen days in prison before admission to a reformatory. As Manton observed, 'Mary Carpenter's tragedy was that her whole life was devoted to the creation of a system, which in eventual practice by others ran counter to her true beliefs.'[170] Scottish reformers were also disillusioned by the period of prior imprisonment before admission to a reformatory. Speaking about the practice some years into the statutory system, when the period of imprisonment had been reduced from fourteen to ten days, Watson commented:

> It can hardly be supposed that the imprisonment of boys and girls for the short period of ten days before being sent to a reformatory school can have any beneficial effect and it may have an injurious one. Can there be any good reason, therefore, for continuing a practice which, to say the best of it, is altogether useless?[171]

THE EARLY YEARS OF THE STATUTORY SYSTEM IN SCOTLAND

With the arrival of the two pieces of legislation in 1854, Scotland had a statutory regime in place with two Acts, each relating to a separate group of children: Dunlop's Act for destitute non-offenders, and the Youthful Offenders Act for children convicted of an offence who were to be sent to a reformatory. However, while this framework seemed to reflect a desire to impose a form of classification on children, this was not what happened in Scotland initially. The terms of Dunlop's Act stated that vagrant children could be admitted to an industrial or reformatory school. The pragmatic Scottish approach referred to above was evident in the full title of Dunlop's 1854 Act, 'An Act to render Reformatory and Industrial Schools in Scotland more available for the benefit of vagrant children'. Clearly, from the Scottish standpoint at the outset of the statutory system there was no obvious need to separate children into different institutions: Dunlop's Act envisaged a mixing of children sent by the courts on offending and non-offending grounds, the approach taken by the pre-statutory schools. Indeed, some Scottish institutions sought official certification as both industrial and reformatory schools, and in the early years of the statutory system children sent to Scottish institutions by the courts continued to be mixed. However, under growing pressure for a uniform UK-wide approach, this state of affairs was not allowed to continue: the practice of mixing non-offenders (sent by the courts under Dunlop's Act) with convicted children (sentenced under The Youthful Offenders Act) was disapproved of by the new national inspectorate set up to oversee the statutory system. In 1856 a statute came into effect which meant that schools could not now be certified as both reformatories and industrial schools.[172]

This growing trend towards uniformity north and south of the border was accentuated by a system of compulsory inspection of reformatory and industrial schools by the national inspectorate. One outcome of this process was the need to establish designated reformatories solely for convicted juvenile offenders in Scotland like those in England. The late 1850s saw the founding of Oldmill Reformatory in Aberdeen in 1857 and Wellington Reformatory Farm School near Edinburgh in 1859.[173] Glasgow, of course, already had established reformatories, the male and female Houses of Refuge.

The arrival of the dual system of separate reformatories for convicted children and industrial schools for the destitute non-offenders marked a significant departure from the pre-statutory Scottish system where there was not seen to be any need to distinguish between children on offending and non-offending grounds by separating them into different institutions and subjecting them to different treatment. The regimes in the newly established reformatories were under the scrutiny of a national inspectorate, which had been responsible for overseeing the development of a network of reformatory schools in England set up after the Youthful Offenders Act of 1854. These institutions were on the whole harsh and penal in nature, requiring children to undertake very arduous work. The setting up of a chain of reformatory schools run on the English principle imported a degree of austerity to the Scottish system which was alien to the ethos of the benign social welfare experiment set up by the pre-statutory Scottish industrial schools. They were very different from the experiment founded by Watson in Aberdeen, which was an initiative founded on humane, compassionate principles that clearly benefited children.

In the next section, the first High Court case in Scotland under the statutory system will be discussed, the case of *Hay and others* v. *Linton* on 15 December 1855.[174]

Hay and others *v.* Linton

This case was brought by a poor law inspector, John Hay, together with the mother of a seven-year-old girl named Susan Guy who had been apprehended by the police for begging in the Grassmarket in Edinburgh. The action challenged the decision of a magistrate in the police court who had ordered Susan to be sent to the Original Ragged School, Edinburgh until the age of fifteen under section one of the new legislation, The Reformatory Schools (Scotland) Act 1854 (Dunlop's Act). Those bringing the case sought a bill of suspension of the magistrate's decision, on the grounds, firstly, that Susan's apprehension and incarceration in a police cell had been incompetent under the Act; and, secondly, that the magistrate should have accepted the security offered by a poor law inspector to prevent her being sent to the school. The court suspended the order and Susan was released.

The details of the case were that when Susan had appeared before the magistrate he decided to proceed under Dunlop's Act and continued the diet till the next day to allow intimation to Susan's mother and the inspector of the poor. A warrant was granted to detain Susan in the police cells overnight, despite the fact that she had a home to go to. The following day the magistrate set security at the value of £4 for Susan's good behaviour for twelve months, again continued the diet until the following day to allow the security to be found and granted a warrant for Susan's continued incarceration. The family were recipients of poor relief and the security was offered by the poor law inspector as an interested party to obtain her release. The inspector took an interest in the action because under the Act the poor law authorities were responsible for paying for pauper children admitted to industrial schools and he wished to avoid being burdened with this cost. Had this security been accepted, then in terms of the Act Susan would not have been sent to the industrial school. The offer was rejected by the magistrate on the grounds that the inspector was not a parent and therefore had no interest recognised under the statute. Susan was then ordered to be detained in the Original Ragged School in Edinburgh until the age of fifteen years.

Suspending the magistrate's order, the High Court accepted that the inspector could offer security and also stated that the warrants granted in the case were irregular. Susan was then released. According to a local newspaper editorial, this was seen as a test case which would affect the fate of a number of other Edinburgh children in a similar position:

> We Report a debate and decision of considerable interest under this Act [The Reformatory Schools Act] respecting principally the validity of caution tendered by parochial officers. Besides the case founded on there had occurred other thirty two similar cases in the city parish at the time the action was raised, and the number has been augmented since. There were six cases in the Canongate parish also awaiting the result of the case tried on Saturday, and likewise a number in St Cuthbert's parish. The decision will also we believe be important in regulating the operation of the Reformatory Schools Act throughout Scotland generally.[175]

An important consequence of this case was that, following this decision, magistrates in Scotland in similar cases (involving children whose parents were in receipt of poor relief) accepted security offered by poor law inspectors, meaning that the children involved were not sent to industrial schools under the Act. To some extent this thwarted the intention of Dunlop's Act because it meant that the statute was implemented by the courts in a way which failed to achieve the objective of compelling the attendance of all destitute and begging children at industrial schools under court order. This was certainly the position in 1857 when Sydney Turner, the first national inspector of the statutory schools, reported on the situation in Scottish industrial schools:

> Scarcely any of the children in them are committed under the Act, the clause enabling parochial boards to withdraw such children on giving security for their better protection having almost neutralized the direct operation of the statute altogether.[176]

Had it not been for this decision, more children would have been admitted under court order in the late 1850s. The next chapter reveals that the practice of poor law inspectors offering security for children under Dunlop's Act was particularly prevalent in Edinburgh, but did not happen in towns where the parochial authorities could not provide alternative education in a poor law school, such as Aberdeen. However, in the next chapter it also emerges that the ability of either poor law inspectors or parents to circumvent the Act in this way was soon to be curtailed by the new Industrial Schools (Scotland) Act 1861, which did not re-enact the section allowing security to be offered.[177] In subsequent chapters it becomes clear that, as the statutory system evolved, very many destitute children were admitted by court order to industrial schools.

It is interesting to read some of the arguments advanced in the Hay case on behalf of the Crown. It was argued that begging was an offence under the Police Acts and that had matters proceeded under this legislation rather than the new Reformatory Schools (Scotland) Act (Dunlop's Act) then imprisonment would not have been open to challenge. According to this view, begging children were in reality criminals and belonged to a category of offenders which it was reasonable to incarcerate. On behalf of the Crown, it was argued in relation to the detention in the police cells:

> In her detention she suffered no unnecessary hardship. It would have been a legal thing for the judge to have punished her under the Police Act by sending her to prison, but instead she was detained so that something might be done for her benefit. Having, therefore, punishment in his option, the judge was entitled to detain her by incarceration.

Dunlop's Act was designed to target vagrant children under the age of fourteen and only applied to Scotland.[178] As already noted, there was no equivalent legislation in England until the Industrial Schools Act of 1857. The proclaimed purpose of this new legislation, and the later 1857 Act, was, as stated by the judges here, the protection of neglected and destitute children. In section one Dunlop's Act refers to the vagrant child 'found wandering *and though not charged with any actual offence*' being 'brought by any constable or police officer before a Sheriff or magistrate'. The statute was framed in diversionary terms. As was argued in the parliamentary debates, this was not intended to be a penal measure. But the children admitted to institutions under this statute would hardly have known this because in practice they were treated as criminals, as this case all too clearly demonstrates.

This case shows that from the outset of the statutory system, children targeted under this Act (ostensibly one which decriminalised juvenile vagrancy) were being *prima facie* cast in a criminal light. Susan Guy was apprehended by the police, brought before a magistrate, detained for two days in police cells and ordered to be detained in an institution for eight years, despite the fact that she had a mother willing to look after her and vouch for her behaviour. Challenges to oppressive criminal justice practices like this were only possible if resources could be found to fund legal action. Although in this case a saviour did appear in the form of the inspector of the poor, his actions were less motivated by pure altruism than by the desire to relieve the parish funds of the burden of having to pay for Susan's maintenance in the industrial school for years on end. Oppressive practices were to be a continuing feature of the system.[179]

The development of the statutory system

The crystallisation of the industrial school system in legislative form was in time to alter substantially the character of the schools from essentially schools at which attendance was in theory voluntary and on a daily basis to residential institutions where children were detained under court order with severe penalties attached for absconding or for those helping children to abscond. The penal character was noted by Sydney Turner, the Inspector of Schools, who wrote in 1870 that the certified industrial schools were 'reformatories of a milder sort',[180] a view similar to that of the Departmental Committee Report of 1896, which regarded the only distinction between the two types of institution as one of age difference.[181]

Watson and Guthrie were disillusioned by the departure from their original vision, which had placed great stress on maintaining the family bond, seeing this as an opportunity to effectively evangelise whole families, as children returning home from school newly imbued with scriptural values imparted the Gospel to their parents. Writing in 1872, Watson spoke about the stigma which attached to children admitted to industrial schools by a magistrate's order rather than attending voluntarily.[182] Watson commented on the change in the character of the schools:

> Great changes have however, been made on the character of the original industrial schools by the operation of these Acts. The children sent to them cease to be free agents. They are under legal restraint, and may be detained for five years and punished for desertion.[183]

Critical of the development of residential schools, on the basis that they broke up families, he added:

> It loosens all family ties, prevents the growth of domestic affections and makes the object of its care a mere cosmopolite without love of home or of country.[184]

As well as being separated from their children under the statutory system, parents were liable to pay for their child's upkeep in the school and were subject to fine or imprisonment for failing to pay. As already noted, if a child was from a family in receipt of poor relief then the Parochial Board was liable. This led to problems as legal disputes sometimes arose as to which parish was liable. Just as the poor law represents the 'forgotten past' of the welfare system, and formed a whole body of legal rights and duties which were endlessly argued over in the courts, so the legislation setting out the conditions under which children could be detained in institutions under court order is a sadly forgotten area of legal history; and both the poor law and this area of child law are inextricably entwined together in a complex morass.[185] It is hardly possible to understand many of the cases concerning the detention of children in industrial/reformatory institutions without having a rudimentary understanding of the intricacies of the poor law, as was demonstrated in *Hay and others* v. *Linton*.

The inspector's interest in the case of *Hay and others* v. *Linton* was to ensure that the parish funds would not be burdened for many years with the liability for Susan's upkeep in the Original Ragged School. This was a taste of things to come. Financial considerations were a huge factor in many ways in the operation of the system, encompassing questions about the extent of state liability for maintenance of children in institutions and the determination to recover contributions from parents to prevent them offloading their responsibilities,[186] which led to parents being prosecuted, fined and imprisoned for up to ten days for non-payment.[187] However, at least in the early years of the statutory system, there appears to have been less of an appetite to pursue parents in this way in Scotland, to the annoyance of the inspectorate.

In addition to the many court battles between rival inspectors of the poor disputing financial liability for detained children, there was also a lot of discussion about the desirability of offsetting the costs of institutions (ideally to the level of institutional self-sufficiency, according to some) by industrial education. Watson's original conception of industrial education[188] was that it would instil in children the habits of honest work, which would make them into respectable citizens and would also have the effect of raising their self-esteem so that they would feel they had earned their bread and were not regarded as charity cases. He wished to avoid at all costs the stigmatising effect of children becoming aware of what he called the 'eleemosynary character' of the schools.[189] Unfortunately, his benign intentions, which envisaged work such as net-making for fishermen, were later translated by others into far more arduous demands being placed on children.

The industrial work undertaken in the Scottish industrial schools set up on Watson's model of Aberdeen schools was usually simple work intended to teach children a trade like shoemaking and carpentry or domestic skills. In the early years of the statutory system in Scotland, the industrial schools were not markedly different from the pre-statutory schools, with many children continuing to attend as day pupils on a voluntary basis. Until the practice was banned in 1856, some schools sought certification as both industrial and reformatory schools, so both offending and non-offending children continued to be mixed. After 1856 and the setting up of a national inspectorate for all statutory schools throughout the UK, children who had been convicted of an offence were directed to separate designated reformatory schools. The effect of this was that these reformatory schools were set up in Scotland under the auspices of the national inspectorate, which attempted to impose a more uniform system. In consequence, the Scottish reformatories followed the lead of the already established system of English reformatory schools. Just as many of the English reformatories were reformatory farm schools, inspired by the farm schools of the continent, including Foucault's prime example of a disciplinary establishment, Mettray in France, so this model was adopted in the development of the Scottish reformatory network, which meant that the inmates were expected to perform similar types of farm work to the work carried out in English institutions.[190]

The industrial tasks allocated to the inmates of the reformatory schools in England (set up after The Youthful Offenders Act 1854) often involved very demanding work. As the inspectors' Reports were to show, the industrial work expected of children varied considerably, from mundane and harmless activities in some institutions to profitable but hazardous outdoor work such as brick-making, which was injurious to children's health; and the desire to maximise profit by some managers led to a reluctance to release early on licence the older boys who had a greater capacity for work.[191] For instance, in the first Report by the inspectorate in 1857, Sydney Turner made it clear there was no fear that reformatories would be viewed as a soft option by the inmates, something that was a source of public concern:

> They work about eight hours and are in school for mental instruction about three hours per day. The field work and other labour, though not always carried on as methodically and skilfully as I could wish, is usually real and entails a full amount of hard practical exertion on the boys engaged in it, and (to town bred lads peculiarly) a considerable degree of self denial and endurance. Many boys have said to me, 'I would rather be in prison than there; I should have more to eat and less to do.'[192]

He described how boys were expected to work extremely hard:

> digging, trenching, brickmaking and stockkeeping, in all weathers, at all seasons, with the scripture regulation in full force – If a man will not work, neither should he eat.

Conditions within reformatories were deliberately kept to a basic level in order to allay public concerns that 'undeserving' children would be treated more advantageously than the children of the respectable poor at a time when there was no compulsory education available for all. Turner was keen to dispel any notion of a comfortable berth, pointing to the frequent attempts to abscond from the reformatories. His reason for doing this was probably because he was one of the architects of the legislation and therefore wished to deflect criticism of the new system.

Most of Turner's attention in his first Report of 1857 was directed at certified reformatory schools in England, but there was a section on Scottish certified schools.[193] At this point there were few dedicated reformatory schools specifically for convicted children in Scotland and Turner referred to the ones in Glasgow, and also reformatories struggling with difficulties of 'first commencement' in Aberdeen and Montrose.[194] All of these were certified reformatories under The Youthful Offenders Act.

The next category he discussed were schools having dual certification under both Dunlop's Act and The Youthful Offenders Act. Four schools fell into this group, being certified as both industrial and reformatory schools, which meant that they could receive from the courts both vagrant children and children who had been convicted. Turner was critical of these institutions for mixing their intake in this way:

> Convicted children are mixed with paupers and day-school scholars, a practice which I cannot think defensible or safe.[195]

Thirdly, he described the fourteen schools certified as industrial schools only, under Dunlop's Act, as being 'industrial feeding schools of a superior description'. In trying to assess the impact of the legislation on Scotland in the initial stages of the statutory scheme, Turner's comments are very important. They reveal that, at least in the first few years after the introduction of the legislation, most of the children attending schools certified under Dunlop's Act were still there on a 'voluntary' daily basis rather than resident inmates detained under court order. This of course was to change in later years as the residential system, strongly criticised by Watson and Guthrie, became the norm.

In 1857, though, it appeared that the industrial schools were still composed mainly of voluntary pupils. Turner stated that the practice by magistrates of accepting security offered by parochial officers when poor, vagrant and begging children appeared in court had undermined the operation of Dunlop's Act. It will be remembered that this was the issue under consideration in *Hay and others* v. *Linton*. As previously noted, Turner's comments suggested that the decision in that case affected the practice of magistrates in a way that limited the numbers of children being admitted as inmates to be detained as residents compulsorily under court order. But, as the next chapter reveals, the practice of offering security was to be curtailed by legislation in 1861.

Turner also observed that the

> indirect operation of the law appears to be considerable and very advantageous; large numbers of children coming voluntarily or being sent by their parents – from the knowledge that if found idling and begging in the streets they can and will be sentenced to the school and compelled to attend it. I think the value of these certified industrial schools in Scotland can scarcely be exaggerated. They seem to offer the cheapest and most effective means for preventing the evil which the reformatory can only cure.[196]

He commended especially the work done in Aberdeen, noting that unlike other towns and cities its streets were free from neglected children, who were instead busy being educated at the city's industrial schools.

CONCLUSION

What has emerged very strongly from this analysis is the criminalising impact of net-widening diversionary approaches to juvenile misconduct in the nineteenth century. The examination of the pre-statutory system of institutions in Scotland has revealed that diversionary approaches were not inherently problematic and could have good results. This was certainly the case when the magistrates in Aberdeen and Edinburgh directed children appearing in front of them to the type of schools set up by Watson and Guthrie in the 1840s. These were, in most respects, admirable establishments which helped a great many children and, according to the accounts of the original reformers, brought about an impressive reduction in juvenile mendicancy and offending. However, although it was not completely evident by 1860, as the statutory system developed, so the gap between the aspirations of the reformers and the practical operation of the system widened, and the ethos of the system changed character.

As the statutory system became embedded, considerable numbers of children came to be detained in the reformatory and industrial schools, residential establishments which were penal in character, often demanding that children undertake arduous work: this harsh ethos prevailed in both the reformatories for convicted offenders and also in industrial schools, where the majority of children had not been convicted of any offence and were detained on grounds such as vagrancy or destitution. It is important to emphasise that the designation of these institutions as schools is more than a little misleading. They were very much part and parcel of the criminal justice system. They were regarded by those incarcerated in them and also by the public as nothing less than a form of imprisonment.[197] Thus, children were subjected to an insidious process of disguised criminalisation in which many were drawn into the system by the net-widening effect of the diversionary strategy, and, once there, were subjected to a penal regime.

Ironically, despite her admirable philanthropic concern for children, there are clear indications that the most ardent proponent of the reformatory movement in England, Mary Carpenter, was aware that children would probably be more likely to be convicted under the system she proposed. Like all of those involved in the reformatory campaign, she was anxious to repel any suggestion that the legislation would in any way lead to young offenders having an easy ride or being treated in any way more favourably than the children of the deserving poor. When she gave her evidence on the subject of reformatory schools to the 1852 Select Committee,[198] she was anxious to show that the system she proposed was not a 'bonus on crime'[199] but would entail real punishment with reformatory effect. In this context she expressed her belief that under a statutory system of reformatory schools the courts would be much more likely to convict children than was the case before. She argued that if criminal justice officials were aware that convicted children would be sent somewhere where they would be reformed, rather than face the futile alternative of prison, then, instead of pursuing a policy of simple non-prosecution of minor offences, it was much more likely that children would be convicted.

This chapter has revealed there were certain key components involved in the criminalisation of children. Watson's writings on Aberdeen in the 1840s help distinguish the variables of criminalisation, the factors which operated together to criminalise children: policing practices, the effect of new criminal prohibitions, procedural changes and sentencing decisions. Firstly, the development of urban policing in Aberdeen created a situation where children's offences would be more likely to be dealt with in criminal justice terms. Secondly, new criminal prohibitions designed to maintain order in the expanding town impacted adversely on children's street activities, bringing them to the attention of the police. Thirdly, the effect of summary procedure was important too and meant that, although children's cases were quickly processed by the new police and justice of the peace courts, there was an ever-escalating volume of children appearing in court. And, fourthly, there was the problem of sentencing inconsistencies by legally unqualified magistrates, which resulted in many children being sentenced to imprisonment for contravening the new prohibitions criminalising minor misconduct. It is important to recognise that this process of criminalisation was occurring in other towns and cities too, as local Police Acts across the country created similar offences.[200] As noted in Chapter 1, the situation in Aberdeen resonates strongly with the developments in Metropolitan London discussed by Susan Margarey.[201]

But, perhaps most interesting of all, Watson's observations on the injustice of people being subjected to criminal sanctions for offences which had no clear moral component underlines his belief that there was an indissoluble connection between criminal law and morality. And, for him, criminal law had to be linked with common-sense notions of morality, of things which people had an innate sense were wrong, such as theft, wife-beating and assault. He strongly objected to the criminalisation of harmless activities, such as flying a kite, and commented that criminal law should be about matters which were 'wilfully injurious to person or property'.[202] His writing shows that in the mid-nineteenth century Scottish lawyers were addressing key issues about the nature of criminal law: issues such as what constitutes harm and the justification for creation of criminal offences.

3

The Dream Fades

INTRODUCTION

The period between 1860 and 1884 witnessed the entrenchment of the statutory system in Scotland. In 1866 there was consolidating legislation regulating certified industrial and reformatory schools across the UK.[1] Although amended in certain respects by subsequent legislation, the 1866 Acts on industrial and reformatory schools remained in force at the end of the nineteenth century and were the principal statutes defining the conditions under which children were admitted to certified schools. With the national inspectorate for certified industrial and reformatory schools continuing throughout the latter half of the century to exert pressure for uniformity of approach in Scotland and England, it appeared that both jurisdictions were adopting a common approach to criminal and destitute children. However, despite the constraints imposed by the overarching UK statutory system and the powerful accompanying trend towards convergence both at a practical level and in terms of ethos, the Scottish approach to juvenile offenders and destitute children remained distinctive in important ways. The focus of this chapter is the way in which the Scottish system adapted to and evolved within the statutory framework between 1860 and 1884, when a Royal Commission set up to investigate industrial and reformatory schools reported its findings.[2]

In a sense, each decade from the 1860s until the 1880s had its own tale to tell. The theme of the 1860s was one of consolidation as the statutory system became thoroughly embedded. The development of the system was well recorded in the pages of the *Reformatory and Refuge Journal*. The *Journal* covered all significant matters related to industrial and reformatory schools. It discussed legislative developments and had notes on visits to institutions all over Britain. It also provided commentary on official Reports by the inspectorate and reported on papers delivered at conferences by important figures in the reform movement, such as Thomas Guthrie from Scotland and the pre-eminent English reformer Mary Carpenter.[3] Much space was devoted to details of debates at meetings such as the Social Science Congress, where the latest ideas were exchanged. The overall impression which the *Journal* sought to convey in the 1860s was a sense of energetic and excited purpose reflecting a desire to create a flourishing framework of schools linked not just by common legislation but to some extent by shared aims and co-operation between institutions, even across borders. For example, at a meeting of managers of Scottish and English institutions in 1862 the possibility was discussed of supplying a reformatory in Yorkshire which had surplus places with reformatory boys from two Scottish counties.[4]

The project definitely had grand ideas, keeping an eye on the international scene and looking towards developments in the United States and on the continent for inspiration.[5] But drawing on ideas from other jurisdictions was nothing new for those involved in the English reformatory movement, particularly Mary Carpenter. As a Unitarian, she looked to New England as her spiritual homeland and was well informed about reformatory institutions developed there, as well as those established on the continental mainland, especially the renowned Mettray in France. And, of course, she was also hugely influenced in her endeavours to establish the statutory system by the success of pre-statutory initiatives in Scotland, particularly the Aberdeen system.[6] Developments in Scotland should be seen in the context of this dynamic of changing responses to juvenile offending on an international scale. This concern with international links was to have implications on a practical level, as those involved in the management of institutions developed programmes of emigration, particularly to Canada, for some children leaving institutions.[7] This chapter examines the way in which, throughout the 1860s, Scottish institutions responded to external pressures emanating from legislative developments and the growing dynamism of the reformatory-industrial movement across the UK.

The contrast between the beginning of the decade and the end was marked. In many ways the 1860s began optimistically for the Scottish reformers. After all, they appeared to have succeeded in securing a major goal by achieving a legislative framework. At this stage it was not entirely apparent that the statutory system they had striven so hard to achieve would eventually subvert their original vision of reform. As in the pre-statutory system, there was still scope for local variation, and in the course of this chapter evidence emerges that some towns, notably

Aberdeen and Edinburgh, managed in the early 1860s to some extent to retain the ethos of the original pre-statutory system.

Ten years later, the picture across Scotland as a whole had significantly altered. By the 1870s the original vision espoused by the Scottish reformers was severely compromised, and the main theme which emerged from this decade was one of attempted restoration of the essential elements and core humanity of the original project. The reformers had witnessed the statutory system taking on a momentum of its own as it flourished and developed in directions they had not anticipated. Residential institutions had become the norm, and the period saw the expansion of the industrial school system. The main architects of the original reforms were becoming advanced in years and they watched with concern as the routine institutionalisation of children under the statutory system undermined their long-held objective to help children in trouble. For example, following the introduction of universal compulsory education in Scotland in 1872, the industrial-reformatory legislation was used to detain children simply found truanting. Developments of this sort were alien to the ideals of the reformers, who placed high value on maintaining the integrity of the family bond. Anxious to preserve the legacy of benign reform, William Watson was determined to redress matters. The key to the success of the original pre-statutory enterprise had of course been the day industrial school, and it was to this idea that Watson returned. For this reason he became active in promoting a campaign for day industrial schools to be run on the lines of the early schools in Aberdeen. The outcome of this final major public intervention by the early campaigners is analysed in the course of this chapter.

If the hallmark of the 1870s was one of attempted restoration of the original vision, the early 1880s were marked by ambivalence and inertia in the face of calls for reform of the system. It was clear to many commentators that the system had developed multiple shortcomings, and yet little was done to tackle the problems. A Report on the state of the law relating to juvenile offenders in 1881 revealed judicial disquiet.[8] Calls for reform came from other quarters too, including Lord Norton in England, who as Viscount Adderley had been one of the prime sponsors in parliament of the original reformatory legislation.[9] Despite this, there appeared to be no official willingness to address the difficulties with root-and-branch reform. The Royal Commission on reformatory and industrial schools which reported in 1884 acknowledged the criticisms.[10] It heard the evidence of the veteran campaigner William Watson, who was still arguing lucidly at the age of eighty-eight that the residential industrial school system should be dismantled and replaced by day industrial schools. Watson was emphatic that it was wrong to separate children from their families, and also wrong to pursue impoverished parents through the courts for financial contributions.[11] However, the Report of the Royal Commission did little more than outline a list of recommendations with the aim of improving the existing system. Radical reappraisal had to wait another twelve years, and the outcome of the Departmental Committee on reformatory and industrial schools in 1896 which exposed and addressed many of the flaws and abuses of the system.[12]

Although it is true that at the level of policy the statutory system resolutely occupied a central position in the official response to children in trouble which remained virtually unassailable until the findings of the 1896 Committee, this did not mean that the system was immune to challenges through the courts. There were several reported cases where recourse to the High Court of Justiciary resulted in the liberation of children sentenced to detention in institutions.[13] In these cases the High Court dealt with bills of suspension and liberation seeking to overturn decisions by lower courts to send children to industrial or reformatory schools. The court's important role in addressing some of the inequities of the system, especially in remedying what it deemed to be abuse of procedure in the practice of the lower courts, is analysed in the course of the present and the following chapter.

At the other end of the court hierarchy were the police and burgh courts, which dealt with most of the committals of children to the institutions. While official case reports exist of some children's cases referred to the High Court of Justiciary, information about cases finally determined by lower courts is less accessible. One important source which sheds light on the practices of the lower courts in dealing with young offenders is the archive of records relating to boys sent by courts in Edinburgh, Glasgow and the Borders to Wellington Reformatory Farm School. These were cases of boys convicted of an offence, most commonly petty theft, and sentenced to a period of imprisonment followed by detention for five years in the reformatory under the Reformatory Schools Act.[14] It is particularly fortunate that these records remain, as Wellington was a very significant reformatory: according to the Inspector Sydney Turner, it held the singular distinction of being 'the Scottish Red Hill'.[15] For Turner this was no mean praise, as Red Hill was his own creation. Set up under the auspices of the Philanthropic Society in 1849, the reformatory at Red Hill in Surrey was the first experimental attempt to transplant to England a farm school based on the system set up by Demetz at Mettray in France, the system which Foucault identified as the pinnacle of the disciplinary ideal.[16] Like the reformatories in Mettray and at Red Hill, Wellington adopted a system of housing boys in small units or pavilions rather than in one large building. Turner clearly approved of this kind of architecture, believing that the smaller family-type unit would facilitate more effective reformation and avoid difficulties associated with some of the large soulless reformatories where many boys were housed under one roof.[17] Economic considerations prevented most reformatories from implementing the Mettray layout but, according to Turner, efforts were nonetheless made by many reformatories to adapt the 'domestic principle' by striving to create a homely environment. With the establishment of Wellington the disciplinary model took firm root on Scottish soil in a way which faithfully reflected the original French conception.

For an insight into cases resulting in admission into industrial schools from the 1870s, the Edinburgh Industrial Schools Complaints Books, containing details of the burgh court process relating to each child, have proved an equally useful source.[18] This archive of records, like those relating to Wellington, helps to flesh out a clearer picture of the statutory system in operation with fascinating detail about the circumstances of the children involved. While these sources are concerned with individual cases, an overview of the whole system in practice is given by reading the annual reports of the Inspector of Reformatory and Industrial Schools. The significance of the inspectorate is covered in the next section of this chapter.

The remainder of this chapter proceeds as follows. The next section considers the issue of centralisation and the role of the inspectorate. This is followed by a discussion of the position of the reformatory and industrial schools within the Victorian criminal justice system. The chapter then moves on to consider developments in each of the decades in turn.

CENTRALISATION AND THE ROLE OF THE INSPECTORATE

The inspectorate played a crucial part in unifying the system. In 1857 Sydney Turner (1814–79) was appointed as the first Inspector of Reformatory Schools, going on to undertake the onerous task of inspecting the developing network of reformatory and industrial schools until his retirement from the role in 1876.[19] Turner was a clergyman in the Church of England and a leading figure in the English reformatory movement. As noted earlier, he was instrumental in the development of Red Hill reformatory farm school in Surrey in 1849, where he served as chaplain.

Examining the role of the inspectorate reveals that it lacked adequate resources to perform its task. Compiling annual reports was an immense

undertaking. It involved visiting all the certified institutions and producing a report, albeit usually a brief one, on the progress of each one. The
preface to the reports contained a lengthy general statement with an
assessment of how the system was developing as a whole, and also contained a large section devoted to statistical analysis. There were pages
of tables recording numbers of admissions and discharges, along with
information about previous convictions of inmates, recidivism rates,
notes on the finances of institutions and details of the destinations of
children leaving the schools, if known.[20] Whether these reports accurately reflected the true nature of the establishments under inspection
has been questioned by some commentators. For instance, one former
inmate of an industrial school described the vigorous scrubbing and pol-
ishing in the days leading up to inspections and he doubted whether any
inspector ever witnessed anything which the managers of the institutions
did not wish him to see.[21] Nevertheless, the reports were far from uncrit-
ical. For example, in one report Sydney Turner accused a Scottish reformatory at Parkhead, Glasgow of forcing young boys to undertake the
arduous task of brick-making, which he described as degrading employment unsuitable for children.[22] In another Report he dealt unflinchingly
with a child sexual abuse scandal which occurred in the Glasgow House
of Refuge for boys in 1867. Far from sweeping the matter under the
carpet, the Report discussed the 'shock to public confidence caused by
the discovery of such corrupting practices'.[23]

Following the 'very searching and painful' inquiry, Mr McCallam,
the Superintendent of the Refuge, resigned and the reformatory's activities were suspended to allow the directors to place 'the institution on a
healthier footing'.[24] In a subsequent report, when the reformatory had
resumed its operations, Turner was critical that so many of the former
staff had been retained and was not surprised that there had been several
cases of absconding by boys.[25] The approach taken by the inspectorate
in these and other cases lends weight to the view that the inspectorate
adopted the role of attempting to protect children from the worst aspects
of the system.[26] It has been argued that Turner may have been ineffective
in confronting mistreatment of children,[27] but it has to be remembered
that the office of the inspectorate was surprisingly small in terms of man-
power. Based in an office in London, the chief inspector was supported
only by an assistant inspector and a number of clerks.[28] With its con-
strained resources and extensive responsibilities for inspecting schools
throughout the UK, the scope the inspectorate had for exerting much
influence over the day-to-day running of establishments must have been

limited, so its capacity for regulating the system should not be over-emphasised. However, it did at least provide a very significant external check on the activities of the institutions.

THE SCHOOLS IN THE VICTORIAN CRIMINAL JUSTICE SYSTEM

While the network of certified reformatory and industrial schools embraced a number of different types of institutions varying, for example, in size, grounds of admission, gender intake, location and types of industrial work carried out, what they all had in common was that they were run on the 'voluntary principle'.[29] Some schools were partially reliant on voluntary subscriptions and all were run by independent managers who exercised a considerable degree of autonomy. In some senses the schools occupied uncharted territory as private organisations which were an integral part of the criminal justice system. They were not state prisons, but as statutorily certified establishments under Home Office direction to which many children were sent to be detained by order of the courts they were central to the operation of the criminal justice system.[30] The ambiguous role of the schools was widely recognised and was the subject of debate in parliament in 1866, when the consolidating legislation was being discussed. One contributor to the discussion succinctly explained the position of the schools, which he described as 'public institutions':

> These schools were originally founded upon the voluntary principle, but they had become in some degree state institutions, and were partly maintained by public money.[31]

Clearly, although the school managers enjoyed a degree of independence in terms of internal organisation, and were subject to only infrequent outside inspection, the consensus was that they served a public function and were part and parcel of the fabric of criminal justice, a perception reinforced when prison authorities were authorised by statute to contribute to, build and maintain schools.[32] The importance of the schools' public function as an arm of the criminal justice system has been under-estimated. Mahood, Cale and Moore have concentrated on the socio-logical importance of the schools as child-saving institutions rather than stressing their significance within the criminal justice system.[33] Similarly, although Garland regards the schools as an influential model of insti-tutionalised reformation, he considers them to be on the perimeter of the criminal justice system: he describes them as 'private institutions, dealing with children and not with citizens, kept formally distinct from the state system of dealing with deviants'.[34] He argues:

> We should note that these institutions meant that the practice of reformation (albeit in an educational and often evangelical form) had a definite foothold in the system . . . they formed a reformative example on the margins of the system and one which would be referred to again and again as a precedent for a much wider (and somewhat different) practice of reform.[35]

This judgment of the schools as marginal fails to recognise the centrality of their role in providing the courts with an alternative to imprisonment for thousands of young offenders in mid-nineteenth-century Britain. Locating the schools at the centre, rather than on the fringes, of the criminal justice system has substantial implications. It suggests that ideas about reformation of individual offenders were widely accepted and put into practice far earlier than the Garland thesis allows. According to Sydney Turner, it was a central aim of reformatory schools to adapt their programmes of reformation to meet the needs of the individual offender:

> Reformatory training is of necessity essentially based upon religious influences. Little permanent impression can be made unless a sense of religious duty is aroused and religious affections awakened. For this simple free Scriptural teaching with careful personal application to the individual character is specially required.[36]

This approach contrasts with the Garland argument that in the Victorian criminal justice system 'each individual was treated "exactly alike", with no reference being made to his or her criminal type or individual character'.[37] This is an argument which is developed more fully in the next chapter in discussing the background to the juvenile court system.

For the moment the main point being emphasised here is that as the statutory system became ever more entrenched in the period 1860–84, it played a far from marginal role in the way the courts responded to criminal and destitute children.

THE SYSTEM IN THE 1860s

Consolidation was the central theme in the 1860s. Pressures to establish a common approach both north and south of the border came from a number of sources. As we have seen, the influence exerted by the inspectorate was important. Another vital factor was the consolidating legislation of the mid-1860s, which will be discussed shortly. But first I will look at a less obvious but also very influential factor in the way the system developed: the effect of funding cuts on voluntary admissions to the industrial schools. I will also look at the issue of variation within the system, focusing on the early 1860s when there continued to be considerable scope for local differences in the way Scottish towns operated. This section reveals that in the early years of the statutory system, in many respects the industrial schools in Aberdeen and Edinburgh were not very different in 1861 from the way they had been in the pre-statutory system. However, this was to change. The period following the consolidating legislation of the mid-1860s marked a time of transition for the industrial schools, as the process of adaptation to the constraints of the statutory system took effect. A new legislative focus on the criminality of industrial school admissions meant they were now regarded by the inspectorate as a form of junior reformatory, which had important consequences for the treatment of children. The final part of this section looks at the role of the reformatories in the 1860s.

Financial problems: funding cuts on voluntary admissions

The 1861 Select Committee Report on Education of Destitute Children addressed the vexed issue of funding. Scottish industrial schools had been affected by a reduction in the levels of state funding for pupils attending the schools as voluntary cases, a policy designed to decrease the number of voluntary attendees and to promote industrial schools as establishments reserved for cases committed by the courts.[38] The 1861 Committee recommended preserving the existing levels of funding, which set allowances per pupil far higher for committed cases than voluntary cases, and also stipulated that grants for general costs were to be restricted to those schools which were statutorily certified.[39] Those involved in the schools complained bitterly about the loss of the educational grants and inadequate support for voluntary cases, arguing that their role in preventing children from resorting to crime was being undervalued. Such a departure from the pre-statutory conception of industrial schools as primarily preventive institutions met with resistance from the original campaigners, especially Guthrie and Watson.[40] This concern was voiced by Scottish witnesses to the 1861 Select Committee.

In his evidence, William Watson stressed the value of the schools as an 'immense boon' to society which had transformed the face of Aberdeen:

> In the town there were 280 children reported by the police in 1840 as living by begging and stealing; there is not a child in Aberdeen living by begging or stealing now.[41]

Arguing that the government should at least support the schools to the extent of meeting the cost of the educational element of the institutions, he pointed to the widespread recognition of the value of the schools in the community, which allowed the schools to rely on regular voluntary subscriptions from local people to meet the costs of food and clothing for the children. Watson was well aware of the risk posed by seeking public funding: there was a fear that receiving public money would undermine the capacity of the schools to raise the voluntary subscriptions on which they depended. However, he felt that in view of the proven capacity of the schools to prevent children at risk from descending into a life of crime, it was fair to expect the government to assist in shouldering part of the burden by paying for the salaries of the teachers, leaving other costs to be met by charitable donations. He stressed that the schools were so successful in producing useful members of society that local businesses were clamouring to employ the children emerging from industrial schools.[42] But despite Watson's very robust plea on behalf of the schools, he did not succeed in improving the level of funding.

Part of the reason for this appeal for increased assistance falling on deaf ears was that the arguments advanced on behalf of Scottish industrial schools with their mixed intake of voluntary and committed cases were undermined by the position adopted by some of the English ragged schools, notably the London ragged schools under the patronage of Lord Shaftesbury. Under Shaftesbury's considerable influence these schools for the destitute children of London spurned the notion of government aid, preferring to rely entirely on charitable donations for fear that their independence would be threatened and their evangelical, missionary focus compromised by accepting public money.[43] This approach was in perfect keeping with the 1861 Committee's evident preoccupation with discouraging 'pauperism' at public expense.[44] However, in the face of hostile questioning, Watson strongly refuted the notion that the schools undermined the self-reliance of the poor, arguing that the experience of Aberdeen had shown they had completely the opposite effect.[45]

Ultimately this governmental financial policy favouring committed cases at the expense of voluntary admissions had a profound impact. Over the course of the 1860s the number of industrial schools in Scotland with a mixed intake of voluntary day pupils and compulsory cases declined in favour of residential institutions, usually single sex, reserved mainly for pupils detained under court order.[46] The change in character in the certified industrial schools in the course of the 1860s was clearly expressed by Sydney Turner in 1868:

> The Certified Industrial Schools are of two classes. The one for both sexes, in which a certain number of the children attending are day scholars, who receive instruction but are only partially fed; the other for either boys or girls exclusively, in which the children are entirely lodged and boarded, and the majority detained under magistrate's warrant. The Scotch schools were generally of the former description, but are now mostly of the latter.[47]

Local variation in Aberdeen and Edinburgh in the early 1860s

The most remarkable aspect of Watson's evidence was that under his influence the industrial schools in Aberdeen in 1861 seemed to be operating very much as they did in the pre-statutory era. Of the four schools involved in Watson's project only two were statutorily certified, and out of a total of 490 pupils attending the schools only forty were committed by magistrates under Dunlop's Act, the remainder being voluntary admissions.[48] Entirely in keeping with Watson's views on the importance of children remaining in a family environment, children committed statutorily were accommodated with respectable local families, not in an institutional setting: clearly, even though the statute required that children under court order should not remain at home, the managers of the schools in Aberdeen interpreted the statute to allow children to continue to live in a family home so far as possible.[49]

It is not clear why only two of the four industrial schools sought statutory certification under Dunlop's Act, but the answer may lie in a desire to retain independence and also in the relatively low number of committed cases: there was obviously no need for more than two schools capable of receiving statutory admissions.[50] As Watson commented, the mere existence of the Act and the knowledge that repeated occurrences of vagrancy would result in a court order forcing attendance and removal of a child from home was enough in itself to keep juvenile vagrancy to a minimum.[51] There had only been five or six committed cases the previous year, and in Watson's view the Act had been successful in reaching the children it was intended for. That did not mean, however, that the legislation could not be improved. Watson approved of proposed legislation extending the category of children who could be committed to industrial schools to children who 'associated with thieves'.[52] The existing categories of children eligible to attend the certified industrial schools were

destitute and vagrant children. Under the amending legislation about to
come into effect, the category of children admissible under court order
to the certified schools would be extended to include children under
twelve charged with an offence and 'refractory' children under fourteen,
as well as those associating with thieves. With this mixing of children
from destitute and offending backgrounds, the intake of the schools was
in legislative terms restored to the pre-statutory position. However, in
practice there is evidence that the Scottish courts had continued to send
young children appearing before them for trivial first offences to industrial schools anyway, just as they had done in the pre-statutory system.[53]

In answer to detailed questioning on the position of children who
had been committed under Dunlop's Act, Watson explained that in some
such cases children had security for good behaviour offered on their
behalf by their parents in order to 'bail out' the children so that the
parents would avoid being pursued in court by the Poor Law Board for
recovery of the costs of child support.[54] Unlike in Edinburgh,[55] there
were no cases in Aberdeen of Poor Law Boards offering security; this
was only permitted in towns where the Board could offer a child a place
at a poor law school, none of which existed in Aberdeen.

The poor law inspectors of Edinburgh were far more active: according to Charles Ferguson, the Superintendent of the United Industrial
School, the policy of poor law inspectors in Edinburgh was invariably to
offer security rather than meet the costs of supporting children committed statutorily to the industrial school. This was done on the basis that
the child would be offered alternative support by the Board, either in the
poorhouse or by lodging out the child with respectable parties. However,
Ferguson reported that in one case a child removed by the inspector was
not offered education in a poorhouse school but instead sent to work in
a colliery in Falkirk.[56] Even when children were provided with education
in the poorhouse, this was likely to have been of a very inferior quality
compared to what was available at the industrial school.[57] The effect
of this cost-cutting policy being adopted by inspectors of the poor was
that there was only one child in the Edinburgh United Industrial School
committed under Dunlop's Act.[58] However, the ability of either poor law
inspectors or parents to circumvent the Act in this way was soon to be
curtailed by the new Industrial Schools (Scotland) Act 1861, which did
not re-enact the section allowing security to be offered.[59]

What emerges clearly from the evidence provided by both Watson from
Aberdeen and Ferguson from Edinburgh is that in the early 1860s there
continued to be scope for local variation in the way different Scottish
towns operated. In many ways the industrial schools in these towns were

very similar in 1861 to how they had been in the pre-statutory system. The main objective of Dunlop's Act, to provide powers to compel attendance at industrial schools in cases where it was deemed necessary, appeared to have operated so well in Aberdeen that Watson could say that the work of the Act had been almost accomplished.[60] In both Aberdeen and Edinburgh, the main work of the schools in providing industrial education for destitute children continued as in the pre-statutory system; the primary focus was still on exercising a preventive role in rescuing vulnerable children from descending into a life of crime. As before, there was a great demand for places in the schools and stringent admissions procedures were adopted to ensure only deserving cases were admitted, with parents of prospective applicants having to complete an admission schedule, followed by a visit inquiring into the home circumstances of the family.[61] However, the activities of poor law inspectors in Edinburgh in offering security for children being committed under Dunlop's Act circumvented the operation of the Act so that few children brought before a magistrate for vagrancy were retained by the schools as compulsory attendees. This practice was curtailed by the legislation in 1861, as noted in the previous section.

Over the course of the 1860s the predominance of this kind of day industrial school gave way in Scotland to a different type of institution, the residential and usually single-sex industrial school where most children were detained under court order. As we have seen, one of the main reasons for the decline in voluntary attendees was the policy changing the way in which schools were funded. Sydney Turner offered some additional insight into the reasons for the change in the schools in his 1870 report. The main reason he gave for the change was the impact of 1860s legislation on industrial schools. In extending the categories of admission to include criminal conduct by young children and defining the grounds of admission to include 'refractory' conduct and children whose 'parents or associates shall be criminal'[62] as well as those who were vagrant or begging, the emphasis had been placed on the criminality of industrial school admissions. He said this had changed the character of the schools so that they had altered from being primarily concerned with the education of the 'ragged and neglected class' to 'houses of detention for the young vagabond and petty misdemeanant'.[63] He added:

> The position of certified industrial schools has thus completely changed, and though still called schools they are in fact reformatories of a milder sort . . . In accordance with this change in character in their objects their locality and their mode of operation have been changing too. Originally they were designed and used as day schools and the majority of the children found in them were day scholars. They were, therefore established in the poorer and

more populous districts of the towns in which they were situated. But for some years past from considerations of health and the necessity of more careful custody and more varied and especially of out-door employment, many of the schools have been moved into the suburbs of the town or country surrounding it; a change which has rendered the attendance of day scholars in most cases impossible or very inconvenient and has confined the inmates almost entirely to children regularly committed by magistrates for detention.[64]

In keeping with this change, two industrial school training ships were established for the first time in Scotland in 1869. One berthed on the Clyde and the other on the Tay, they received boys from various towns and cities with a view to training them in nautical skills. This pattern of relocation of children far from their homes was to continue, with, for example, many cases of Edinburgh girls being committed to Nazareth House[65] Industrial School in Aberdeen from the late 1870s onwards, as will be discussed later. However, it should be recognised that despite the overarching pressures towards conformity of approach, there still continued to be evidence of diversity within the system in the late 1860s. By this point most children in Scottish industrial schools were under court order but in some towns, such as Edinburgh, some detainees were lodged out rather than accommodated in the schools;[66] there continued to be a number of mixed-sex schools, although over the next decade they were to become increasingly substituted by single-sex schools;[67] and similarly, although the Inspector's Report[68] records that in 1869 some day scholars were attending industrial schools, for example in Edinburgh and Aberdeen, several years later this was no longer the case.[69] The transformation taking place in the 1860s was a process continuing into the 1870s. The role that major pieces of consolidating legislation had to play in this change in the certified industrial schools will be explored more fully in the next section.

LEGISLATION IN THE 1860s

Legislation admitting young offenders to industrial schools

The 1860s were characterised by consolidating legislation. As we have seen, when Watson gave evidence to the 1861 Committee he was anticipating the introduction of new legislation on industrial schools, the Industrial Schools (Scotland) Act 1861. This consolidating Act repealed Dunlop's Act and the Act of 1856.[70] The Act extended the category of children admissible under court order to industrial schools to include not only vagrant and destitute children but children under twelve charged with an offence, children who were associating with thieves, and also 'refractory' (uncontrollable) children under the age of fourteen, but not any who had previously been imprisoned for more than thirty days. If a parent applied to have a 'refractory' child admitted, then the parent could be ordered to make the maximum parental contribution of five shillings a week; this was intended to discourage parents from offloading their responsibilities. By admitting children under twelve who had offended to industrial schools, the Act allowed very young offenders to be dealt with under the industrial schools legislation rather than that applying to reformatories, which meant that they were no longer required to endure a period of prior imprisonment. As discussed earlier, this also meant that there was legislative authority for both destitute and offending children to be admitted under court order in certified institutions, and there is some support for the view that this reflected existing practice in schools.

Significantly for localities such as Edinburgh, where poor law inspectors had undermined the operation of Dunlop's Act by offering security for good behaviour of children, the power to offer security was not re-enacted. The Act also empowered managers of schools to lodge out children under detention with their parents or respectable parties, although as we have seen this was in practice what happened in Aberdeen already.[71] Framed in similar terms to the Industrial Schools (Scotland) Act 1861, the English Industrial Schools Act was greeted with enthusiasm by Sydney Turner:

> We cannot have a better model for our English Industrial Schools than those of Scotland, and especially those in Aberdeen, whose success laid the foundation of the system which the Industrial Schools' Acts recognise.[72]

UK legislation on industrial schools

The Industrial Schools Act 1866 consolidated the Scottish and English legislation, placing the certified industrial schools of both countries within the same statutory framework. According to Turner, the Act gave 'an increased stability and fresh impulse to the most useful movement which it is designed to strengthen and direct'.[73] The statute set out the categories of children who could be sent under court order to an industrial school when brought by 'any person' before a magistrate in Scotland or two justices in England.[74] The Act provided that children under fourteen found begging could be sent to an industrial school: children included here were those 'found begging or receiving alms (whether actually or under the pretext of selling or offering for sale any things) or being in any street or public place for the purpose of so begging or receiving alms'. This definition was interpreted by the courts to apply to children selling objects such as matches or bunches of heather on the street.[75] The Act also applied to children 'found destitute, either being an orphan or having a surviving parent who is undergoing penal servitude or imprisonment'. As before, children were eligible to be admitted to a certified industrial school if 'found wandering and not having any home or settled place of abode or proper guardianship or visible means of subsistence' and, also as in the earlier legislation, the Act included children thought to 'frequent the company of reputed thieves'.[76] As in the 1861 legislation, the managers retained the discretion to lodge children out of school either with parents or any 'trustworthy and respectable person'.[77] Under section twenty-seven, managers of a certified school were given power to grant a licence to a child after not less than eighteen months' detention.[78]

The Act retained the provision that children under twelve charged with an offence could be sent to an industrial school provided that they did not have a previous conviction.[79] It also re-enacted the section providing that parents or guardians 'unable to control' refractory children under the age of fourteen could apply to have them admitted, a widely used ground of admission.[80] A further section related to children in a poorhouse brought before a magistrate by managers of the institution: where they were either found to be refractory or had a parent convicted of a crime punishable by penal servitude or imprisonment, the court could, 'if it is satisfied that it is expedient', order the child to be sent to a certified industrial school.[81]

There was also an important section in the Act concerning liability for upkeep of children in industrial schools. Section thirty-eight applied only to Scotland, and its effect was that if a child was in receipt of parochial relief within three months of being brought before magistrates, then the local authority would have to repay the Treasury for the cost of his upkeep while in the school. This section re-enacted section twenty-one of Dunlop's Act, so it had been part of the Scottish legislation from the outset of the statutory system. Sydney Turner saw this as a 'most valuable provision' and regretted that it had not been extended to England: in his view, many of the children eligible to attend industrial schools under court order should not be maintained at the expense of the general taxpayer because they belonged to 'the half-destitute and ill-trained classes for whom the local authorities should justly and naturally be responsible'.[82] However, this section was the source of much conflict in Scotland between the Treasury and parish authorities about which body was responsible for maintenance.[83] The ramifications of this section were seen throughout the whole period in which the Act applied. For example, in the later decades of the century, when the Royal Scottish Society for the Prevention of Cruelty to Children (RSSPCC) was active in rounding up destitute, vagrant children from the streets of Scottish cities, they often gave children refuge in shelters prior to appearing before a magistrate to be sent to an industrial school. The ostensible reason given for the retention might be to have time to complete inquiries or to negotiate with the authorities of a school for their admission. However, this was not the whole story. The 1896 Report on Reformatory and Industrial Schools heard evidence that when children were detained in the shelters the true reason for such detentions was to keep the child for the period of time required to ensure that the child would be admitted to the industrial school without the obstacle of a reluctant local authority being encumbered with the responsibility of having to pay towards the child's upkeep while in the school.[84]

To summarise the main differences between this and the previous Scottish legislation: apart from the section allowing licensing out of children after a minimum of eighteen months, the chief difference was the extension of the categories of admission to include children with a parent in prison, and children guilty of refractory conduct in a poorhouse. This emphasis on bad conduct and criminal parentage, combined with the fact that young child offenders and those associating with thieves were already candidates for admission, added to the changing perception and position of the industrial school in Scotland through the 1860s. As noted earlier, Turner now regarded industrial schools as the preserve of the 'young vagabond and petty misdemeanant', or a 'milder' sort of reformatory for younger children.[85] It is clear that this consolidating legislation had important consequences for the criminalisation of children in Scotland: from being a place of refuge for the poor and destitute, the industrial school was in the process of becoming a place of detention for the budding criminal.

Consolidating Reformatory Legislation

Like the Industrial Schools Act 1866, the Reformatory Schools Act 1866 repealed previous Acts and placed the legislation in both Scotland and England on the same statutory footing. There were two important changes with respect to both countries. First, the Act provided that young offenders under the age of sixteen could be sent to a reformatory after serving a prison sentence of ten days, again for not less than two and not more than five years. This meant that the Act reduced the period of prior imprisonment from fourteen to ten days. The second main change introduced by the Act was that children under the age of ten were not

to be sent to reformatory unless they were previous offenders.[86] Sydney
Turner summarised the 'chief improvements' of the Act as:

> a power of apprenticing their inmates after being out on licence was given
> to the managers as a check on the interference of unworthy parents; that
> the managers were empowered to detain such offenders as were committed
> for absconding or insubordination to prison for an additional period corre-
> sponding to the time during which they had been absent from the school;
> that the process of enforcing the payments of parents was made simpler and
> more direct, especially in Scotland; and that on this as on the other points of
> licence and apprenticeship the law was made uniform for both Scotch [sic]
> and English schools. The minimum age at which children should be received
> into reformatories was fixed at ten years, except in cases of second conviction
> or of sentence by a superior court.[87]

REFORMATORIES IN THE 1860s

For the Scottish reformers, the primary focus had always been on prevention of crime. For Watson and Guthrie, the reformatory was the last
resort, almost an admission of failure to rescue a child.[88] As discussed
in the previous chapter, the notion of the residential reformatory for the
convicted young offender was not part of the original Scottish vision.[89]
The Scottish reformers had been motivated by a far more holistic,
welfare-focused approach which embraced both destitute and offending
children in a project based on the day industrial school. In some respects
the 1861 amending statute on industrial schools which made children
under twelve charged with an offence eligible to be sent by court order
to a certified industrial school represented a legislative concession to the
idea of combining both types of children in one institution, although
there is some evidence that this was happening in practice in Scottish
industrial schools anyway.[90]

By the early 1860s, reformatories were well established within the
system. Watson was asked by the 1861 Committee about the reformatory in Aberdeen, Oldmill. He explained the circumstances under which
a child could be admitted to the reformatory:

> If a child has become delinquent and has committed a theft, he is brought
> before a magistrate; the magistrate finds that the child has been living a
> vicious life and has no proper person to take care of him, he is then sent to
> prison with a view to him being taken into a reformatory for a period of five
> years. Almost all children now sent to prison are sent to prison for the pur-
> pose of being sent to a reformatory.[91]

In giving this answer Watson was remaining diplomatically silent about his own personal opinion on the prior period of imprisonment required before admission to a reformatory; elsewhere, he was scathing about the practice of imprisoning children at all.[92] Watson's response here demonstrates his perception that in Scotland imprisonment for children was by 1861 regarded chiefly as a prelude to detention in a reformatory. However, this may be an overstatement by Watson of the effect of reformatories: according to the Inspector's Reports, there was still a considerable proportion of children undergoing sentences of imprisonment alone.[93]

Some indication of the types of cases which resulted in children being sent to a reformatory is given by the Wellington Reformatory Farm School records.[94] The Superintendent of the reformatory, Mr Craster, spoke at a meeting of reformatory school managers in 1861, and his description of the basis on which the school operated was recorded in the *Reformatory and Refuge Journal*:

> The managers refused to admit any boy for less than five years . . . If they found it was his first offence they did not regard him as a criminal and advised his being sent to Dr Guthrie's Industrial School.[95]

Wellington admission records suggest that the requirement that detention was to be five years in all cases was for the sake of uniformity, but boys were usually sent out on licence 'after one half or two thirds of the period'.[96] Before leaving, boys were required to show some evidence of numeracy and literacy, particularly ability to read the Bible, and to have acquired skills to enable them to find employment, either related to farm work or a trade such as tailoring, shoemaking or carpentry.[97]

In almost all cases, the boys sent to Wellington had previous convictions, normally for petty theft, and were being sent to Wellington for a further act of theft. However, where a boy had committed an offence which was regarded as serious, he could be admitted to the reformatory even if he had no previous convictions.[98] The age restriction of twelve was adhered to in most cases but there were some exceptions, where, for example, young boys aged eleven were already detained in an industrial school on offence grounds and received a conviction for committing a further offence in the school; in this case, the Superintendent of the industrial school requested that they should be sent to the reformatory despite being under twelve.[99]

Twelve-year-old James Eagle was a typical admission to Wellington. His case was heard at the Police Court in Edinburgh in March 1861 before Magistrate John Boyd. James was convicted of the theft of two bottles of ale from a shop at Market Street, Edinburgh. He had one pre-vious conviction for assault when aged nine, for which he was admon-ished and sent to the ragged school at Castle Hill. James was sentenced under the Youthful Offenders Act 1854 to fourteen days at the prison in Edinburgh, to be followed by detention for a period of five years in Wellington Reformatory. In accordance with the policy of inquiring into details of a child's background, the admission records of the school provide information about James's circumstances, recording that he was one of five children, that his parents were both of 'intemperate habits' and that his father, a cap maker, had convictions for theft and assault.[100]

In a later case dealt with under the consolidating statute, the Reformatory Schools Act 1866, which reduced the period of prior imprisonment from fourteen days to ten days, thirteen-year-old Thomas Collins was convicted of theft committed along with his brother and two other boys.[101] He was sentenced at Musselburgh Police Court in June 1867 to ten days in Musselburgh prison, to be followed by three years at Wellington.

For an insight into the judiciary's view of the role of Wellington Reformatory, we can look to the reported case of *HMA* v. *Beattie and Kelly*.[102] James Kelly was a thirteen-year-old boy convicted of the theft of carpenter's tools by housebreaking and opening lockfast places, and sentenced by the High Court of Justiciary to ten days' imprisonment followed by five years in Wellington. He had acted along with an older boy of sixteen who was sentenced to penal servitude for seven years. James had no previous convictions and his counsel produced a letter commending his good character from the headmaster of James's school, New Greyfriars' School in Edinburgh. The Lord Justice General pro-nounced on the gravity of the offence, which he said would normally merit 'a serious sentence', but in view of James's plea of guilty, his youth and previous good character he stated:

> A consideration of these circumstances, and that you may yet become a better boy, and a hope that you may still lead an honest and industrious life, has led the court to consider what sentence should be pronounced against you . . . these objects would best be secured by your being subjected to a confinement in a reformatory school during a lengthened period of years, previous to which it is necessary that we pronounce sentence of imprisonment for a short period.[103]

James's case was unusual in that most boys who were admitted to Wellington had appeared before lower courts, most commonly the police or burgh courts or sometimes the sheriff court for fairly minor thefts.

Theft by housebreaking, however, was regarded as a serious crime, as seen by the severe sentence imposed on James's co-accused, who was not eligible to be sent to a reformatory as he had attained the age of sixteen. The comments addressed to James by the Lord Justice General suggest a new interest in securing the best means of reforming the individual young offender, turning him into 'a better boy'.[104] Clearly it was no longer simply a matter of judges administering punishment; there was now a focus on the best way of ensuring that young offenders would become 'honest and industrious'. The influence of Mary Carpenter, the guiding spirit of the reformatory movement, was palpable in this new judicial attitude. It appears that a decade after the Youthful Offenders Act, the rhetoric of the reformatory campaigners had thoroughly permeated even the highest echelons of the Scottish judiciary.

THE 1870s: A PERIOD OF RECLAMATION

In the 1870s it was abundantly clear that the statutory system in practice was diverging significantly from the original conception of the Scottish reformers. The pre-statutory system had been based on the success of day industrial schools, first in Aberdeen and then in other Scottish towns. However, as the statutory system had evolved the predominance of industrial schools containing a mix of boys and girls and both day pupils attending on a voluntary basis and pupils under court order, whether residential inmates or lodged out, had been eclipsed. By the 1870s, most Scottish industrial schools were single-sex residential boarding establishments where the majority were detained under court order.[105]

As the schools were residential there was no perceived necessity to locate schools near children's families, and the system expanded to include a new form of industrial school, industrial training ships for boys sent under court warrant: the *Mars* on the Tay and the *Cumberland* on the Clyde. The Edinburgh Industrial Schools Complaints Books record many cases of boys being sent to *Mars* from the early 1870s onwards.[106] The frequency of committals from Edinburgh certainly lends weight to the view expressed by the Inspector's Report that admissions to *Mars* were 'much too rapid'.[107] He had a similar comment to make about the *Cumberland* training ship.[108]

The Inspector's Reports of the early 1870s were the last written by Sydney Turner. They make interesting reading. As one of the most significant figures in the English reformatory movement and Chaplain of Red Hill, he had devoted many years to overseeing the development of the statutory system. In these final Reports he was clearly keen to offer his evaluation of how the system had evolved and to suggest improvements for the future. With the retiral of Sydney Turner in 1876 and the death of Mary Carpenter the following year, there was a definite sense of handing the baton on and trying to ensure that the legacy of reform was left in good order.

The Report of 1875 is particularly interesting in its review of the development of the system over the years. Commenting on the UK system as a whole, Turner noted that in the period since 1864 the number of reformatory schools had not increased and the number detained in them had not increased significantly, from 4,300 in 1864 to 5,000 in 1874. This contrasted with the expansion of industrial schools over the same period, both in terms of number and size. He noted that in 1861, when 'the first effective Industrial Schools Act was passed for England', there were thirty-eight schools, mainly in Scotland, containing 488 children, while at the end of 1874 there were 104 schools throughout the UK, with 11,400 children. He attributed this increase to the schools being used 'as asylums for children who should naturally have been placed under the care of parish authorities or as a means of relief and charitable assistance for those whom the poverty or carelessness of their parents left without adequate protection or support'.[109] He added that 'so long, indeed, as children can be freely sent at any age under fourteen for six or seven or more years detention in these schools as being orphans or "without proper guardianship", that is practically because their parents are too poor or too indifferent to maintain and control them properly, new schools will be required and existing schools will be pressed to enlarge their accommodation to an almost unlimited extent'.[110] In his view, the schools had achieved a great deal in reducing juvenile crime and juvenile vagrancy but they had been overused and should have been reserved for 'the vagrant, the vicious and the half criminal'.[111] This attitude was far less inclusive than that of the original Scottish reformers: when they had established the first industrial schools they were happy to embrace all genuinely destitute children, although of course their vision was centred on the idea of the day industrial school, not residential institutions.

By the mid-1870s, the original reformers were ready to attempt to reclaim their central vision of the day industrial school. Watson recorded in his autobiography that he attended a conference in Edinburgh of managers of industrial and reformatory schools in May 1875 where he spoke on a subject close to his heart, that of the importance of 'powers of parents to custody of their own children'.[112] He also noted that he discussed the issue of day industrial schools with the wealthy and influential English philanthropist Baroness Angela Burdett Coutts:

> She entirely agreed with my view on day industrial feeding schools as it was impossible by the Certified Board and lodging schools to undertake the class of children for whom the industrial school was originally intended.[113]

Spurred on by such support, Watson engaged enthusiastically in a campaign to introduce day industrial schools to Glasgow. Despite his advanced age, he put in a valiant effort in writing to newspapers, publishing papers and supporting campaigners. He also rallied support for a parallel campaign in England run by the elderly but still indomitable reformer, Mary Carpenter.[114] Glasgow responded to the call for reform by recourse to local legislation, as it had in the 1840s when the Houses of Refuge were set up. In 1878 local legislation was used to provide a statutory basis for day industrial schools much like the original schools set up in Scottish towns in the 1840s, a significant development for the city and one which set Glasgow apart from other Scottish cities in some respects.[115] This was another successful appeal to the Glasgow ethic of local civic responsibility and accountability. It took a further fifteen years for Scotland to implement national legislation providing for day industrial schools.[116]

THE EARLY 1880s: CALLS FOR REFORM

Calls for reform came in the early 1880s from a number of sources. Even the architect of the original reformatory legislation, Lord Norton, formerly Viscount Adderley, questioned the role of reformatory and industrial schools: in 1881 he was advocating that they should be replaced by 'schools for neglected and destitute children'.[117]

A Report in 1881 on the state of the law relating to juvenile offenders revealed that sheriffs had concerns. In particular they were critical of the statutory provision requiring prior imprisonment of juvenile offenders before admission to a reformatory.[118] This concern was said in the Report to be shared by Scottish reformatory managers and more generally by 'enlightened public opinion', which 'condemned' the provision contained in section fourteen of the Reformatory Schools Act 1866 requiring a period of ten days' prior imprisonment.[119] Objections were also raised that in some cases children were sentenced to detention in reformatories after being convicted of very minor offences which were not even offences under general statutes or common law, but simply trivial transgressions under local statutes, such as stone-throwing or vagrancy. Questions were raised as to the competence of this procedure under section fourteen.[120] This issue was subsequently dealt with in the case of *Maguire* v. *Fairbairn*, where the High Court of Justiciary held that section fourteen was not applicable to cases where children had committed police offences.[121] This case was discussed by Sheriff Substitute Spens of Lanarkshire.[122] He recounted the number of children who had been sent to reformatories in Scotland for police offences in the years leading up to this decision: seventy-two in 1879 for vagrancy; eight in 1880 for breach of the peace, and fifty-one for vagrancy; in 1881 fifty-seven were sent for vagrancy and two children were sent for sleeping in a close. The *Maguire* case involved a fifteen-year-old boy who was sentenced to ten days' imprisonment followed by five years in a reformatory for breach of the peace. The High Court passed a bill of suspension and liberation, suspending the order to send him to the reformatory and granting liberation. The Lord Justice Clerk said: 'I do not think that clause fourteen was ever intended to apply to the minor grades of crime, but only to those of graver complexion, such as theft or similar offences.'[123]

In 1882 a Royal Commission was issued to investigate all aspects of the operation and management of reformatory and industrial schools.[124] Taking two years to amass and consider evidence, the Commission reported in 1884. For critics of the system, the report was disappointing. Although it recommended an end to the practice of imprisonment prior to admission to a reformatory, the alternatives it suggested were harsh. It recommended that instead, magistrates should be empowered to order that boys should be whipped.[125] For girls it recommended the alternative of solitary confinement, the length of which was to vary according to age: a maximum of seven days for those under twelve and not more than fourteen days for older girls. Its suggestions to improve education were more enlightened: for example, that the prospects of teachers at the schools should be placed on an equal footing with teachers in public elementary schools. In relation to inspections it recommended that the educational aspect of the schools should be inspected by the Education Department but that all other aspects should remain under Home Office direction. It advised that children should not be detained beyond the age of sixteen and proposed that licensing out for children should be used more often.[126] However, the Commission singularly failed to address fundamental questions about the nature of the system. This was despite hearing evidence extremely critical of the system from, for example, William Watson.

Giving remarkably lucid evidence even in his late eighties, William Watson was characteristically forthright. He strongly advocated returning to the original principle upon which his early schools in Aberdeen had been founded, that of the day industrial school. Questioned about the potentially adverse influence that parents could have on children, he responded that this was of small concern when children were returning home at seven o'clock in the evening tired out after being occupied all day at the day industrial school. In his view there was little opportunity for parents to exercise a bad influence in these circumstances and he had come across many cases where the children had been able to exert 'a great change in the character of the parents' as a result of the good influence of the school. He vehemently denounced the residential industrial schools for destroying familial affection, leaving children with no home to return to when they were eventually discharged from the schools:

> they must have a home, and that is the great objection to those sleeping places where children are kept all night. You break up at once the tie between parent and child. The parent sometimes is very glad to get quit of it; but at the same time when a child is kept for two or three or four or five years locked up in an industrial school it loses all natural affection, and his parent forgets it, and does not care about it, and the consequence is that when it comes out it really has no home to go to. Therefore, I think that these day and night schools ought to be utterly abolished. I never found that any evil whatever resulted from children going to their parents' home.[127]

Referring to the period when Dunlop's Act came into effect, Watson explained that in Aberdeen there was discussion about whether committed cases should be kept overnight, but the schools adhered to their principle of day attendance for both voluntary and committed cases. In cases where children had no homes they usually had no difficulty in finding homes for them, particularly for the girls, though there were sometimes problems finding people willing to take the boys in; it was this he believed that led some institutions to house homeless boys overnight but he deplored the fact that 'now they all sleep there, I believe in many schools'.[128] Watson advocated that all certified industrial schools should be converted into day schools, and that government aid should be withdrawn from those that refused to comply. He also argued that managers of schools should be given discretion to discharge pupils when they considered they were ready, rather than be restricted by a definite period of detention; this would mean that the children leaving the schools could take advantage of employment opportunities when they arose.

Asked if his opinion that the existing industrial schools system should be abolished applied also to reformatories, Watson replied that reformatories were a different matter. He was of the view that they should be retained for older children who had become 'delinquent' and were beyond the age when they could be sent to an industrial school, for those beyond thirteen or fourteen. There was a need for them in such cases as otherwise magistrates would not know what to do with the children, but he argued that prior imprisonment should be abolished as it was 'a great mistake'.[129] For Watson, the central focus was not on the reformatories, which he viewed as an adjunct to the main enterprise of prevention to be carried on in the day industrial schools.

Watson was pressed on his views about the clause in the Industrial Schools Act 1866 'which deals with children who might be convicted of crime but against whom no conviction is made or recorded in order that they may be sent to an industrial school'.[130] Asked if he regarded a day industrial school as appropriate for these children who had offended, he replied that children's offences were usually very minor matters and that the day industrial school should include children brought before the court on offending grounds. In answer to a further question on the issue of whether all children under twelve should be excluded from reformatories, Watson commented on his practice as a Sheriff dealing with children's cases and also on the impression that his many visits to institutions had made upon him:

> Yes, I think that every child under twelve might be sent to an industrial school, and that reformatories might in general be found for the delinquent children. I look upon children's offences in general as comparatively trifling. I never had a case in which I thought it necessary to send a child to reformatory, or at least very few instances, as far as I recollect, but my recollection is not quite as good as it was some years ago. I visited the schools over and over again and was very much interested with what I saw in most of them; but I was very sorry to see a child taken away from its parents, and kept in a certified industrial school, and who perhaps for three years never saw its parents. I think it was very cruel, and I was very unwilling to break up the family connection.[131]

This passage clearly conveys Watson's distress and disappointment with the way the industrial schools system had departed from his original project. From the very outset he had been motivated by the best of humanitarian ideals and had devoted much of his life to the cause of assisting children in trouble. As the passage suggests, he spent much time visiting institutions, always interested in how they were developing. He also attended many conferences of the Social Science Congress, the sounding board of those interested in reform in this area, often delivering papers expounding his ideas. A key element of his philosophy had always been supporting not just the children but also trying to improve the lot of whole families: by elevating the condition of children he sought to use them to raise the values and expectations of parents too. This core idea had been undermined by the development of a system removing children from their homes, breaking up family ties to such an extent that children leaving institutions after several years' separation from their families were effectively estranged with no real homes to return to. From Watson's viewpoint this was a complete reversal of what he had set out to do.

This appearance at the Royal Commission was to be Watson's last major contribution in the public arena. Even in the very twilight of his life he was fighting the corner for the destitute and disadvantaged, promoting the value of compassion. He was clearly bewildered by the continuing concentration on pursuing parental contributions for the upkeep of children. Responding to a question on this issue, he commented that he had never found any parents he thought were in a position to pay. He also stressed the point which seemed to have long been lost sight of by everyone else in the endless arguments over funding, that the children attending these schools applied themselves diligently to industrial work which was of economic benefit, and their efforts should be appreciated and valued:

> I always understood that in an industrial school the children paid for their education, and that the parents did not require to pay for them. I knew very well that they did not, but at the same time I was anxious to impress upon the minds of the children that they paid for what they got. They gave five hours to labour very willingly, and in many cases their earnings amounted to a considerable sum.[132]

This was an important point of principle for Watson, that the dignity of children should be respected by ensuring that they were not made to feel like charity cases. Unfortunately this core idea was far from uppermost in the minds of those running the schools in the 1880s.

CONCLUSION

By the early 1880s the statutory system had followed an interesting trajectory which in many respects had veered in a quite different direction from the original route planned by the early reformers. In the early 1860s there was still considerable scope for local variation in the operation of industrial schools. The later years of the decade witnessed the consolidation of the statutory system as the influence of a national inspectorate, consolidating legislation and national policy decisions regarding funding created pressures for increasing uniformity within the system. Although there was still evidence of some diversity in the late 1860s, the next few years saw the demise of the day scholar. The transformation taking place in the 1860s continued, and in the 1870s most Scottish industrial schools were single-sex residential boarding establishments where the majority were detained under court order. The main theme of the 1870s was one of reclamation, as the original reformers attempted to restore the essential elements of the original project with a campaign proclaiming the centrality of day industrial schools. Calls for reappraisal and re-evaluation continued into the 1880s and were met with no more than token changes and a lack of official willingness to address fundamental issues. Radical re-assessment had to wait for the next decade.

4

New Horizons?

INTRODUCTION

Watson's appeal to the 1884 Royal Commission to abolish all residential industrial schools fell on deaf ears.[1] He made clear then that his ideal system would have been a flourishing national network of local day industrial schools on the model established in Aberdeen and other towns in the pre-statutory period. The one Scottish town which came close to achieving what he had striven for was Glasgow, with its locally funded day industrial schools. As we have seen, these were set up under local legislation as a result of the successful campaign sponsored by Watson in the 1870s.[2] These were the exception. By the end of the century, the statutory system had evolved into a net-widening diversionary mechanism under which thousands of children were subjected to prolonged detention in penal establishments. As will be discussed in this chapter, this entailed criminalisation of children, particularly Scottish children, on an immense scale. However, it will also be argued that despite the undeniable extent to which the statutory system departed from the original holistic principles on which Watson had based his scheme, there continued to be a residual element of humanitarianism evident in the approach adopted by the Scottish courts. As we have seen, the distinguishing feature of the pre-statutory system was a pragmatic approach based on religious philanthropic principles. This legacy of humanitarianism left its hallmark on the Scottish system, surviving in the abhorrence of child imprisonment demonstrated by many Scottish judges. It also survived in the tendency of judges to view the schools as a refuge for children in need, particularly industrial schools where there was no period of prior imprisonment. There was a degree of ambivalence in this approach by the judges, as they were well aware of the penal nature of the schools under the statutory system, but in many cases they took the view that the lack of alternative welfare provision for these children left them with little alternative.[3] These underlying tensions are revealed in the 1896 Report of the Departmental Committee on Reformatory and Industrial Schools, which is discussed fully in the first section of this chapter. The Report presented a radical appraisal of the reformatory-industrial school system and in doing so produced an extensively detailed and critical account of the way it operated in Scotland. There is no doubt that Watson would have been disillusioned that, despite the criticisms contained in the 1896 Report, the statutory system continued much as before, with large numbers of children being admitted to residential schools.

An important aim of this chapter is to consider the impact of the legislative changes which occurred in the period marking the transition, from the closing decades of the nineteenth century to the early twentieth century. According to one influential school of thought, this period was transformative for the criminal justice system.[4] The question addressed here is what this meant for children and for the legacy of the original Scottish reformers. On one reading of the evidence, there was an unstoppable momentum for change at the turn of the century. For children, the most important statute was the Children Act 1908. Against a background of Liberal welfare initiatives and new concern for the health and well-being of children, the Children Act, also known as the Children's Charter, created the statutory basis for juvenile courts and removed children from prisons in all but exceptional circumstances. Both of these developments were entirely in keeping with the humanitarian legacy of the original Scottish reformers, who were primarily concerned with recognising the special position of children within the criminal justice system. However, despite the promise encapsulated in the creation of juvenile courts, a great advance on one level, in practical terms the courts failed to deliver much that was of benefit to children. The 1908 Act has been regarded as laying the foundation for juvenile justice in pre-Kilbrandon Scotland,[5] but, in spite of its significance in many ways, the Act was not the decisive break with the past that has been supposed. This argument is developed further in the third part of this chapter.

In pointing to the ongoing continuities, particularly the fact that the Act did not greatly extend the grounds on which a court could intervene, this chapter challenges Garland's influential argument that the juvenile court was a significant element of a new penal landscape.[6] It was argued in the previous chapter that there is a need to reassess the importance of industrial and reformatory schools within the Victorian criminal justice system, recognising them as an integral part of the criminal justice system. Children were sent to the schools under court order. Although run on the 'voluntary principle', they were regulated by statute, subject to statutory inspection, in receipt of public funding and under Home Office direction. This challenged Garland's view of the schools as being marginal, private institutions, a theme evident in much scholarship which fails to emphasise the centrality of their role in the fabric of criminal justice.[7] As also argued in chapter three, a central part of the ethos of the schools from the 1850s onwards was adapting programmes of reformation to suit individual offenders.[8] Re-evaluating the significance of the schools within the criminal justice system suggests that ideas about reformation of individual offenders were widely accepted in the mid-nineteenth century rather than at the turn of the century, as Garland and many other scholars suggest.[9] The present chapter continues to question certain aspects of the existing literature, particularly in relation to the juvenile court.[10]

Earlier chapters of this book have identified pragmatic, organised and religiously inspired philanthropy backed up by civic support as the primary force for change in juvenile justice in mid-nineteenth-century Scotland. Although later decades of the century witnessed a transformation of the original project, there was always an abiding current of humanitarianism in the approach adopted by the Scottish courts. Humanitarianism was also the driving force at a grass-roots level. As will become clear from the cases discussed in this chapter, it was this that motivated the Royal Scottish Society for the Prevention of Cruelty to Children (RSSPCC) and bible missionaries in Scottish cities in facilitating the admission of large numbers of destitute children to industrial schools. At the level of policy change, humanitarianism was a potent factor in removing children from prison and developing juvenile courts. It was a consistent element, always present to some degree, and an important catalyst in the reform of juvenile justice throughout the nineteenth and early twentieth centuries. This emphasis on humanitarianism poses a challenge to the Garland argument, which accords great significance to positivist scientific discourses in describing a move from the uniform discipline of the Victorian penal system to a different focus on individual reformation and specialised categorisation of offender types.[11] However, as Victor Bailey points out, this period at the turn of the nineteenth century is 'simply not intelligible in terms solely of an emerging positivism or medicalism'.[12] Instead, Bailey makes a case for other factors contributing to penal change, including radical humanitarianism.[13] The history of the development of juvenile justice in nineteenth-century

Scotland supports this position: it indicates that a plausible and convincing case can be made for radical humanitarianism as one of the main motors for change in the Scottish criminal justice system. This chapter also presents evidence that the influence of scientific discourse has been overstated: the first section of the chapter questions the argument that a late nineteenth-century scientific, positivist focus on understanding the child, together with a new recognition of the psychology of adolescence, significantly altered responses to the young offender in practice.[14] In Scotland a far more pragmatic approach was taken.

To summarise the layout of this chapter: the first section considers the 1896 Report, while the second section examines legislative developments and in particular the 1908 Children Act and the juvenile court. The third and final section of the chapter examines some cases of children brought before the courts. This analysis of court practice is conducted on two levels: firstly by considering cases of children sent by police and burgh courts to industrial schools and to Wellington Reformatory, and secondly by considering the role of the other end of the court hierarchy, the High Court of Justiciary, in dealing with bills of suspension and liberation relating to children sent to the institutions. The examination of the cases provides a very useful insight into how the courts dealt with children at the turn of the century, giving some indication of how changes in legislation regulating admission to the schools were implemented in practice.

REAPPRAISAL OF THE SYSTEM

Background to the 1896 Departmental Committee Report

This section examines the 1896 Report in some depth. The reason will become clear later in the chapter: much of the discussion of the 1896 Report relates to the situation in Scotland and the way the industrial-reformatory legislation was applied there. The Report described a number of abuses, and it is important to examine these issues. In the final part of the chapter, where the case material is analysed, reference is made to the points raised in the discussion of the 1896 Report, and it is possible to see the system in operation and to offer some explanation for the patterns which emerged.

At one level, the 1896 Report was a radical reappraisal of the system. It pointed out long-practised abuses, underlined the detrimental effect on children of lengthened periods of detention in residential industrial and reformatory schools, and argued that such detention should not occur as a matter of course, but should be reserved for extreme circumstances. Watson had died nine years before this Report and, though he was no longer around to comment, it is likely that he would have found it disappointing. Admittedly, there were aspects of the Report which were in line with his approach, such as its emphasis on preserving the integrity of the family, and the expressions of compassion for children detained in institutions. However, by not embracing the ideal of the pre-eminence of the day industrial school, the 1896 Report diverged from Watson's vision. In failing to focus on day industrial schools, the Report ignored the issue which, for the original Scottish reformers, was the main one. This was, after all, essentially a pre-statutory Scottish ideal.[15] And it only came to partial fruition in the statutory period thanks to Glasgow's sense of civic responsibility, as will be discussed next.

Three years before the 1896 Report, a general statute had provided for the setting up of day industrial schools in Scotland, giving the capacity to extend this provision beyond Glasgow where, as we have seen, there were day industrial schools funded under local legislation.[16] In practice, though, this Act made little difference: Glasgow continued to be the only centre for day industrial schools in Scotland until Edinburgh established one in 1898, and by 1908 there were still only five day industrial schools operating in Scotland, four in Glasgow and one in Edinburgh. While financial constraints may have hindered the development of day industrial schools in other parts of Scotland, this was not the case in Glasgow, which was able to use the fundraising provisions of local legislation to support its day industrial schools.[17] The Glasgow Juvenile Delinquency Board was empowered under the local legislation in 1878 to levy a rate of a penny in the pound to fund the schools and did not receive assistance from the school board rates. Following the 1878 Act, certified day industrial schools were opened in Green Street in 1879, certified for 250 children; in Rottenrow in 1882, certified for 250 children; in Rose Street in 1889, certified for 250 children; and in William Street in 1902, certified for 100 children. This enterprise was said in the 1908 Report to be 'managed with warm hearted enthusiasm worthy of all praise', and despite the need for the Glasgow schools to exercise strict economy they were described as 'most useful and interesting schools'.[18] This was a very limited realisation in Scotland of Watson's ideal of a network of day industrial schools; for most of Scotland there was to be no return to the holistic idealism of the humane pre-statutory day industrial schools.

For most children, diversion to industrial schools meant residential detention. It is important to appreciate the excessive impact that diversion to the residential reformatory and industrial schools had upon

Scottish children by the end of the nineteenth century. In 1894 the daily average population of the Scottish reformatory and industrial schools was double that of the entire Scottish adult prison population. This compared unfavourably with England, where the 1894 figures show the number detained in the schools was slightly less than the adult prison population.[19] In the closing decade of the century, there were about 24,000 children under detention in the 141 industrial schools and fifty reformatories across Britain, with around 5,500 of these detained in forty-three Scottish institutions.[20] This entailed criminalisation of children, particularly Scottish children, on a vast scale.

As will be discussed shortly, the 1896 Report offered some insight into the reasons for the extremely high volume of committals in Scotland. The analysis provided by the Report revealed that the situation in Scotland was complex and that Scottish judges faced with difficult choices were often motivated partly by humanitarian considerations in dealing with children. Underlying this response was the legacy of the pre-statutory reformers, which meant that the schools were still regarded as a refuge for children in need, even though judges were aware that the regime in the schools was penal in nature.

Set up to examine the reformatory-industrial school system throughout the UK, the membership of the 1896 Committee spanned a spectrum of opinion, with some members viewing the reformatory-industrial schools system as inherently flawed and others generally supportive but still critical of aspects of the system. This conflict was reflected in the nine memoranda containing disclaimers on various aspects of the Report.[21] Half of the Committee members (four out of eight) were of the view that instead of isolating children in institutions they should be boarded out with 'respectable' families. This, they argued, would be more effective in nurturing the qualities needed to turn them into upstanding citizens; it would avoid contact with the 'prison tradition' with which the schools were historically imbued; and it would also mean that the children received the wholesome benefits of family life rather than have to endure the depressing effects of institutionalisation, which meant they were exposed to the influence of 'other bad boys'.[22] The Memorandum cast doubt on the accuracy of the 'optimistic' statistics provided by the schools themselves on the success of children leaving the institutions, arguing that assessments from more independent sources had revealed that the figures produced by the schools should be taken with a pinch of salt.

On the other hand, a rival Memorandum by three remaining Committee members expressed support for the general principle of the reformatory-industrial school system and rejected the idea that the schools were tainted by prison traditions; they also supported the veracity of estimates given by the schools, claiming that 73 per cent of children from reformatories and 83 per cent from industrial schools were 'leading good honest lives'. These members wished to point out that although they had signed the Report because there was much in the system that they disapproved of, they considered that the Report 'exaggerated the conditions which we find to be less satisfactory'.[23]

What all the Committee members agreed on was that change was required. The Report took the view that reformatory and industrial schools in the UK formed part of a single system and that in practice there was little to distinguish between the two types of school:

> the children in the two institutions are, in the main, of the same class; and, as a fact, there is no substantial difference in the discipline and regime beyond what can be accounted for by difference of age.[24]

The Report stated that before an order was made compulsorily detaining a child in either a reformatory or industrial school for a number of years, it should be shown that this was necessary both for the child and for 'the public advantage', and that 'nothing short of such necessity can justify detention in one of these schools'.[25] The Report contrasted this approach with the 'asylum theory' it said was adhered to by 'a large number of justices on the bench, especially in Scotland'.[26] (This very significant observation on Scotland will be discussed more fully shortly.) According to the asylum theory, the only question to be asked was whether a child would be better off in such a school. The Report criticised this as a flawed approach. While there were obvious benefits in committing a child to a school in terms of ensuring that the basic physical welfare of the child was safeguarded, this approach failed to weigh in the balance other important issues, which the Report described as the 'evils'[27] of institutional life: such as, the risk that the child might not be reformed, but, in fact, be 'made worse'[28] by his companions in the school; the stigma of having been in such an institution; and the risk that the child might not be able to earn a living on leaving the school. The Report considered that it was not to a child's advantage to be sent to such an institution 'unless the home or the child itself is very bad indeed'.[29] It argued:

> the presumption has hitherto been in favour of detention as providing an asylum where the child will be better off, in future the presumption should be in favour of liberty.[30]

By challenging the residential approach the Report offered a different view of welfare from that which had become the norm under the statutory system and one more in tune with the ideas of the original Scottish reformers; Watson would certainly have agreed with the Report's denunciation of residential schools. But despite the emphasis of the Report on the need to move away from detention, in practical terms the system continued much as before, with the same high numbers of committals. By 1910 there were 25,786 children in residential schools in the UK, some 5,136 of them in Scotland, very similar to the figures for 1893–4.[31] Although the reclassification of schools according to age recommended in the Report did not take place, there was one important area where the Report did have a practical effect: its criticism of the practice of imprisonment prior to admission to a reformatory was influential in paving the way for its abolition in 1899, removing the main difference between industrial schools and reformatories.[32] The way in which the requirement for prior imprisonment affected Scottish children in particular will be discussed in the next two sections.

An undercurrent of humanitarianism in Scotland

Despite the large numbers of children being diverted into prolonged detention in penal residential establishments, there is evidence that the legacy of the original reformers and their compassionate welfare-based system continued to have an influence in Scotland. Like the early reformers, many Scottish judges abhorred child imprisonment: the 1896 Report referred to 'a strong repugnance to the imprisonment of children'[33] in Scotland. This feeling was widespread in Scottish society: the Report also referred to 'aversion felt by the Scottish people to the imprisonment of children'.[34] This explained why reformatories were so few in number in Scotland, as judges were reluctant to impose the periods of prior imprisonment required when a child was convicted and sentenced to a reformatory. In cases where young children appeared before the courts on offence grounds, judges might decide not to convict but to deal with the case by means of an order for detention in an industrial school instead. This could be done if children were under the age of twelve at the date of the order and had no previous convictions.[35]

The Scottish distaste for child imprisonment felt by both the judiciary and 'enlightened public opinion'[36] resulted in the flourishing of industrial schools north of the border at the expense of reformatories. As the 1896 Report pointed out, industrial schools had of course originated

in Scotland: 'they took their origin in Scotland and have always com-
manded attention and interest'.[37] As we have seen, they were the central
aspect of the Watson vision. However, the original day industrial schools
created under the pre-statutory system were establishments designed
to support vulnerable children and their families in a holistic, humane
environment supported by local communities. The residential schools
operating at the close of the nineteenth century were very different institutions imbued with a penal atmosphere, a fact of which judges were
well aware.[38] Despite this, they did resemble the original schools in some
respects: as under the pre-statutory system, Scottish magistrates were
inclined to use the industrial schools both as an alternative to imprisonment and as a refuge which accepted both neglected and offending
children. It has to be recognised that, harsh as the schools may have
been, there were few alternatives in terms of social welfare provision for
children in need. Unlike England, where a considerable proportion of
children who might equally be candidates for industrial schools were in
workhouse schools, Scotland had a lack of poor law schools; boarding
out of pauper children was the favoured option and this did not meet the
high level of need. With the exception of private philanthropic initiatives
such as William Quarrier's homes in the west of Scotland, there was a
desperate shortage of support networks available to destitute children.[39]

In Scotland, children were more likely to be detained in residential
schools at a younger age and for longer periods, again indicative of the
shortage of alternative provision. The likelihood is, as the 1896 Report
concluded, that in many cases magistrates felt that they were doing children a favour by sending them to industrial schools. This continuing
humanitarianism – the tendency to view the schools as a place of refuge
for children in need – was based on the legacy of original pre-statutory
schools. However, the 1896 Report was not impressed by this approach.
The Scottish judges came under fire for their particularly strong adherence to the 'asylum theory' referred to in the general Report.[40] This was
interpreted as evidence of a misplaced sense of benevolence, leading to
'lax administration of the Acts'[41] in Scotland. The Report criticised the
way in which the Acts from the outset had been applied in Scotland as a
means to usher impoverished, neglected children into industrial schools
more as an act of charity than because they were genuinely likely to fall
into crime:

> There exists in the Scottish community a widespread and genuine feeling of
> commiseration towards the numerous children in the large towns who grow
> up wild or drift into crime because they are neglected and have bad homes.

The remedy is thought to be in schools as substitute for home, as asylums; and this would apply in a certain measure to reformatories as to industrial schools were it not for the fact that until lately the only entrance to a reformatory was through a prison.[42]

All of this supports the view that, despite the degree of criminalisation entailed in the diversion of large numbers of children to residential schools of a penal nature, the original humane legacy of the Scottish reformers continued to be influential. It also provides some explanation for the disparity between the Scottish and English statistics referred to earlier: it indicates that the differences were attributable in part to the approach of the Scottish judges and the shortage of alternative welfare provision for the poor in Scotland.

Recommendation to end prior imprisonment

The recommendation to end prior imprisonment was, as already noted, significant. The subject of prior imprisonment as a requirement for admission to reformatories had been a source of controversy right from the outset of the statutory system. While those inspired by true humanitarian motives, such as William Watson in Scotland and Mary Carpenter in England, had always strongly disapproved of the use of prior imprisonment, many others had been staunch advocates of its use, particularly the managers of English reformatory schools. Sydney Turner too had thought it was an indispensable feature of the system, needed both to administer punishment and to deter others from crime.[43] It was the main feature which distinguished the reformatory schools from industrial schools, apart from the age differential between the categories of children admitted to the two types of school. The fact that a period in prison was required before a child could enter a reformatory was also widely thought to be the reason that the reformatory system failed to expand at the same exponential rate of the network of industrial schools: as we have seen, to avoid sending a child offender to prison a sympathetic magistrate might decide not to convict a child and instead impose an order committing him to an industrial school, a practice especially common in Scotland.[44] This trend was demonstrated in some of the cases referred to later in this chapter.

In 1893 there was an important statute which gave magistrates discretionary power to send children to a reformatory without imposing a period of preliminary imprisonment. This Act also raised the minimum age of reformatory admission from ten to twelve, except in the case of previous offenders.[45] The 1896 Report recorded that this statute had been 'very widely acted upon':[46] out of 1,487 children sent to reformatories in Britain in 1894, 1,107 were sent without prior imprisonment. It also noted that 'the Act has helped the reformatories to fill, especially in Scotland'. Clearly the previous requirement to impose a period of imprisonment had acted as a disincentive for Scottish magistrates to send children to reformatories. The 1896 Committee was not impressed with the traditional arguments put forward to support prior imprisonment, dismissing the idea that this was needed to provide an element of punishment. The main argument against prior imprisonment, according to the Report, was that it added to the 'reformatory stigma'. The Committee also disapproved of the 'inequality' between Scotland and England in the greater tendency for Scottish magistrates to dispense with prior imprisonment under the 1893 Act. For these reasons, the Report recommended the abolition of prior imprisonment. Three years later, in 1899, prior imprisonment was finally abolished altogether,[47] removing the primary distinction between industrial schools and reformatories.

The Report was remarkable for its empathy with the circumstances of the institutionalised child. It adopted a noticeably psychological approach in its references to the detrimental effect on the 'inner life'[48] of the child: it contrasted the situation of poor, but nonetheless free, children attending ordinary schools with the isolation and confinement experienced by children detained in institutions: cut off from their families and not allowed to go home, even for a day in some cases, despite being under detention for a number of years. There was also the penal atmosphere of the schools to contend with, a continuing legacy which the schools had never shaken off. This owed its origins to the type of prison regime which Turner found in some schools when he first began making his reports on these 'juvenile houses of correction' and 'houses of detention for the young vagabond and petty misdemeanant'.[49] Turner had described the discipline in some reformatories where 'a routine scheme of regulations was enforced and the building fenced with walls, the windows grated and the inmates clothed, confined and watched as they would have been in prison'.[50] The 1896 Committee reported that 'relics' of this type of discipline remained 'either as rules savouring of repression or, more often, as general traditions without a name which insensibly affect the spirit of the management and the life of the school'.[51] The main point the Report emphasised here was that the knowledge that they were detained under court warrant gave the children in these schools a sense of being disgraced and imprisoned, creating a depressed atmosphere which might have long-term implications for their future success and happiness.[52]

While the Report adopted the language of psychology in its talk of inner life and depression, it was not prepared to accept the new scientific discourse which suggested that the children detained in the institutions were different from other children or in need of specialised treatment.[53] The vehemence with which ideas about the depravity of child offenders was rejected by the Report indicates that such notions were far from being universally accepted. As discussed earlier in the book, the late nineteenth century saw the advent of new scientific notions about the young offender.[54] In relation to this, it has been argued that a late nineteenth-century scientific, positivist focus on understanding the child, together with a new recognition of the psychology of adolescence, altered responses to the young offender. The impact of new knowledges has been emphasised by Garland.[55] In his view, they had a significant role in an altered penal landscape where professional expertise in areas such as psychology and psychiatry was an important factor. He argues that psychology was especially influential in relation to juveniles;[56] and professional advice was sought on this area of scientific knowledge and other matters, with courts being provided with 'social background reports, character judgements or the certification of experts'.[57] In this context, he argues, judicial decision-making was framed in accordance with 'extra-legal' criteria[58] rather than classical concepts about criminal responsibility, and this provided the basis for extensive intervention into the lives of offenders.

However, there is evidence which undermines Garland's argument. As we have seen, the 1896 Report was very robust in rejecting the concept of the inherent deviance of young offenders, dismissing as completely unfounded the notion that these children were anything other than 'ordinary'. Instead, the Report referred again to the words of Turner:

> Nothing has been more certainly demonstrated in the practical development of the reformatory system than that juvenile crime has comparatively little to do with any special depravity of the offender, and very much to do with parental neglect and bad example.[59]

In refuting the idea of 'depravity', the Report emphasised that the children in these schools were victims of neglect who needed kindness and attention to bring about their 'reclamation'.[60] It was clearly absurd to label as depraved, reformatory children often committed for 'venial' offences or young industrial school children detained because of poverty, 'petty delinquencies' or the faults of parents.[61] The Report added that the sheer numbers of children in these schools also meant that it was very unlikely that they were different from other children.

This common-sense approach to the question of the criminality of children was similar in tone to the attitude adopted by the Report of the Gladstone Departmental Committee on Prisons in 1895 in its assessment of ideas of criminal anthropology as an 'embryo' science and its cautious approach towards scientific investigation, which it considered valuable but far from conclusive and beset by 'conflicting theories'.[62] The Gladstone Report stated that 'the great majority of prisoners are ordinary men and women amenable, more or less, to all those influences which affect persons outside'.[63] These sources indicate that there was a strong current of resistance to the new scientific discourses on criminality. The foreign origin of much of this type of theory probably did little to assist its acceptance.[64] There is also evidence that the judiciary was unimpressed by the new ideas and disinclined to have regard to them in their sentencing of offenders.[65] Certainly the 1896 Report had little time for theories of this kind. It gave no credence at all to the results of a system brought to its attention by witnesses, explaining an elaborate and extensively tested method that had been tried out to examine children for evidence of 'abnormality'.[66] The Report defiantly declared that the Committee was 'not at all prepared to admit the theory' that the children were physically and mentally different from others.[67]

This suggests that the influence of scientific discourse in Britain in the late nineteenth century has been overstated. It indicates that new scientific theories about criminality were treated with scepticism and, ultimately, pragmatic common sense was far more influential in practice.

The system in operation in Scotland

One of the most valuable aspects of the 1896 Report is that it provided a very detailed insight into the way the reformatory-industrial school legislation was applied in Scotland. In this section the focus is on the criticisms made of the Scottish system.

Criticisms of procedure

The Report was critical of cases where laxity of procedure had occurred, and on this point had much to say about the way that industrial and reformatory schools statutes were applied by the courts in Scotland. The Report recommended that evidence should be taken down in writing and that a transcript of the evidence and any hearsay information should be forwarded to the Secretary of State. But it noted that adherence to strict standards of legal procedure varied according to the courts involved and the types of cases they heard. The Edinburgh Police Court dealt only with cases involving an offence, 'whether under the general or under the local law'. These were either reformatory cases or industrial school cases brought under section fifteen (the offence section) of the Industrial Schools Act. The only criticism levelled at this court was that the evidence was not taken in writing.[68] The Glasgow Police Court was also said to be generally satisfactory in providing 'numerous safeguards for justice', apart from failing to ensure that proof of the child's circumstances was taken on oath.[69] However, the Report was extremely critical of the casual approach to procedure taken in the courts dealing with those industrial school admissions which were on non-offence grounds. While the Burgh Court at Edinburgh, consisting of one Baillie sitting alone, did adopt some procedural safeguards, in the Justices of the Peace Court at Glasgow, constituted by two Justices, 'all such safeguards are dispensed with'.[70] The Committee accepted that there was no strict 'irregularity' in this: these were not criminal cases and therefore did not require the same high standard of proof as even the most 'venial' criminal offence by a child that only merited a fine. Nevertheless, decisions made by the courts in these cases had extremely serious consequences for children and their parents, and the Report regarded it as 'strange that such lax procedure should be tolerated in cases where the result may be that for four years a child may be deprived of its home and its liberty'.[71]

Professional interests

There were other factors in addition to judicial attitudes and lack of alternative provision for children which contributed to the volume of committals. For example, there were professional interests involved in ensuring that the schools were supplied with fresh new recruits. In Scotland, the managers of industrial schools had agents to procure children for the schools. This was the case in Glasgow, Dundee and probably other towns. This did not happen in England, where school boards had agents but not individual schools. According to the evidence of a Glasgow witness the Scottish agents were zealous in their rounding up of likely candidates:

> But the agents of the schools do not go about collecting boys to go to the schools?
>
> *Certainly.*
>
> They do?
>
> *Certainly.*

If a school is under private management, do its managers appoint an agent to scour the streets to collect children who may be sent to the school?

Certainly, to keep their schools full.[72]

Another witness, the superintendent of a children's centre in Glasgow stated:

in my experience, which extends over nine years, of attending the courts and dealing with children for industrial schools, if they had no paid officers there would be fewer children in the schools, and those that do not require to go or should not be in the schools would not be there.[73]

In addition to the schools' agents, there was the very active Royal Scottish Society for the Prevention of Cruelty to Children (RSSPCC). Though affiliated to the English branch of the organisation, the Scottish society adopted a different approach from its English counterpart. The policy of the English society was to avoid committal to industrial schools, taking action against neglectful parents where appropriate but keeping the family together where possible. The Scottish society, on the other hand, vigorously took advantage of the legislation to institute proceedings in industrial schools cases. The evidence of an official of the RSSPCC assured the Committee that they made 'full inquiry into each case to consider what is due not only to the child but to its parent and the State',[74] but the Report felt it fair to highlight the evidence of Mr MacDonald, the Edinburgh agent to the reformatory office:

Do you think the society wish to take away the children? – *In many cases they have done so; they make no secret of it.*

You are distinctly of the opinion that it is not the policy of the society, then, to keep the home together? – I *say so and have objected to many children being committed, with that in view myself.*

The extent to which the RSSPCC was involved in arranging committals of Edinburgh children to industrial schools will be demonstrated later in the chapter in the analysis of case material.

Often, of course, the activities of these groups were affected by financial considerations. In the case of the school agents, there was not only a self-interested concern to keep themselves in employment but to ensure that the schools were 'large and kept full'.[76] At the root of much of the preoccupation with money was the problem that schools were often lacking in resources, partly because they received inadequate support from the local and also school authorities. The need for more money had unfortunate consequences for children: the schools had to exercise stringent economy; they had to be filled to capacity; and the children were detained for longer to receive the full benefit of treasury allowances and ensure that 'full advantage was obtained from the labour of the inmates'.[77]

Truants

The section of the 1896 Report describing the treatment of truants is complex, but important in exposing the detailed workings of the industrial school legislation and the way the various provisions were applied and contorted. It reveals the way in which the manipulation of industrial school legislation resulted in children being detained for years, simply for truanting. It shows that there was a very significant difference in practice in the way that children truanting from school were treated in Scotland, compared to England.[78] It indicates that abuse of procedure occurred for financial reasons, with schools keen to maximise the allowance they received for each child. It also shows that in some cases school boards disposed of their truants by colluding with parents wishing to get rid of their children. Enlisting the help of parents enabled them to have troublesome children admitted to industrial schools for long periods of detention. All of this is very helpful in understanding the cases from the Edinburgh archives discussed later in the chapter, especially those where parents sought to have their children admitted to industrial schools as 'uncontrollable'.

The reason for the divergence of approach between Scotland and England in the treatment of truants stemmed from the complicated relationship between the Education Acts and industrial school legislation in both countries. In England the Act which made education compulsory was the Education Act of 1870. This Act created school boards with the power to establish industrial schools and to contribute towards the upkeep of children sent to the schools. However, while parents could be fined under the Act for failing to send children to school, there was no power given to school boards under education legislation to send truant children in breach of an attendance order to an industrial school until amending legislation in 1876.[79] This Act created certified day industrial schools in England, authorising truants to be sent either to these new schools or to residential industrial schools. This meant that, between 1870 and 1876, English school boards wishing to send truants to an industrial school did so by resorting to section sixteen of the Industrial Schools Act 1866, which permitted children to be committed as 'uncontrollable'. Children admitted under this section were only eligible to receive the lower rate of weekly allowance from the treasury of two shillings, rather than the full rate paid for children admitted as begging or wandering under section fourteen.[80] The school boards only succeeded in having the children accepted by the industrial schools as uncontrollable by using their power to contribute to make up the difference between the lower rate and the full treasury allowance. This manipulation of the industrial school legislation resulted in children being detained for years simply for truanting. However, in 1876, when the amending legislation authorised English school boards to send cases to industrial schools on the grounds of truancy alone, it was envisaged that any detention of education cases for truancy would be relatively short: power was given to managers of the schools to release children on licence after one month instead of eighteen months.

For Scottish truants, the agony was far more prolonged. In Scotland, compulsory education was introduced by the Education (Scotland) Act of 1872. Like the English Act of 1870, this statute allowed school boards to establish industrial schools but did not authorise them to send education cases to industrial schools. However, the Scottish Act differed from the English in that under the Scottish education legislation there was no power to contribute towards the upkeep of children in industrial schools. Scottish school boards had to wait until 1893 to receive this power under an Act authorising the establishment of day industrial schools by general statute.[81] This meant that between 1872 and 1893, Scottish school boards wishing to rid themselves of truants resorted to the Industrial Schools Acts, as the English school boards had done between 1870 and 1876. The important difference between the way that Scottish and English school boards manipulated the legislation was that since the Scottish boards had no power to contribute to upkeep, they could not avail themselves of section sixteen admitting children as uncontrollable. This would only have given the schools two shillings a week and they would not accept a child for that. Instead, the school boards blatantly contrived to have truanting children admitted under section fourteen as begging or wandering, thus enabling the industrial schools to claim the full treasury allowance of five shillings. The effect of this was that truanting children regarded as a nuisance by school attendance officers found themselves confined to industrial schools for years.

According to the evidence of an agent for the reformatory office who had worked in Glasgow for twenty-three years, the school boards elicited the help of parents in having their children sent to industrial schools:

Every child sent to an industrial school is one forever got rid of. That is just what seemingly actuates them in following up cases, and inducing the parents to get them sent to industrial schools . . . they take advantage of the Industrial Schools Acts, and prove some sort of wandering and want of guardianship and that sort of thing, and get them sent under the better paying sections of the Act.[82]

The problem appeared to be alleviated by the 1893 legislation permitting school boards to send education cases to industrial schools for truancy on condition that the detention for truanting was limited to three months, after which a licence had to be granted. However, this was not the end of the problem.

Despite the 1893 legislation, the practice of detaining truants for years continued in Edinburgh, and probably in other towns too, although the Report only gives details of the situation in the capital. The reason for this was the lack of a day industrial school in Edinburgh until St John's Hill was opened in 1898; at this point the only day industrial schools in Scotland were those in Glasgow created by local legislation in the 1870s.[83] Under the 1893 Act, children in breach of an attendance order could be sent either to a day industrial school or a residential industrial school, but if the magistrate exercised the option of the residential school then, as with the English legislation, the order could not be for longer than three months. This posed a problem for Edinburgh magistrates, as residential industrial schools would not accept a child for so short a period as three months and there was no day industrial school. Effectively this made the relevant section of the 1893 Act 'inoperative'.[84] Faced with this situation, the Edinburgh school board resorted to manipulating the provisions of the Industrial Schools Act 1866: eliciting the help of parents, they used section sixteen to present truant children before the court as uncontrollable in exactly the same way as happened in England between 1870 and 1876,[85] with the same severe consequences for children:

> A child thus committed under section sixteen of the Industrial Schools Act, for what is virtually a breach of the Education Act, will be committed for a term of years, probably until he is sixteen . . . whereas if proceedings for breach of an attendance order had been taken under the Day Industrial Schools (Scotland) Act . . . the child could not have been detained for longer than three months, as at the end of that time the grant of a licence is, under the Act, imperative.[86]

The absence of day industrial schools in other Scottish towns apart from Glasgow meant that similar practices probably occurred elsewhere too. With the establishment of St John's Hill Day Industrial School in Edinburgh in 1898, children in breach of an attendance order could be sent to a day industrial school under the Day Industrial Schools Act and granted a licence after a short period of attendance. However, as we have seen, by 1908 the concept of day industrial schools had not been extended beyond St John's Hill in Edinburgh under the 1893 general Act and the four in Glasgow established under the 1878 local Act.

Although there were not many day industrial schools in England either (only sixteen in operation by 1908), there were fourteen residential specialist truant industrial schools which were set up following the 1876 Elementary Education Act to deal specifically with truanting boys sent for short periods of detention.[87] But the idea of a school especially for truants did not take root in Scotland, with the exception of one opened at Shettleston in Glasgow in 1905.[88] Financial constraint was probably the reason for the lack of other truant schools in Scotland.[89] It is likely that this was also the reason for the lack of day industrial schools, although this was not the case in Glasgow which, as has been discussed earlier, responded to Watson's appeal in the 1870s by using the fundraising provisions of the local Act to support day industrial schools. Certainly the issue of expense was given in the 1908 Inspector's Report as being the main reason there were so few day industrial schools in England: the treasury grant for day industrial schools was small and the schools were costly for school boards to run. The result was that it was 'soon found that it was really less expensive to the rates to pack a child off to an industrial school and be done with him than to maintain a day industrial school specially for his benefit'.[90] This history of the treatment of truants is extremely useful in shedding light on the case material which will be discussed later in this chapter and helps to explain why so many of the Edinburgh industrial school admissions occurred at the instigation of parents claiming their children were uncontrollable.

Young children in reformatories

As well as the abuses which occurred in relation to truant children, the 1896 Report referred to the unacceptable manipulation of statutory provisions which led to very young children being inappropriately placed in reformatories for older children rather than industrial schools more suitable for their age group. Again, this involved complex machinations under statutory provisions. Under the Reformatory Schools Act 1866, convicted offenders under the age of sixteen could be sent to a reformatory and those under ten should not be sent to a reformatory unless they were previous offenders. This was amended by the Reformatory Schools Act 1893,[91] which raised the minimum age of admission to a reformatory to twelve, except where a child was a previous offender. A young child convicted of an offence was therefore eligible to be admitted to a reformatory if previously convicted. Alternatively, and this is what often happened, young child offenders were charged under section fifteen of the Industrial Schools Act and the court did not proceed to convict but instead made an order sending the child to an industrial school. However, if the child had a previous conviction it was not possible to use section fifteen and the court might instead opt to make an order committing him under another section, such as the section fourteen provision permitting committal where a child was associating with thieves. In these circumstances, where a child had been receiving poor relief within the previous three months the parish was liable for his maintenance under section thirty-eight of the industrial schools legislation which applied only to Scotland.[92] One of the witnesses spoke of his experience of very young child offenders from country districts and also from Glasgow being committed to reformatories under the reformatory statute rather than being sent to industrial schools, as would be the normal practice, simply to avoid them becoming chargeable to the local authorities; he gave the example of children of eight, nine or ten sent to 'pilfer' by their mothers and caught by school board officers who wished to avoid encumbering their employers, the parish council, with the cost of maintenance. These children would be presented to the court as a reformatory complaint and committed to a reformatory despite their young age, a practice 'cruel to the children'.[93]

The effect of section thirty-eight also influenced the practices of RSSPCC officers. It was alleged that when they picked up abandoned children and took them to rescue shelters before presenting them to a court for admission to an industrial school, they sometimes detained children in receipt of poor relief longer so that they would fall outwith the period when the local authority would have to pay for them. Often the reason given for this delay was to find time to complete inquiries or to arrange their admission to a school, but the true purpose was to avoid encountering any problems with parish authorities, who resented this drain on their resources.[94]

Although the 1896 Report was forthright in its criticisms of the abuses which occurred in Scotland, it concluded that 'the existence of such a state of things is well nigh inconceivable except on the assumption that all concerned in bringing these children before the courts are persuaded in their own minds that what they are doing is best for the children'.[95] This supports the view that underlying the attitude of many judges was a continuing current of humanitarianism. And this tendency to see the schools as a place of refuge owed its origin mainly to the ongoing legacy of the original reformers.

THE CHILDREN ACT 1908

Background to the Children Act 1908

In many ways the Children Act 1908 was very significant for children in the criminal justice system. It effectively removed the option of child imprisonment in all but exceptional cases and it created the statutory framework for the juvenile court. However, although it was undeniably important in many respects, it will be argued here that it was not the radical break with the past that has been supposed, and that in fact there were many continuities with the Victorian system.

The Act was known as the Children's Charter. It was hailed as the culmination of a gradual process of recognition of the special position of children.[96] The measure should be seen in the context of a developing social-welfare programme in which children were accorded special significance: for example, there was a new focus on infant welfare and health, concerned with issues such as the provision of school meals and school medical inspection.[97] Against this background the Act set out to deal with a wide range of matters relating to children, consolidating and amending the law in areas as diverse as infant life protection, prevention of cruelty to children and prohibitions on the sale of tobacco to children.

Despite its reputation as a radical measure, in some respects the Children Act simply introduced amendments to existing law. This was the case with the section of the Act concerned with holding parents to account financially for their children's misconduct. The Act which first crystallised this concept statutorily was the Youthful Offenders Act 1901. This set out in section two that, where a child or young person under fourteen was charged with any offence for which a fine, damages or costs could be imposed on him by a court of summary jurisdiction and there were grounds for believing that neglect by a parent had 'conduced to the commission of the alleged offence', then the parent could be charged with contributing to the commission of the offence. Also under section two, a parent could be made to pay a fine, damages or costs and ordered to give security for the good conduct of the child.[98] The liability of parents was further enforced by section ninety-nine of the Children's Act 1908, under which parents were assumed to be responsible for fines imposed on their children unless the court was satisfied that the parent could not be found or 'that he has not conduced to the commission of the offence by neglecting to exercise due care of the child or young person'.

Many years later, Lord Kilbrandon, in his famous report on juvenile justice in Scotland, was to comment that this penalising of parents for actions committed by their children was a foreign import into Scottish criminal law, a punitive measure which was a form of vicarious liability.[99] However, as we have seen in earlier chapters, this concept was very well established in nineteenth-century Scotland. In the earliest days of the pre-statutory system, the Child's Asylum Committee in Aberdeen summoned neglectful parents before it and ordered them to meet their obligations. Under the early statutory system, parents could give financial security for the good conduct of their children.[100] One of the main aspects of the statutory system was that parents were required to make financial contributions to the upkeep of their children in institutions.[101] They were penalised if they helped their children to abscond from the schools,[102] and under the Education Acts they could be fined if their children were truants. The 1901 and 1908 Acts encapsulated this familiar concept by holding parents to account financially in a very direct way.

Child imprisonment

The Children Act 1908 removed the option of child imprisonment in all but exceptional cases. Under the terms of the Act, children and young people below sixteen appearing before the courts charged with an offence were to be given bail,[103] and if they were remanded in custody were not to be detained in prison but in an appropriate place of detention.[104] Any child under fourteen who was convicted was not to be sentenced to imprisonment or penal servitude[105] for any offence and could not be committed to prison for failure to pay a fine, damages or costs.[106] Penal servitude was also abolished for convicted children aged between fourteen and sixteen, and a child of this age could only be committed to prison if the court was satisfied that he was so 'unruly' or 'depraved' that the normal arrangements provided for in the Act could not apply.[107]

These provisions represented the culmination of a long process. There is no question that the Scottish reformers Watson and Guthrie would have been delighted to see the demise of child imprisonment. Watson's primary objective was to provide children in trouble with the means to reconstruct their lives in a wholesome environment. Like Mary Carpenter, Watson deplored the imprisonment of children and argued strongly against the provisions of the reformatory school legislation, which imposed prior imprisonment as a requirement of reformatory admission. As discussed in earlier chapters, this humane approach was not one which was universally accepted by all of those involved in the early reform movements. Particularly within the English reformatory movement there were many who advocated prior imprisonment as appropriate and necessary, both as an expression of retributive punishment and as a means of deterring future misconduct by others. This was the clear view of Sydney Turner and many reformatory managers such as the influential reformatory founder, Thomas Barwick Lloyd-Baker.[108] However, by the end of the nineteenth century the humanitarian argument had won the day. The end to prior imprisonment in 1899[109] was followed by the Youthful Offenders Act 1901, which gave courts an alternative to remanding a child in prison, placing him with 'any person willing to receive him'.[110] All of this pointed the way towards the effective end of child imprisonment enshrined in the 1908 Act.

In Scotland, as we have seen, in keeping with the humanitarian tradition of the original reformers, the judiciary, those involved in running the schools and 'enlightened public opinion'[111] all shared a 'strong repugnance' to the imprisonment of children. The previous section discussed the way in which this aversion to child imprisonment impacted on the development of the statutory system in Scotland, with Scottish judges being reluctant to send children to reformatories until the Act of 1893 made prior imprisonment optional.

The humanitarian influence was significant in England too. As one scandal after another about young children imprisoned for very minor offences entered the public domain, the sympathetic reaction led to policy directives to magistrates to consider alternatives to imprisonment of children.[112] This had a dramatic effect on reducing the levels of child imprisonment: in the wake of official directives discouraging the imposition of prison sentences for children, the number of juvenile committals to prison dropped from between eighty and ninety-nine a week in April 1880 to about ten a week in November of that year.[113] But, nonetheless, the Gladstone Committee still considered the retention of child imprisonment a necessity in some circumstances.[114]

However, the humanitarian pressure to end child imprisonment continued. In an early example of the media influencing the direction of criminal justice policy, another important development was the effect of a letter written to the *Daily Chronicle* on Friday 28 May 1897[115] by Oscar Wilde highlighting the plight of children in prison. Wilde wrote in protest at the dismissal of a prison warder who had contravened prison rules by giving a young child prisoner some biscuits:

> The cruelty that is practised by day and night on children in English prisons is incredible, except to those who have witnessed it and are aware of the brutality of the system.

Arguing that no child under fourteen should be sent to prison, he described the 'limitless terror' experienced by children kept locked up in a dimly lit cell for twenty-three out of every twenty-four hours. Their misery was compounded by hunger as they were only offered 'coarse, horrible food'. He also railed against what he termed the ignorance and stupidity of justices and magistrates who sent children to prison on remand. In a challenge to the view that children were contaminated by contact with other prisoners, he added that the only humanising aspect of prison life was the camaraderie and kindness of fellow prisoners. For Wilde, the source of contamination was 'the whole prison system – the governor, the chaplain, the warders, the lonely cell, the isolation, the revolting food, the rules of the Prison Commissioners, the mode of discipline as it is termed, the life'. Wilde returned to this theme when he published *The Ballad of Reading Gaol* in 1898:

> For they starve the little frightened child
> Till it weeps both night and day[116]

Wilde's writings had the desired effect. In response to the letter to the *Daily Chronicle*, Ruggles-Brise, the Chairman of the Prison Commission, issued a memorandum undertaking to do all that he could to put an end to child imprisonment.[117] This helped cultivate the climate in which the following year prior imprisonment as a condition of reformatory admission was abolished in the UK, paving the way for the effective demise of child imprisonment in 1908. Without wishing to overstate the significance of literary works, the impact made by Wilde's writing underlines the point made in chapter one on the importance of cultural influences both as a barometer and catalyst of change in the criminal justice system.

The Juvenile Court

The Children Act 1908 created the statutory basis for juvenile courts in the UK. Under the Act, courts of summary jurisdiction hearing children's cases were required to sit as juvenile courts 'either in a different building or room from that in which the ordinary sittings of the court are held, or on different days or at different times from those at which the ordinary sittings are held'.[118] Except by special leave of the court, only those directly concerned with the case were allowed to attend.[119] In some respects the juvenile court can be interpreted as a very significant step, setting the seal on the recognition of the special position of children in the criminal justice system and, accordingly, a development entirely in keeping with the spirit of the original Scottish reformers. It has been seen as laying the foundation for the governance of juvenile courts in pre-Kilbrandon Scotland,[120] being hailed in the Kilbrandon Report as a 'major landmark'.[121] However, it is argued here that the Act was less of a watershed than has been supposed.

The move to introduce juvenile courts in the UK should be seen in the context of the development of juvenile courts in other jurisdictions.[122] As we have seen in earlier chapters, there was a constant exchange of ideas about juvenile justice reform between different countries throughout the nineteenth century, and this continued to be the case in the early twentieth century, with patterns of reform following similar trends to some degree. The juvenile court movement in the US was of particular influence. Like the English reformatory movement, those advocating juvenile courts in America promoted their cause by courting the great and the good, appealing to a broad range of interests.[123] Similarly, in England, Mary Carpenter relied on the patronage of Lady Byron to support her endeavours;[124] and others in the English upper classes jumped on the bandwagon of reform for their own reasons.[125] But there was important variation in the way reforms such as the juvenile court were received in individual jurisdictions. The juvenile justice culture in which the first juvenile courts operated in Scotland had its own unique qualities derived in part from its history of pragmatic philanthropy. In Scotland, the early reforms in pre-statutory Aberdeen, for example, depended on philanthropic support at a community level. This Scottish approach relying on local cohesiveness was in evidence under the statutory system in the successful appeal to Glasgow's civic conscience in the 1870s to fund day industrial schools under local legislation; it was also evident in the continuing undercurrent of humanitarianism in Scotland. All this meant that the Scottish juvenile court was very different from the American version.

The background against which the first American juvenile court was created in Cook County, Chicago in 1899 was one in which the new social sciences reigned supreme.[126] There was huge interest in understanding the social causes of crime, in 'socialising justice'.[127] And the juvenile court was the perfect place to experiment with medical-therapeutic ideas of individualised treatment of juvenile 'delinquents' and 'dependents'.[128] The courts were informal, there was an absence of procedural constraints,[129] and an array of specialists was on hand to deliver the treatment required in each case. A crucial aspect of the American juvenile court was its overarching paternalism crystallised in the concept of 'parens patriae',[130] which meant that the child was regarded as a child of the state and the court acted as a parental court. For 'dependent' children the kind of social welfare delivered was 'dual track', varying according to their parental situation:[131] the courts administered mothers' pensions so that where a mother was bringing up children alone, the state stepped in to provide financial support as it was considered a father should have done, and the family remained together but was subject to close supervision by probation officials. On the other hand, where the mother was the absent parent the children were sent to be cared for in state institutions.

The Scottish juvenile courts had little in common with the American conception: the magistrates in the Scottish courts had no special expertise in children's cases, and medical-therapeutic ideas about individualised treatment of children were of little, if any, influence. The courts were formal and bound by procedural requirements. Essentially they continued to deal with matters much as before, the main difference being that the juvenile court separated children off from adults appearing in court by being conducted at a different time from the adult courts.[132] But one thing the Scottish and American juvenile courts had in common was that on a conceptual level the existence of juvenile courts was an important recognition of the special position of children in the criminal justice system.

There are conflicting perspectives on the effect of the juvenile court in practice. While some commentators invest the establishment of the juvenile court in the UK with great significance,[133] others are a little more circumspect. Radzinowicz and Hood conclude that ultimately the juvenile court that emerged in practice was 'far short of the radical version of a true family welfare court . . . The legislation was little more than a device to dissociate young delinquents from adult criminals.'[134] To assess the difference the juvenile court made in Scotland it is instructive to look ahead a few years to the Report of the Committee on Reformatory and Industrial Schools in Scotland in 1914.[135] In evidence to the Committee, the Chief Constable of Dundee, John Carmichael, responded to a question as to whether there was a special magistrate for the juvenile court in Dundee:

> No, the ordinary magistrate. The sitting is heard in the ordinary police court room, but at a different hour from the ordinary police court, and the children do not meet with adult criminals coming to the court . . . and do not rub shoulders with the ordinary criminal at all.[136]

Judging from this, one of the main objectives of establishing the court, the segregation of children appearing in court, had been achieved, while that of ensuring that the procedure was presided over by someone with specialist expertise in dealing with children had not. According to evidence given by Edinburgh magistrate James Rose, there was no special magistrate for the children's court in Edinburgh either:

> *Are you in any sense a magistrate of the children's court? Is there a children's court in Edinburgh with separate magistrates?*
>
> No, we all just take our turn.[137]

James Rose expressed extreme dissatisfaction with the use of the juvenile court to deal with child offenders, particularly as most of the offences were extremely trivial, such as playing football in the street or 'hanging on to tramway cars'. He argued that appearing in court was an ordeal for children which stigmatised them as criminals:

> To describe them as children's courts only means that the children brought before them are not now brought into contact with the demoralising sights and disclosures of the ordinary police or criminal courts. This is certainly an improvement, but the institution of these courts has not removed to an extent the difficulty felt by most judges in dealing with children . . . I think an effort should be made to remove from our courts the prosecution of children.[138]

This appraisal shows the frustration and disappointment felt by some magistrates, and indicates that while the juvenile court certainly improved matters for children by keeping them separate from adult offenders, it fell very far short of being a genuinely specialist forum. There was little improvement by the 1920s, when the Morton Committee was set up to investigate the treatment and training of young people and young offenders needing care and protection in Scotland.[139] Published in 1928, the Report criticised the continuing lack of specialist magistrates. It was also critical of some failures to abide by the principle of segregating juveniles from adults, such as when children were allowed to remain in court during the hearing of adult cases.[140] To remedy this, the Morton Report recommended a system of specially constituted justice-of-the-peace juvenile courts composed of people particularly qualified to hear children's cases. The 1932 Children and Young Persons (Scotland) Act allowed such courts to be set up under the authority of the Secretary of State, but only four areas took advantage of this opportunity: Aberdeen, Ayrshire, Fife and Renfrewshire.[141] In England, on the other hand, similarly constituted courts were established across the country under the Children and Young Persons Act 1933. As the work of Logan and Bradley on London's juvenile justice system shows, London led the way with the creation of specialist juvenile court panels under the Juvenile Courts Metropolis Act 1920.[142] But it was only from the 1930s that the idea of specialised juvenile courts fully took root in England. Regretfully, this idea was only realised to a very limited extent in Scotland for the first half of the twentieth century.[143]

In practice, as the Morton Report indicated in 1928, the early juvenile courts in Scotland fell short of the ideals of the Children Act 1908. The evidence here supports the conclusion that the chief importance of the creation of the juvenile court was on the conceptual level in its recognition of the special position of children. The juvenile court did not greatly alter the treatment of children. For example, a close examination of the grounds of admission to industrial and reformatory schools indicates that they were not significantly changed by the Children Act 1908. There was little that was new in section fifty-eight listing the grounds of admission to industrial schools. It re-enacted the terms of the 1866 Act concerning begging, wandering, being found destitute, frequenting the company of thieves, being 'refractory' in a workhouse or poor law school and being beyond control. It also replicated section one of the Industrial Schools Amendment Act of 1880 concerned with a child found residing with prostitutes.[144] There were only two entirely new provisions. The first provided that a girl was eligible to be sent to an industrial school if she was the daughter of someone convicted of a sexual offence in respect of his daughters under sections four or five of the Criminal Law Amendment Act 1885.[145] The second was section 58(1)(d), which stated that a child was liable to be sent to an industrial school where his parent was 'by reason of criminal or drunken habits unfit to have care of the child'.[146] In relation to children who had offended, there was some modification of the earlier provisions: where a child under twelve was charged with an offence, he could be sent to an industrial school but the requirement under section fifteen of the 1866 Act that there should be no previous conviction was removed.[147] In addition, a child of twelve or thirteen with no previous conviction could be sent to an industrial school if the court was 'satisfied that the character and antecedents of the child are such that he will not exercise an evil influence over the other children in a certified industrial school'.[148] In relation to reformatory admission, a child convicted of an offence between the ages of twelve and sixteen could be admitted to a reformatory, as previously; but the minimum age of admission was twelve, so that younger children with a previous conviction were no longer admissible.[149]

Generally, though, the provisions were much the same. Even the addition of the new condition in section 58(1)(d), empowering magistrates to remove children where they considered parents unfit by reason of criminal or drunken habits, had a familiar ring about it. Criminality of parents had been a long-standing ground of admission. Under the Prevention of

Crimes Act 1871, children under fourteen of a woman twice convicted of 'crime' could be sent to an industrial school;[150] and children in a workhouse or poorhouse school with a parent who had been convicted of a crime punishable by imprisonment, or penal servitude, had been liable to be admitted to an industrial school since the 1866 statute.[151] The point to be emphasised here is that, in setting out grounds on which children could be admitted to industrial schools, the 1908 Act was largely consolidating earlier legislation and adding one or two amendments.

Clearly these provisions were nothing very new. There was still great continuity with existing legislation and practice. The significance of this underlying stability is that it poses challenges for scholars like Garland, Wiener and others who adhere to the view that there was a radical change of emphasis in this period. Garland's interpretation of the court's significance acknowledges the importance of the juvenile being accorded a special position. However, like Donzelot and Lasch in the international context, he sees in this an avenue for extensive social intervention into the private domain of the family, particularly the working-class family.[152] For Garland, the principle of special juvenile courts 'endorsed the conception of the child or juvenile as a special category and promoted a separate institutional basis for the future development of social work and criminological initiatives . . . Thus if the juvenile was the tactical point of entry established in criminological discourse, the juvenile court provided its institutional equivalent in practice.'[153] According to this view, the 1908 Act was highly influential in introducing the idea[154] that family problems were 'to be administered not solely by charity and voluntary social work but through a series of public channels, presided over by the specialist juvenile court'.[155] In Herbert Samuel's statement that the state intervention was justified where domestic discipline had failed, Garland saw an extension of intervention 'beyond the limits of offence behaviour stipulated by the criminal law'.[156] Clarke also supported the idea that from its inception the juvenile court had wide powers of intervention in the domestic sphere.[157] With this Foucault-like observation also being made about juvenile courts in France and America, this has been a familiar theme in juvenile court studies internationally.[158] In Garland's view, then, the juvenile court marked the opening of a new vista of interventionism, a world of probationary inspection, expert knowledges and increased surveillance. This view is reflected in much of the existing literature.[159]

But the evidence does not all point in this direction. The enduring elements of continuity with existing legislation and practice point to considerable underlying stability rather than radical departure. It has to be conceded, of course, that there were very significant developments around

this time. For example, the 1908 Act states that where a child is presented
to the court by a parent as beyond control, the court may decide to place
the child under the supervision of a probation officer instead of sending
him to an industrial school.[160] And, of course, as well as the development
of probation,[161] the creation of juvenile courts and the virtual end of child
imprisonment were enormously significant. However, it is important not
to underestimate the ongoing links with the Victorian criminal justice
system. In many respects as far as children were concerned, the juvenile
court was conducting business much as usual. This observation is clearly
supportive of Victor Bailey's position, which also underlines the continuities with the past. More directly in point, it also resonates strongly with
Platt's observation on the introduction of the juvenile court in the US: he
argues that the American juvenile court has been wrongly construed as a
radical innovation. He maintains that it was a 'politically compromised
reform which consolidated existing practices'.[162]

Referring back to chapter three, the argument was developed there
that ideas about reformation of individual offenders were widely
accepted and put into practice far earlier than the Garland argument
allows.[163] Garland argues that the Victorian criminal justice system
treated offenders in a uniform fashion, with no account taken of 'criminal type or individual character'.[164] In his view, the focus on individual
reformation developed at the turn of the century. However, there is evidence that the ethos of the reformatory school was from its inception
based on adapting programmes of reformation to meet the needs of the
individual offender.[165] All of this points to a pattern of underlying stability in many respects, rather than one of radical change.

EVIDENCE FROM THE ARCHIVES

Industrial School Admissions

In this section my aim is to examine archival material, with the intention of shedding some light on the practices of the courts. Analysing the
records of children admitted to industrial schools in Edinburgh brings to
life many of the observations made in the 1896 Report discussed earlier
in the chapter.

The material here is drawn mainly from the Industrial Schools
Complaints Books for Edinburgh, large volumes concerned with admissions to industrial schools complete with details of the burgh court process relating to each child.[166]

The volume for 1901–4 relates to complaints under the Industrial Schools Act 1866 regarding 'uncontrollable or abandoned children', which were cases under sections fourteen and sixteen. Normally the cases resulted in the children being sent to a residential industrial school until the age of sixteen.[167] Most of the cases concerned children who were destitute and found wandering with no visible means of support. Often children had been found on the streets selling small objects such as matches, white heather or papers. In these circumstances the complaint was in terms of the children being found begging for alms 'under the pretext' of selling these items. These children fell under section fourteen of the 1866 Act.[168]

The majority of cases were brought at the instance of an inspector of the RSSPCC, who initiated the legal process before the magistrates at the burgh court in Edinburgh. Commonly known as 'the cruelty', the society originated in the 1880s. It is clear that the RSSPCC inspectors were embarked on a moral crusade. Following legislation making cruelty to children a criminal offence, they assumed the responsibility of intervening in cases involving possible neglect. They were particularly vigilant in inspecting even the personal cleanliness, beds and bedding, home conditions, character and earnings of families.[169] According to an account based on the records of the society:

> The RSSPCC was the only family welfare agency in Scotland from its foundations in 1884 until well into the 1960s. During this period no other organisation daily engaged with the consequences of poverty and parental neglect for children.[170]

The overall impression gained from reading the cases is that the RSSPCC, sometimes assisted by other associations such as missionary groups, was tremendously active in Edinburgh. Their role involved rescuing neglected children either reported to them or discovered by them. Often they placed children temporarily in a 'shelter' at the organisation's base at 121 High Street until they could be brought before the magistrates. As the 1896 Report noted, their *modus operandi* was sometimes questionable. Unlike their English counterparts, which supported vulnerable children in a family context while ensuring neglectful parents were appropriately dealt with, the Scottish society adopted the policy of vigorously promoting removal of such children to institutional care.

A typical example where a child was brought by the RSSPCC inspector before the court under section fourteen was provided by the case of Angus McKay on 28 January 1901. The record notes that Angus, aged thirteen, was 'found destitute, being an orphan'. Angus was committed to Liberton Industrial School until the age of sixteen. Similarly, on 29 September 1903, James Turnbull, an RSSPCC officer, presented twelve-year-old Thomas Duffy to the court on the ground that he had 'been found begging or receiving alms under the pretext of selling or offering for sale white heather'. In this case, Thomas's father signed his consent to his son being sent to the *Mars* industrial training ship until the age of sixteen.

On 2 March 1904, James Turnbull presented an eleven-year-old boy named David Herbert Scotland to the court after he had been 'found wandering and not having any home or settled place of abode or proper guardianship or visible means of subsistence'. This time the child's mother signed her consent to her son being sent to the *Mars* until the age of sixteen.

In another case presented by James Turnbull, on 2 April 1904, a ten-year-old girl named Mary Fox was found 'wandering in the Canongate, Edinburgh having no home or proper guardianship or visible means of subsistence, her father being a soldier in India and her mother a woman of bad character'. Mary was committed to Nazareth House, Aberdeen, until the age of sixteen. The institutions to which children were committed depended on their religion. Catholic girls like Mary were often sent to Nazareth House in Aberdeen, while Catholic boys were sent to St Joseph's in Tranent. Protestant children were sent to a number of different schools, usually in Edinburgh, such as the original ragged school in Liberton or schools in Leith. For older children or often those 'beyond control', the *Mars* training ship in Dundee was a common destination. Some children were sent to schools in other areas, such as Stirling or Newton Stewart. It was not unusual for siblings to be sent to separate industrial schools.

In exercising their role to protect children, the RSSPCC inspectors also presented many children who were living in houses with known or reputed prostitutes. Often there was a note of written evidence provided by an RSSPCC inspector with details of visits he made to the residence of the children investigating their situation. Cases of this sort were dealt with under section one of the Industrial Schools Amendment Act 1880,[171] and the circumstances in which the children were found were usually well corroborated by two police constables.

The case of the three Rafferty children was one in point here. Mary Agnes, aged twelve, Hugh, aged ten, and six-year-old James were presented to the court on 15 July 1904. In addition to the testimony of James Turnbull, there was evidence from another RSSPCC officer and two police constables testifying to the children being found in a house resided in by prostitutes. The court was provided with evidence of the circumstances of the children when officers visited them on eleven separate occasions; evidence was given that on eight out of eleven visits there were prostitutes in the house. Details were also given of the number of men in the house on each occasion. Mrs Rafferty was described as a deserted wife who was 'very much addicted to drink' and reliant on the earnings of prostitutes for her income. All three children were committed to an industrial school until the age of sixteen. Mary Agnes was sent to Nazareth House in Aberdeen and both boys were sent to St Joseph's in Tranent.

A surprisingly large number of children also appeared before the magistrates at the instigation of their parents, often a single parent, more usually a father, or perhaps another relative, such as a grandparent. The allegation in these cases was that the child was uncontrollable in terms of section sixteen of the 1866 Act. Usually this charge would be made about a boy of eleven, twelve or thirteen, but in one case this charge was made by a father about his six-year-old daughter. Another case involving a girl, Emma Cooper, was presented by her father Robert on 11 November 1901. He stated that ten-year-old Emma 'resides with him, wanders away from home for nights at a time and his wife being dead he is unable to exercise proper control over his said daughter'. In this, as in the earlier cases, the child was sent to be detained in an industrial school until the age of sixteen. Sometimes there was a short statement signed by the parent to the effect that they consented to the child being sent to an industrial school, and sometimes there was an undertaking by the parent that they would contribute a certain amount to the child's upkeep.

Some insight into the reason for so many children being committed under section sixteen was given by the evidence presented to the 1896 Committee. At first sight it seems strange that so many children were presented to the court by their parents or guardians as uncontrollable. The answer lies in the complicated manipulations of process that took place to deal with truant children, as discussed earlier. As the 1896 Report noted, the school board sought to elicit the support of parents to present truant children as uncontrollable. Sadly, it appears that many parents were willing to co-operate with this.

The cases discussed so far do not involve children committed to an industrial school on offence grounds. Some examples of this type of case appear in general Edinburgh burgh court and police court records. For instance, in the volume for February 1909 there are cases of children sent to an industrial school having appeared in court on charges of theft. They were not convicted, but an order was pronounced committing them until the age of sixteen under section fifteen of the 1866 Industrial Schools Act.[172] One such case was that of nine-year-old William Stead, sent to Liberton Industrial School after being charged with stealing a pack of cigars from a shop.

Turning to the Industrial School Complaints Book for 1908–10, it is interesting to note that the front of this volume contains a loose-leaf sheet with a table recording the 'number of children committed to Industrial Schools under section 58(1) [of The Children Act 1908] from the Burgh Court, Edinburgh, during the year 1910'.

Under the Act of 1908, the Burgh Court was operating in these cases as a juvenile court. The table is reproduced below.

These fifty-seven children were some of the 787 children admitted to the thirty-two Scottish industrial schools in 1910, making a total of 4,323 children under detention. This was a much larger intake than that to the now reduced number of seven Scottish reformatories operating at this date, which admitted 185 children and had 813 under detention in 1910.[173] Nationally the UK figure for industrial schools was 19,857 children under detention in 143 industrial schools,[174] while the reformatory figure was 1,462 admissions and 5,929 under detention in forty-three schools.[175] The 1910 Report gives the figure for all classes of residential schools within the system, including short-term residential schools, as 25,786 (20,726 boys and 5,060 girls). There were also 3,320 children in the UK attending day industrial schools at the end of 1910.[176]

Again, post-1908, many of the Edinburgh industrial school cases proceeded at the instance of an inspector of the RSSPCC, and a considerable number continued to be instigated by parents alleging that children were 'uncontrollable'. Post-1908, the wording of the crave by the complainer was different, simply asking that the court order the child to be sent to a certified industrial school, rather than the previous practice of framing matters 'according to justice', with the requirement that the child 'answer this complaint' before the court. There was evidence of more detailed particulars and details being recorded about the child and his family circumstances, often moralistic in tone, denouncing the parents for being addicted to drink.

An interesting example, showing the implementation in practice of section 58(1)(d) of the Children Act 1908, making it a ground for being sent to an industrial school if a child is 'under the care of a parent or guardian who, by reason of criminal or drunken habits, is unfit to have care of the child', is provided by a case from 1909 concerning Mary Ann and James Sutherland.[177] The case was initiated by the RSSPCC inspector after he had received a complaint that the children, aged eight

Table 4.1 Number of children committed to Industrial Schools under section 58(1) of the Children Act 1908 from the Burgh Court, Edinburgh in 1910

Industrial Schools for Boys

Mars Training Ship, Dundee	St Joseph's Tranent	Lochend Rd, Leith	Fernie Park, Perth	Dr Guthrie's, Liberton	Total
7	13	9	11	4	44

Industrial Schools for Girls

Victoria, Restalrig Rd	Nazareth House, Aberdeen	Dr Guthrie's, Gilmerton	Total
6	3	4	13

Total number of boys and girls = 57.

and six, were being neglected and appearing at school in an unkempt condition. The parents did not accept the basis of the complaint and had two witnesses to support them. The inspector argued that they had previous convictions for theft, fraud and assault, were of intemperate habits and had neglected their older children, who were in industrial schools already. The case was sisted pending further reports and there are extensive notes of further visits and investigation by the RSSPCC, as a result of which the parents appeared to have made a concerted effort to impress. The notes record that,

> The house was clean and tidy and also the children. The children are attend-
> ing school and the mother signed the pledge on the fourth of January. The
> father is working constantly and keeping straight and gives his wife his wages
> of 15s a week.

This sober state of affairs was corroborated by visits by two other officers over the following two months, and the case was ultimately deserted. According to Garland, this case could be interpreted as an example of the extent to which the 1908 Act allowed extensive scope for intervention in the domestic sphere, allowing close surveillance and invasive control of family circumstances on welfare grounds. However, as the discussion of the earlier cases relating to children committed under section one of the Industrial Schools Amendment Act 1880 amply demonstrates, intrusion into the private domain was already a well-established feature before the Children Act 1908.

Reformatory admissions: Wellington cases

As was discussed earlier, Wellington Reformatory near Edinburgh was in many ways the Scottish incarnation of Mettray: Sydney Turner's description of the school praised the architecture adopted, a number of pavilion-type buildings each designed to house a small number of boys in family-style units; he also noted the resemblance to the first English reformatory, Red Hill in Surrey, where he had been instrumental in cre-ating a school based on Mettray but intended to be attuned to English culture.[178] I wish to focus now on the children admitted to the 'Scottish Mettray' at the turn of the twentieth century.

As in earlier decades, most of the boys admitted had been convicted of minor offences. Usually the offence was one of theft. One case that was slightly different was that of fourteen-year-old Thomas Wardrop, who was convicted of malicious mischief at Linlithgow Sheriff Court on 17 February 1893. He was sentenced under the 1886 Reformatory

Schools Act to ten days' prior imprisonment followed by three years in Wellington. He was charged with having broken six panes of glass in an office window and throwing four stones onto a railway line from a bridge 'to the danger of the lieges'. Thomas had a previous conviction for theft, for which he was admonished. In the section of his admission form where comments on the child or his parents could be added, his mother was condemned as 'mother loose – given to drink'. Thomas was described as 'quite neglected and in danger of becoming a confirmed criminal'.

Some of the boys were convicted of the crime of intending to commit theft. For example, the charge relating to thirteen-year-old Charles Blumont stated that 'being a known thief he was found in a shop with intent to commit the crime of theft'. On 17 March 1893 he was convicted at Edinburgh Police Court and sentenced under the 1866 Act to ten days' prior imprisonment followed by five years at Wellington. Charles had a previous conviction for theft, for which he had been admonished. The notes on his admission recorded that his father was at sea and his mother said that he was 'beyond control', that he was prone to staying out at night and would not attend school. There was also a note that the police believed that since his last conviction he had been 'associating with bad characters'. Clearly the 'beyond control' formula was taken into account in reformatory admissions as well as those to industrial schools.

Another case where a boy was convicted of intent to commit theft and was condemned by his parents as 'beyond control' was that of fifteen-year-old Charles Thom. The offence with which he was charged in the police court was that 'being a known thief he was found on the Bridge at Canonmills, Edinburgh with intent to commit theft'. As in the previous cases, Charles had an earlier conviction for theft, for which he had been admonished. On 27 March 1893 he was sentenced under the 1866 Act to ten days' imprisonment followed by five years in Wellington (although under the amending Act of 1893 the offender was not in any case to be detained beyond nineteen).[179] The admission records stated that Charles's father was 'poor', a 'gas worker' and that 'nothing was known against him'. As in the previous case, Charles's parents made matters worse for him by detailing behaviour designed to demonstrate that he was beyond control:

> His parents state that this boy is beyond control, will not work, keeps bad company, and has not resided with them since December 1892. The police state that since his last conviction he has been an associate of thieves.

A further case where a parent apparently wished to have a child admitted to a reformatory was that of twelve-year-old John Dick, convicted on 8 April 1893 at Edinburgh police court of 'theft aggravated by his having been previously convicted of theft'. Again, under the 1866 Act he was sentenced to ten days' imprisonment followed by five years in Wellington. As in the previous cases, he was said to be beyond control, a poor attender at school and in the habit of keeping bad company. The record stated that his mother, described as poor and a widowed housewife of good character, 'wishes him sent to a reformatory school'. These reformatory cases were like the industrial school cases where parents of truanting or troublesome children facilitated the admission of the children to institutions.

By the early 1900s, the admissions to Wellington were being sent there directly without a period of prior imprisonment. As discussed earlier, this requirement had been removed by the Act of 1899. Although prior imprisonment had not been compulsory for reformatory admissions since the amending Act of 1893, which gave magistrates discretionary power to dispense with it, the Wellington records suggest that between 1893 and 1899 the children being sent there were sent to prison first.

In the early 1900s, the convictions and sentences of the boys were dealt with under the Reformatory Schools Acts 1866 and 1893, as amended by the Act of 1899. An interesting case from 1902 which exemplifies this was that of fifteen-year-old Daniel Oliver, who was convicted of theft of clothes. He was sentenced at Stirling Burgh Police Court to four years in Wellington with no prior imprisonment. The notes recorded that his father was a labourer, poor and of good character. Daniel was said to be associating with bad characters, committing petty thefts and failing to attend school. The history of his previous three convictions is interesting in illustrating the types of sentences young offenders were likely to receive before they reached the stage of being candidates for admission to Wellington. The punishment imposed for his first offence of theft was '2s 6d or five stripes';[180] on his second conviction he was admonished and on his third appearance in court he was imprisoned for seven days.

The boys sent to Wellington did not always remain in the school for the full time stated in the sentence. Sometimes they were discharged earlier. This is what happened in the case of fifteen-year-old James Ferguson, who was convicted of theft at Glasgow Central Police Court on 30 October 1902. James had been convicted earlier the same month for 'using obscene language' but had been admonished for this. The assessment given of James's father in the notes was that he was poor, a

blacksmith, 'of indifferent character said to be cohabiting with a prostitute'. James was recorded as having 'no fixed place of residence' and
lacking in 'parental supervision'. Although he was sentenced to three
years in Wellington, he was discharged from the school on 25 August
1903, having been detained for ten months. The warrant authorising his
release was issued by the Secretary of State at the Home Office.

Early discharge was also the outcome in another case from 1902,
that of twelve-year-old Donald Davidson, convicted of a minor theft in
Hawick Sheriff Court on 12 November 1902. He had a previous conviction for petty theft and was sentenced to five years in the reformatory
school. The records show that he was declared eligible for discharge in
May 1903 after six months' detention. As in the previous case, no reason
was given in the records for the early release. There was an exchange of
correspondence regarding Donald's placement on release. The school
wrote to the poorhouse governor in Hawick asking for Donald to be
admitted 'as a pauper'. The governor responded that he would require
permission from the inspector of the poor. Replying to the request, the
letter from the inspector of the poor stated:

> My council would not wish him to go to the poor house where the stamp of
> pauperism would be more firmly impressed upon the child. We board all our
> children out in comfortable homes.

He undertook to make inquiries to see if Donald's grandmother would
be able to look after him, so that 'the boy may not go near the poorhouse at all'. This response was not surprising. While the school authorities were seeking to transfer Donald from one institution to another,
those administering the poor law in Scotland preferred to board children
out with suitable families rather than detain them in poorhouses.

Turning to the cases of boys admitted to Wellington under section
fifty-seven of the Children Act 1908, it is interesting to note that the case
notes continued to refer in many cases to children being beyond control. For instance, thirteen-year-old James McEwan, who had no previous convictions, was convicted of theft at Edinburgh Police Court on
22 March 1913 and sentenced to five years in Wellington. The details
of his background recorded that his father was dead, his mother was a
domestic servant, and he had been living with an aunt and uncle who
claimed that he was beyond their control.

One interesting difference in these later cases is the reference to probation in the records of some children, such as fourteen-year-old James
Liddle. He was convicted of theft of a wrap shawl on 20 February
1913 at St Rollox Police Court, Glasgow and sentenced to five years in

Wellington. His history of convictions began with an offence of theft at the age of nine, for which he was cautioned by a police superintendent. When he was twelve he was admonished for malicious mischief, and when aged thirteen he stole an overcoat and was on probation for twelve months.

It is also worth noting that as well as new forms of response to juvenile offending such as probation, there were still cases where corporal punishment was administered. Thirteen-year-old William Sutherland was convicted for five acts of theft at Leith Police Court on 1 February 1913. He was sentenced to five years in Wellington. William's background was that he was the son of a dock labourer, his mother was dead and he was described as neglected. His notes recorded that 'the boy has been previously birched (six stripes) in the Sheriff Court for theft by housebreaking'. Clearly probation was at one end of a range of penal responses which also incorporated less enlightened approaches.

The discussion of these Wellington admissions, and also those referred to in the previous chapter, has given some indication of how changes in legislation regulating admission to reformatories were implemented in practice by the courts. It has illustrated, for example, the changes in relation to prior imprisonment from the period of fourteen days under the Youthful Offenders Act 1854 through to the eventual demise of the practice in 1899. The remarkably constant feature throughout the whole period was that boys continued to be admitted for usually very minor offences, often with the complicity of parents. This parental complicity in the process of removing children was not just a feature of the Scottish system. It was a pattern which was repeated in schools for young offenders throughout Europe at this period.[181] On a theoretical point, it has been argued that this detracts from the Foucauldian interpretation of such institutions as being the embodiment of disciplinary power.[182] The Foucauldian focus on discipline fails to account for the agency of the actors involved in the process, in this case the choices made by parents who helped to have the children admitted.[183]

Cases in the High Court of Justiciary

In contrast with the cases where parents were complicit in the referral of children to industrial schools, there were situations where parents strongly objected to their children's removal. And in some cases the admission of children to institutions was challenged in the High Court of Justiciary. There are several reported cases where the High Court considered bills of suspension and liberation, asking the court to quash decisions of lower courts and order the release of children. Two of these cases were referred to briefly in chapter three. In *Maguire* v. *Fairbairn*,[184] the High Court passed a bill of suspension and liberation in the case of a fifteen-year-old boy who had been sentenced to ten days' imprisonment followed by five years in a reformatory for breach of the peace. The reason given by the High Court for its decision to pass the bill was that admission to reformatories was not intended by the legislature to apply to 'minor grades of crime',[185] only those of 'graver complexion'[186] such as theft. The second case referred to in the previous chapter was that of *Wilson* v. *Stirling*,[187] where the High Court passed a bill of suspension and liberation freeing a nine-year-old boy who had been sentenced to an industrial school for begging without due notice having been given to his mother. In this case and others, the High Court was extremely critical of irregular or unfair practices. Criticising the magistrate's actions, Lord Neaves said:

> Such a proceeding is at variance with common justice and humanity, and cannot be approved by the court.[188]

The High Court was also vigilant in rectifying abuse of procedure in the case of *McKenzie* v. *McPhee*.[189] In this case, the High Court suspended an order sending a girl of ten, Margaret McPhee, to Maryhill Industrial School for five years and ordered her liberation. The child and her mother had both appeared in Glasgow Police Court on charges of theft. The mother was convicted of theft and sentenced to thirty days in prison. The girl was not convicted but an order was made under section fifteen of the Industrial Schools Act 1866 committing her to the industrial school. The procedure followed in the police court in respect of the mother was irregular in terms of the Glasgow Police Act 1866: no citation was served by the police, no intimation was provided of the charge and no advice was given of a right to adjournment. The mother's conviction was quashed and the Lord Justice Clerk was scathing about the conduct of the police as public prosecutors here, accusing them of having perpetrated 'a travesty of legal proceedings in a civilised country'. In relation to the girl, the irregularity arose because her father had not been informed. Lord Adam said:

> The Magistrate pronounced the order in the absence of the proper guardian of the child, and in the face of remonstrance by the mother. It humbly appears to me that this was a proceeding of a most oppressive kind, and if such proceedings are common in the Police Court of Glasgow the sooner they are put a stop to the better.[190]

For an insight into the judicial understanding of the Industrial Schools Act 1866, Lord Traynor's comment was revealing:

> The Industrial Schools Act is intended to provide for the case of children who have no guardians, or whose guardians are neglecting them. But it is a new idea to me that children of law-abiding citizens, whatever their position in life, may be sent to an industrial school in this way. It is admitted that the order was pronounced in the absence of the girl's father, and without intimation to him that such an order was to be pronounced. We cannot sustain such an order.[191]

Adopting a similar line, the Lord Justice Clerk objected to the child of a 'law-abiding citizen' appearing for the first time on a charge of theft being sent away for five years with no intimation being given to the father:

> If that is the practice it is high time that the court should interfere to stop it. The object of such an Act as the Industrial Schools Act is to provide for the case of children who are not expected to be dealt with in their own homes.[192]

It is important to note that the emphasis here is on the status of the father as a person of good character, a law-abiding citizen. In other cases where the child was not fortunate enough to have a parent regarded by the court as an upstanding citizen, then the absence of notice was not held to be a material factor. This was the situation in the case of *Hunter* v. *Waddell*,[193] which concerned a boy of eleven named Isaac Hunter and his four friends who appeared in the burgh police court in Troon on a charge of stealing twenty-four cakes of sweetmeats from an automatic machine. The boys all entered pleas of guilty. Isaac's friends all had their parents in court to support them and promise to take charge of them. The boys were fined two shillings and sixpence each, with an alternative of twenty-four hours' imprisonment. The fines were all paid. Isaac Hunter had no one with him in court and the prosecutor decided to withdraw the charge of theft and he was dealt with instead under section fifteen of the Industrial Schools Act 1866.[194] He was ordered to be detained in the certified industrial school in Kilmarnock until the age of sixteen. Again in contrast with the earlier cases where parents colluded with children's admission, in this case Isaac and his father William Hunter brought a bill of suspension of the order for detention in the industrial school and for Isaac's liberation. They complained the order had been pronounced without notice to the father and was oppressive. It was held that the order was not in the circumstances oppressive and the suspension was refused. Unfortunately for Isaac, the judges took a dim view of the lack of parental presence in court. Mention was made of Isaac's irregular attendance at school, and the opinion was formed that Isaac was not being properly cared for. He was therefore regarded as a proper candidate for an industrial school. Lord McLaren emphasised that an important factor to be considered in determining whether a parent should have received notice was whether he was a 'well conducted person'. This comment underlined the importance of the respectability of parents in the court's decisions on such issues.

It is clear that, while in some cases the High Court was willing to step in and intervene to remedy what it saw as oppressive or abusive practices, in others it upheld the decisions of lower courts. Another example of this was provided in the 1901 case of *Taylor* v. *Tarras*.[195] This case concerned a thirteen-year-old boy, John Taylor, who was charged with theft in Fraserburgh Police Court on a complaint under the Burgh Police (Scotland) Act 1892. He was convicted and sentenced to a reformatory school for three years under section fourteen of the Reformatory Schools Act 1866. No complaint was served on John in advance of the trial and the magistrate failed to advise him of his right under the Burgh Police Act to ask for an adjournment. In addition, his mother, his only surviving parent, had not been informed of the proceedings, although his uncle knew of the matter and was present in court. With his mother's consent, John sought to suspend the conviction, but the High Court upheld it on the ground that under the Burgh Act there was no absolute duty on a magistrate to inform the accused of his right to an adjournment. In reaching this decision, the High Court took into account that in the interim John's mother had died and that he had no relatives willing to care for him. As the Lord Justice Clerk put it:

> Accordingly, if we were to sustain this suspension we would practically turn the poor boy adrift on the streets, whereas under the education and discipline of the reformatory school it is to be hoped that he may ultimately become a useful member of society.

This approach lends weight to the observation made by the 1896 Committee Report on the judicial attitude to the schools in Scotland, that in some respects judges regarded committing children to the institutions as a benevolent act. But, on the other hand, there is also evidence that judges were well aware of the 'penal element', as Lord Neaves put it in the case of *Wilson* v. *Stirling*.[196]

CONCLUSION

What is clear from this chapter is that by the end of the nineteenth century the statutory system had evolved into a net-widening diversionary mechanism under which thousands of children were subjected to prolonged detention in penal establishments, entailing criminalisation of children, particularly Scottish children, on an immense scale. As we have seen, the 1896 Departmental Committee Report revealed many abuses, but the system continued much as before into the early twentieth century. Despite this departure from the original holistic principles on which Watson had based his scheme, there continued to be a current of humanitarianism evident in the approach adopted by the Scottish courts: this remained in the abhorrence of child imprisonment demonstrated by many Scottish judges; it also survived in the tendency of judges to view the schools as a refuge for children in need, particularly in the absence of adequate alternative provision for the poor. As we have also seen, the period saw the virtual end of child imprisonment and the introduction of the juvenile court, both developments in the spirit of the original Scottish reformers who were mainly concerned with recognising the special position of children within the criminal justice system in a pragmatic way. However, although juvenile courts were a great advance on a conceptual level, in practical terms they failed to deliver much that was of benefit to children.

Although it was significant in many ways, the 1908 Act was not the decisive break with the past that has been supposed. In fact, there were very strong continuities with the Victorian criminal justice system. The evidence points to the juvenile court being little more than a mechanism to separate children appearing in court from contact with adult offenders. And the Garland argument in *Punishment and Welfare* that the juvenile court presided over a new field of expanded intervention appears overstated in the light of the evidence that the grounds for intervention were not greatly extended by the Children Act 1908. Indeed, the evidence from the examination of case material points to there being considerable capacity for social intrusion into domestic circumstances accompanied by wide scope for removal of children to institutions long before 1908. On the question of the influence of scientific theory on developments, there is also ground for caution. Despite its psychological talk of 'inner life' of children and the effects of depression on child development, the 1896 Committee Report was not amenable to the idea that children who were committed by the courts to institutions were in any way different from ordinary children or in need of specialised 'treatment'. Taking all this into account, it is fair to conclude that, although the period witnessed important changes, the underlying theme was one of continuity with the statutory system.

5

The Road to Kilbrandon

INTRODUCTION

In 1887 William Watson died, disillusioned, at the age of ninety-one. As the century was drawing to its close the gulf between the humanity of his original project and the austerity of the statutory system was immense. His early achievements in Aberdeen in the 1840s had inspired him to forge ahead with the development of the pre-statutory Scottish system, the first successful attempt in Britain to create a national diversionary system for juvenile offenders. But in subsequent decades the demands made by the UK statutory system altered his system beyond recognition. In the final decade of the nineteenth century there were about 24,000 children under detention in reformatory and industrial schools in Britain, usually detained for many years and subjected to a penal regime.[1] Sadly, Watson did not live to see the Children Act 1908. However, the Act's provisions virtually ending child imprisonment and creating the juvenile court set the seal on the recognition of the special position of children in the criminal justice system. Finally, the special case for children was enshrined statutorily, even if, in practice, the juvenile court failed to deliver much of an improvement for children.

This final chapter brings the historical account up to date and draws some overall conclusions. It is not the intention in this chapter to explore the twentieth-century history in depth, but rather to point to the connections between the period studied in detail here and later changes. With this in mind, this chapter opens with an attempt to flesh out the account offered in the book by examining developments in the inter-war years and then moves on to consider the Kilbrandon Report. This includes discussion of the background to the Report and argues that in important respects William Watson can be seen as foreshadowing Kilbrandon.

The following part of the chapter presents key conclusions in the following areas: the impact of diversionary systems; childhood in the nineteenth century; the underlying tensions, conflict and compromise within nineteenth-century juvenile justice reform; and the areas in which the book poses challenges to existing thought. The focus of the penultimate section is on research conclusions in relation to criminalisation and the key factors which operated together to criminalise children. The final section discusses transjurisdictional issues which have emerged in the book, and draws together topics of concern and debate which recurred throughout the period studied and which remain highly relevant to contemporary juvenile justice.

THE INTER-WAR YEARS

Although this book does not provide a detailed account of the twentieth-century history, it is important to have some sense, even if necessarily sketchy, of the path taken by Scottish juvenile justice in the years from the Edwardian period until the Kilbrandon Committee received their remit in 1961. As with many areas of life, the aftermath of the First World War proved a decisive period for the industrial and reformatory school system in the UK. The war years were marked by a high level of admissions to the schools.[2] This was attributed by some commentators to increasing numbers of children getting into trouble because of lack of parental supervision when their fathers were on military service or their mothers were working, concerns which were to re-emerge during the Second World War.[3] However, by the 1920s there was a marked decline in admissions.[4] For a number of reasons, predominantly social change, the schools fell out of favour. The classic Victorian solution of institutionalisation seemed old-fashioned in a brave new world where much that had seemed inevitable before the war was now open to challenge.[5] Widely publicised revelations uncovering abusive treatment of children had over time eroded public faith in the system.[6] In addition, there was much-improved social welfare, education and health provision to support the poor and their children.[7] There was also a change in criminal justice culture as judges opted for other solutions such as probation instead of sending children to the institutions.[8] All of these factors combined to reduce the role of the schools, which had, after all, been created as essentially a response to the problems of children in the mid-nineteenth century, when no viable safety network of social services existed. By the 1930s the distinction between industrial and reformatory schools had been erased. Following the Children and Young Persons

(Scotland) Act 1932 they became known as 'approved schools' catering for both children who had committed offences and those in need of care and protection.[9] This Act embodied most of the recommendations made by the Morton Committee set up in 1925 to review juvenile justice in Scotland, including the raising of the age of criminal responsibility from seven to eight.[10]

As in the nineteenth century, the inter-war years were marked by heated debate as to how best to treat children brought before the courts. On one level, the widespread use of probation orders for young offenders seemed progressive. In 1933 orders of probation were made in 1,225 cases in Scottish juvenile courts, while 258 children were committed to institutional schools.[11] However, while most children convicted by the courts were dealt with by way of admonition or a fine, there were also those in the Scottish judiciary who still believed in the value of corporal punishment for juveniles, something which was resorted to far less frequently in England.[12] There were 207 children sentenced to birching in Scotland in 1933. The reasons for the continued adherence to the practice of birching in Scotland are not clear, but there was considerable public concern about this issue in the inter-war years.[13] There were objections too from professionals, such as magistrates, and also the police, who were charged with the unpleasant task of delivering the punishment. A vocal anti-birching lobby emerged supported by the labour movement and feminist groups. Women's organisations fiercely objected to the class bias in what they perceived as a brutal form of punishment being inflicted almost exclusively on the sons of the working class, a similar argument to that often heard in the nineteenth century when reformers stressed the vastly different responses to misconduct by the children of the wealthy.[14] Pressure from opponents of corporal punishment succeeded in securing a Departmental Committee on the issue in 1937, which recommended an end to the practice throughout the UK.[15] Moves to introduce legislation to this effect were shelved with the outbreak of war in 1939, and the use of corporal punishment was not finally abolished until the Criminal Justice Act of 1948.

The leap from a criminal justice culture in which birching was practised to one which only a relatively short time later was able to accept the recommendations of the Kilbrandon Committee seems extraordinary. And yet it is also perfectly consistent with one of the main points to emerge from this book: that the alteration in penal patterns in juvenile justice results to a large degree from the outcome of the recurrent battle between conflicting positions on what might be termed the care/control continuum. There is always a vying for supremacy between differing perspectives, and sometimes the cogency of a radical and persuasive agenda is what changes the direction of criminal justice policy. Like William Watson, Lord Kilbrandon offered a visionary new approach to juvenile justice based on holistic values, and both were able to lead Scottish juvenile justice in a new direction.

KILBRANDON

The road to Kilbrandon

In examining the origins and working of the pre-statutory system, the book has presented evidence of a fully functioning welfare-based approach to juvenile justice in Scotland well over a century before the Kilbrandon Report.[16] In many ways, William Watson can be seen as foreshadowing Kilbrandon and there are strong grounds for arguing that the road to the children's hearings system mapped out by Kilbrandon was in a sense a route along which Scottish youth justice had travelled long before. The Kilbrandon Committee was appointed in 1961 'to consider the provisions of the law of Scotland relating to the treatment of juvenile delinquents and juveniles in need of care or protection or beyond parental control'.[17] Published in 1964, the Report highlighted the failings of the existing juvenile court system and recommended that juvenile cases under sixteen should be referred to a children's hearing, a panel of three lay members charged with the responsibility for deciding on the child's need for 'special measures of education and training'.[18] The recommendations paved the way for the Social Work (Scotland) Act 1968, which came into effect on 15 April 1971. The children's hearings provide an informal and child-friendly setting in which children themselves can participate, along with others interested in their welfare. Under this system the courts are only involved in juvenile cases in very limited circumstances, either those involving serious offences where the Crown retains discretion to prosecute, or where contested grounds of referral are heard by a Sheriff.[19] Additionally, orders made by a panel are subject to appeal to the Sheriff Court.[20]

There are striking echoes of William Watson's approach in the Report. It strikes a chord with Watson in the following ways in particular: firstly, in its holistic approach to children in trouble, seeing all such children as having the same basic difficulty of being in a situation where 'the normal up-bringing processes' have, 'for whatever reason, fallen short'.[21] In adopting this view, Kilbrandon, like Watson, rejected the idea of distinguishing between children who had offended and those presenting other sorts of problems. The second striking similarity is the focus on the need to provide children with special measures of education and training.[22] And, equally resonant of Watson, is the Kilbrandon notion of the centrality of supporting families and encouraging parental co-operation in improving life for children, thus fostering a sense of responsibility in an inclusive manner.[23] Watson could almost have written the lines of the Report discussing the system in place for removal of children to residential training institutions, where the infrequent contact meant that parental responsibility was 'extinguished' and parents were reduced to 'passive spectators'.[24] And the Report's emphasis on community involvement in decision-making about children reflected in the lay membership of the hearings' panels has parallels in the important role played by the Child's Asylum Committee in Aberdeen and the admissions committees to the pre-statutory industrial schools throughout Scotland in the 1850s. It is hard to escape the conclusion that Kilbrandon emerged as a worthy successor to Watson, imbued with a vision very much in the spirit of Watson's radical approach.

In its appraisal the Kilbrandon Report reviewed the background to juvenile justice in Scotland, making reference to the significance of the Children Act 1908 as a 'major landmark' which laid the foundation for the governance of juvenile courts: although amended by later legislation, the core principles of the system operating in 1961 remained those set out in this Act.[25] This assessment of the 1908 Act reflects the importance of the statute but overlooks the extent to which the system in operation in Scotland in the first half of the twentieth century still adhered to nineteenth-century conceptions. As discussed in the book, the 1908 Act was not an unambiguously decisive break with the past. And elements of the nineteenth-century framework survived into the mid-twentieth century. This was particularly evident in the categories of grounds under which children could be brought before juvenile courts. At the time Kilbrandon was appointed these included delinquency, care and protection issues, truancy or 'refractory' conduct.[26] This has a very familiar ring about it to anyone immersed in Victorian juvenile justice and can clearly be traced back to the nineteenth-century statutes regulating admission to reformatory and industrial schools. Similarly, as I shall discuss in more depth shortly, the idea of holding parents to account financially for their children's misconduct, a notion which Kilbrandon considered alien to Scots law, is one rooted in the nineteenth-century approach which applied throughout the UK.

The Kilbrandon Report

Kilbrandon assessed the existing system of juvenile courts in terms of their capacity to meet the needs of children, and concluded that a completely new approach was required, one which did not centre on the traditional court model. He found that dealing with children by way of absolute discharge or admonition, as happened in many cases, did not get to the root of the problem, which was how to deliver supportive measures to help such children. For similar reasons, he rejected the imposition of fines. In 1962, 8,428 young offenders under seventeen were fined. Of these, 5,788 were under sixteen, and in 746 of these cases the fine was imposed on the parent (although in practice it was normally the parents who paid fines imposed on children). The Report referred to fines on parents as a 'punitive' measure which was essentially a form of vicarious liability.[27] Kilbrandon argued that penalising parents for actions committed by their children was a foreign import into Scottish criminal law.[28] He traced the genesis of the provisions on fining parents back to the Children Act 1908, as re-enacted by section fifty-nine of the 1937 Children and Young Persons (Scotland) Act. However, as has been discussed earlier in the book, this concept had in fact first been crystallised statutorily in section two of the Youthful Offenders Act 1901. And the idea of holding parents to account financially was also embodied, although not in such a direct way, in the provisions of the nineteenth-century reformatory and industrial school legislation where parents were liable to contribute to children's upkeep in the institutions. This notion, therefore, was arguably very well established in Scottish juvenile justice historically.

In any case, as Kilbrandon rightly pointed out, fining parents did nothing to train children, and it was far more useful to attempt to encourage parental co-operation in a more inclusive manner. Looking at the history of the courts, he lamented the fact that as far back as 1932 the opportunity had been missed to seize the chance to set up a widespread system of specially constituted justice of the peace juvenile courts manned by those particularly qualified to deal with children's cases.[29] The 1932 Children and Young Persons (Scotland) Act had allowed for such courts to be set up by the authority of the Secretary of State in areas where the local authorities requested them. Only four areas elected to introduce these courts. Faithful to the innovative tradition of William Watson, one of these was Aberdeen. The other areas to opt for the new courts were Ayrshire, Fife and Renfrewshire. Kilbrandon admired this type of specialist court, comparing it to similarly constituted courts set up as juvenile courts in England and seeing it as possessing some of the same qualities to be found in the membership of the proposed children's panels.[30] He observed:

> The importance, to my mind of this apparently almost abortive provision in the practice of Scotland is that one might well expect that the people who are to man the new panels will be the same, to a large extent, as those who sat in the statutory juvenile courts. It is greatly to be hoped so. We can ill afford to lose the services of informed and public-spirited people.[31]

The failure to set up more of these types of court meant that in most of Scotland juvenile cases were heard by sheriff courts, the burgh (or police) courts and ordinary justice of the peace courts rather than the specially constituted type. The main problem with this system was that it was incapable of addressing the critical point, that, as Watson recognised long before, most children in trouble were essentially facing similar difficulties. This was the case whether they came before the court on grounds of delinquency, care and protection issues, truancy or 'refractory' conduct, terminology with a pedigree stretching back to the nineteenth-century cases discussed earlier in the book. But, in contrast to Victorian judges who were prepared to accept the credibility of parents arguing that their children were guilty of refractory conduct and so 'beyond control', Kilbrandon rejected the appropriateness of parents being able to use this ground to institute proceedings: in his view, such situations indicated the presence of familial problems requiring 'careful inquiry into the home background and parental attitudes'.[32] Clearly the time was ripe for an overhaul of juvenile justice and this is what Kilbrandon succeeded in achieving for children under the age of seventeen:

> In the broadest sense this means the revocation of the jurisdiction of the criminal courts, except in rare cases . . . over young people between the ages of eight and sixteen, or seventeen after the year 1971.[33]

This summed up the ethos of post-Kilbrandon juvenile justice: for most children in trouble the arrival of the children's hearings system in Scotland heralded an era of radical decriminalisation. The children's hearings system was established in 1971 and still deals with the vast majority of children in trouble, forming the basis for the uniquely Scottish approach to youth justice.[34]

What has emerged from the discussion in this section is that the historical perspective has enabled us to look at Kilbrandon in a new light, highlighting the connections between nineteenth-century conceptions and twentieth-century developments. Very importantly, it has shown the parallels between Watson and Kilbrandon, suggesting that in many ways William Watson can be seen as foreshadowing Kilbrandon.

KEY RESEARCH CONCLUSIONS

This section presents the key conclusions of the research in four different areas: the impact of diversionary systems; childhood in the nineteenth century; conflict and compromise in juvenile justice reform; and challenges to existing thought.

The impact of diversionary systems

One key research finding is that by the end of the nineteenth century, diversionary systems for juveniles within the criminal justice system had evolved into a mechanism for diverting large numbers of children into prolonged detention in penal residential establishments, a development which had a particularly excessive impact on Scottish children. As noted in the previous chapter, in 1894 the daily average population of the Scottish reformatory and industrial schools (about 5,500) was double that of the entire Scottish adult prison population. In England and Wales, on the other hand, the 1894 figures show the number detained in the schools (about 17,500) was slightly less than the adult prison population.[35] At the close of the century there were about 24,000 children under detention in the 141 industrial schools and fifty reformatories across Britain, with around 5,500 of these held as inmates in forty-three Scottish institutions.[36] This was criminalisation of children, especially Scottish children, on an immense scale.

Not only do these statistics underline another theme running through the book – the uniqueness of the Scottish dimension and the need to investigate this; they also highlight the complexities involved in any such investigation. On one level, the high number of Scottish children held in institutions represented a complete distortion of the idealism of the original Scottish reformers and their pre-statutory system founded on principles of compassion, civic co-operation and local cohesion. But it would be wrong to suggest that the legacy of the reformers was completely abandoned. By that I mean that some Scottish judges were still clearly influenced by humanitarian considerations in their responses to children appearing before them. To that extent, they acknowledged the spirit which motivated the first attempts at reform in Scotland and there was always an abiding current of genuine altruism flowing through the

Scottish system. However, under the statutory system judges faced the difficult dilemma of reconciling their humanitarian inclinations with a punitive statutory regime.

As the 1896 Report of the Departmental Committee on Reformatory and Industrial Schools demonstrated, not only did Scottish magistrates cling to the vestiges of humanitarian idealism by their abhorrence of child imprisonment, they were also wedded to the 'asylum theory'. This too had a humanitarian imperative, derived to a large degree from the history of the welfare-based pre-statutory schools. It was based on 'a widespread and genuine feeling of commiseration towards the numerous children in the large towns who grow up wild or drift into crime because they are neglected or have bad homes'.[37] Such attitudes accounted for the tendency in Scotland to view the schools as a refuge for children in need of help.[38] This was associated with an over-readiness to commit children to the schools, especially industrial schools where prior imprisonment was avoided. But at the same time there was judicial awareness of the now penal nature of the establishments to which children were being sent.[39] It is also important to recognise that in many ways judges considered that despite the penal aspect of the schools they had little choice but to commit children in need as there were inadequate alternative support systems available in Scotland.[40] Under the English poor law, pauper children were commonly admitted to poor law schools.[41] This did not happen in Scotland, where the practice was to board out pauper children,[42] a scheme which did not meet the needs of the large numbers of destitute children. Apart from notable exceptions, such as Quarrier's enterprise in the west of Scotland, there was a widespread shortage of viable support networks for destitute children.[43] Scottish magistrates were presented with children whose presence in court was often associated with this lack of welfare provision. All of this offers some explanation for the high volume of committals to the schools: it points to the disparity between the Scottish and English figures being attributable to the approach of the Scottish courts, and also the inadequacies in Scottish social provision for the poor.

The child in the nineteenth century

One key finding of the book is the central role played by new ideas of childhood in the reform of juvenile justice. In the nineteenth century, childhood was pictured through a new cultural lens. This vision of childhood derived from an amalgam of different sources, including the Romantic ideal of childhood portrayed in literature, religious ideas and the Victorian domestic ideal of family life. According to this new cultural configuration, the child was regarded as innocent and in need of protection. But for those children who came to the attention of the criminal justice system the realities of life were far removed from the idealised conception of childhood. The heightened sensitivity to the position of children emphasised the need to make special provision for children in the criminal justice process: it highlighted the inappropriateness of imprisoning children alongside adults, underpinning moves to extend summary procedure for young offenders. This processed children's cases quickly, thereby avoiding long periods on remand with adult prisoners. The recognition of the special position of children also lay at the heart of diversionary developments, providing for children to be sent to reformatory and industrial schools instead of prison; and it was also the basis for the creation of juvenile courts.

In the hands of philanthropic evangelists who initiated reform of juvenile justice, the new emphasis on the vulnerability of children was a powerful concept. The notion of the child as in need of care and protection was put into practice in the day-to-day running of the pre-statutory day industrial schools in Scotland. It could be seen in the concern to ensure that children received adequate food every day of the week; that they were educated; and that they were turned out looking clean and tidy, even to the extent of insisting that their hair should be 'bone combed'.[44] As noted in chapters one and two, this concern with respectability was a defining feature of the schools, with huge stress being placed on children being God-fearing and hard-working as well as of respectable appearance. The notion of respectability shaped intervention in the lives of children in a way which can be linked to Eliasian ideas of the civilising process. Effectively, the schools sought to transmit the values and manners of upright citizenry from the respectable classes to the most marginalised, impoverished and degraded in society. An article in the journal edited by Dickens, *Household Words*, described this group of children as having 'a raggedness and dirtiness which defied classification, and demanded an establishment of their own'.[45] The day industrial schools were, in essence, engaged in a genuine civilising exercise, an attempt to elevate the poorest children into the ranks of acceptability, sobriety and citizenship. Only in this way, by emulating and adopting the lifestyle of the respectable orders of society, could children free themselves of the stigma of criminality. But this was not a mere concern with outward aspects of civilised existence such as acceptable appearance. The primary goal was to instil moral values. This was an outreach to vagrants and offenders who were, by virtue of their mode of life, excluded from society: the project was energised by a missionary agenda where children were seen as a means of raising the moral condition of their wider families. They were tasked with being miniature evangelists who would return to their homes each evening and impart to their parents the scriptural values they had absorbed in the day industrial school.[46] If the ultimate aim was moral transformation of families, this could only be achieved by placing the child in a pivotal role at the centre of family life. This echoes the theme expounded by Aries, who talked about the central position of the child as the focus of family life. For the pre-statutory Scottish system, supporting the child in this position at the heart of their families was of prime importance. This emphasis on maintaining the integrity of the family explains why Watson was so critical of developments under the statutory system, which saw children separated from their families in residential schools. Like Aries, Watson argued that residential education was, by its nature, detrimental to children. There are definite parallels between Aries's theory and the disciplinary nature of reformatory education.

With regard to the application of Elias's theory, there are two further points to be made. Firstly, as noted in the previous section and discussed in depth in chapter one, the idea of civilising and decivilising is useful for understanding the contradictory forces, progressive and regressive, present in the history of juvenile justice. As we have seen, throughout the nineteenth century there was a tension between irreconcilable perceptions of children in the criminal justice system. On the one hand, there were the progressive developments. This was exemplified by Watson's civilising mission, which saw children in trouble as vulnerable and in need of care and help. On the other hand, under the punitive regime in statutory reformatory and industrial schools, regressive, decivilising, harshly disciplinarian features were in evidence.

Secondly, as noted in chapter one, Elias's theory has been widely applied in the analysis of the relationship between violence and civilisation. In this context, it has been used to explain a relative pacification of society occurring in the course of the civilising process. This idea has been applied to account for a decline in homicidal violence over time.[47] But, as the cases discussed in this book illustrate, in the nineteenth century the focus of concern for juvenile justice in Scotland was not violent offending by the young. The cases discussed in the previous chapters were almost exclusively to do with very minor, non-violent, offences: vagrancy, trivial thefts or low-level disorder. If we compare this to the contemporary situation where there is much anxiety about violent offending by the young,[48] it is indicative of an important shift of emphasis, with the focus now on more aggressive conduct.[49] This presents a challenge for those who argue that there was a process of pacification over time. It points to the need for a more nuanced interpretation of Elias's theory which can incorporate both civilising trends such as pacification over time and those in the opposite direction, as I argued in chapter one.

To sum up this section on childhood, the main point being reinforced here is that over the course of the nineteenth century it is possible to detect abstract ideas and new conceptions of childhood reflected in practice in the reform of juvenile justice, affecting the lives of children in a very tangible way.

Conflict and compromise

Underlying the account presented in this book has been the tension involved in balancing different interests and perspectives, in addressing issues of both care and control, dealing with contrasting perceptions of children as vulnerable and in need of love on the one hand and yet somehow also posing a threat or presenting challenges to order on the other. Inevitably, addressing these issues caused division and debate, as was shown in the first chapter in the context of the discussion on the civilising process. Later chapters demonstrated that conflict was evident at every stage, from the very first attempts at reform, and this was sometimes resolved by compromise on the part of the reformers. As we have seen, William Watson in Scotland and Mary Carpenter in England were both eager to gain parliamentary support for their ideas of reform. However, to advance their cause they had to concede certain key principles, notably their resistance to prior imprisonment of children under the reformatory legislation. Public opinion demanded to be assured that the children of the undeserving poor, and especially those of the 'dangerous classes',[50] would not receive special privileges at a time when many children of the respectable poor did not have access to adequate education. The obvious wish to satisfy critics of the new reforms that there was no 'bonus on crime'[51] was evident in the earliest Reports by the influential Inspector Sydney Turner, in which he emphasised the hardships imposed on juvenile offenders.

It is important to appreciate that those involved in reform of juvenile justice were far from being united in their approach. Part of the argument presented here has been that one of the main reasons for the change in ethos in Scotland under the statutory system was the introduction of a punitive dimension influenced by developments imported from the English reformatory system. But supporters of the reformatory movement in England were not all of a punitive mindset. Far from it. The movement was deeply influenced by the disciplinarian model of Mettray in France but it encompassed a broad spectrum of views.[52] At one end was the formidable humanitarian philanthropist Mary Carpenter, with her focus on the child's need for love idealised in her idyllic Red Lodge Reformatory for girls in Bristol.[53] Bought with money gifted by her patron Lady Byron, the reformatory was housed in a splendid Elizabethan mansion. This was the glorious setting in which Mary Carpenter could put into action her dreams of nurturing wayward children, allowing them to reclaim their childhood with games, picnics and pets to look after, although of course in practice she faced plenty of challenges and things were not quite so ideal. But there were also those who complied with popular demands for retribution by speaking approvingly of prior imprisonment as a condition of reformatory admission, notably Inspector Sydney Turner.[54] To Carpenter's dismay, the retributive mindset ended up holding sway. And the punitive approach found a very receptive audience among upper-class English landowners who were doubtless motivated by a degree of self-interest in (apparently magnanimously) welcoming reformatory establishments on their country estates as a useful source of labour.[55] All of this blend of mixed motives was enshrined in the UK legislation.

Often the rather pejorative term 'child-savers' has been applied to nineteenth-century juvenile justice reformers.[56] This labelling is suggestive of the paternalistic and superior attitude sometimes attributed to Victorian reformers who, it is argued, for their own reasons attempted to impose their values on those they set out to help. As has become clear, those involved in reform were far from being a homogeneous group with a fixed agenda: there was a range of personalities with differing viewpoints and intentions. Some were exemplary, while others were less than noble. But it is important to recognise that it was genuine humanitarianism which primarily motivated the initial reform of juvenile justice in nineteenth-century Scotland, and despite the later transformation of the original project and the extent to which children were criminalised, the Scottish approach always retained a continuing current of humanitarianism.

The point being reinforced in this section is that juvenile justice reform entailed constant conflict between differing perspectives on the care/control continuum. And, to advance their cause, reformers sometimes resolved this conflict by compromising on key principles, such as opposition to prior imprisonment.

Challenges to existing thought

The sheer scale of the system of reformatory and industrial schools raises a host of important issues. Firstly, as discussed in chapter three, it calls for a reassessment of the relative significance of reformatory and industrial schools within the nineteenth-century criminal justice system.[57] The schools were far from being simply private marginal institutions on the fringes of the system, as Garland maintains.[58] Although the schools were run by independent managers on the 'voluntary principle', they were regulated by statute, children were sent to them by court order and they were under Home Office direction. They were subject to statutory inspection, received public funding and were very much seen as an integral part of the criminal justice panoply.[59]

As statutorily certified institutions in which thousands of children were detained by order of the courts, they played a very important role, exercising a public function as an arm of the criminal justice system. Recognising this involves re-evaluating their position, locating them firmly in the centre rather than at the fringes of the system, as Garland suggests.

Understanding the importance of the schools in this way also has implications for the development of ideas about individual reformation of offenders. It was a central aspiration of the highly influential first national Inspector of reformatory and industrial schools, Sydney Turner, that children should receive 'reformatory training' of a scriptural nature. He wrote that reformatory schools aimed to adapt their programmes of reformation to meet the needs of the individual offender, a strategy where 'careful personal application to the individual character is specially required'.[60] That such an agenda was being promoted as the ideal method by Turner, who sought to set his stamp on the schools throughout the UK from his appointment in the mid-1850s, does not fit at all easily with Garland's assertion that in the Victorian criminal justice system 'each individual was treated "exactly alike" with no reference being made to his or her criminal type or individual character'.[61] Turner's comments suggest that ideas about individual reformation had wide currency far earlier than is usually assumed – in the mid-nineteenth century rather than at the turn of the century.

The second research conclusion which challenges existing thought concerns the juvenile court. While recognising that the creation of the juvenile court was a significant step on a conceptual level, the book has argued that in many respects the juvenile court did not change the way children were treated. It has been shown that the grounds of admission to the schools were not greatly expanded by the 1908 Children's Act, which largely consolidated the earlier legislation governing admissibility and added one or two amendments. Even the section empowering magistrates to admit children where their parents were deemed unfit by reason of criminal and drunken habits was not entirely new, as criminality of parents had been a ground of admission since the mid-nineteenth century.[62] Under the 1866 industrial school legislation, children in a workhouse or poorhouse school with a parent in prison had been liable to be admitted.[63] Similarly, under the 1871 Prevention of Crimes Act, children of a woman twice convicted of crime could be sent to an industrial school.[64] As discussed in chapter four, this emphasis on underlying stability conflicts with Garland's view that the juvenile court was an important part of a new penal landscape where there was extended capacity for interventionism and control over family life. And on this interventionist point, the case material in chapter four has shown there was considerable scope for judicially sanctioned intrusion into domestic circumstances long before 1908. The evidence points to considerable continuity with existing practice.

The third research finding which conflicts with existing approaches concerns the influence of scientific theory. The book has presented evidence that scientific notions of the young offender[65] were questioned and greeted with scepticism by, for example, the 1896 Report. This evidence of resistance to new scientific ideas poses challenges for Garland's claims about the far-reaching impact of new knowledges.[66] He argued that expertise in the human sciences occupied an important role in a new penal realm where judicial intervention was influenced by the investigations of professionals, such as psychiatrists, psychologists and other experts, rather than purely in accordance with classical legal criteria concerned with criminal responsibility. This 'extra–legal'[67] expertise was often concerned with issues such as evidence of deviation from normality, and psychological knowledge was of particular influence in cases involving juveniles.[68] The input of experts to the court process was provided by 'social background reports', or 'character judgments'.[69] However, it has been argued in this book that, while there was certainly general awareness of new scientific disciplines such as psychology and interest in them, there was also considerable scepticism about them. Such resistance to scientific ideas about the deviance of offenders undermines the suggestion that they were greatly significant in altering judicial decision-making.[70] It is argued here that common-sense notions about the causes of youth offending were more influential. For example, although the 1896 Report made psychological references to the 'inner life'[71] of children and the effects of depression on child development, it stoutly rejected the idea that young offenders were different from other children or in need of specialised treatment. It robustly refuted any notions of depravity, pointing instead to other causes, such as parental neglect and the effects of poverty. The Report defiantly declared that the Committee was 'not at all prepared to admit the theory' that the children were physically and mentally different from others.[72]

This indicates resistance to new scientific ideas about criminality, suggesting that the influence of scientific discourse in late nineteenth-century Britain has been overstated. It undermines the argument that a scientific, positivist focus on understanding the child together with a new recognition of the psychology of adolescence altered responses to the young offender.[73] It suggests that while new scientific ideas were widely circulated, ultimately pragmatic common sense was still the predominant influence.

CRIMINALISATION

One striking feature of this study is that the historical perspective has allowed us to see that over the course of time there have been certain key factors involved in the criminalisation of children. These were outlined in chapter one: policing, procedural changes, judicial decisions and legislation. In chapter two these elements emerged as critical for the criminalisation of children in Aberdeen in the 1840s. In Watson's writings, these were the four predominant variables, each of which played its part and worked together in criminalising children. These critical cogs in the wheel of criminalisation were not only important on a local level; they were equally relevant on a much wider scale. As we have seen, Susan Margarey's work shows parallels in Metropolitan London.[74] In both Scotland and England, changes in criminal administration had far-reaching consequences for children within the criminal justice system.

As Watson's observations make clear, the development of urban policing was crucial. Under new local police Acts there were many criminal prohibitions designed to create order in public spaces in the industrialised centres of population, and some of these impacted on children's outdoor pursuits, criminalising their normal activities on the streets. More vigorous policing made it more likely that children's breaches of criminalised conduct would come to police attention. The development of summary procedure in the new police and justice of the peace courts meant that children's cases were dealt with expeditiously, but created an ever-escalating volume of children appearing in court. And the situation was compounded by inconsistencies in sentencing by magistrates unqualified in the law, which led to some children being sentenced to spells in prison for breaching trivial prohibitions.

Over the course of time, the same type of variables highlighted in Watson's account affected the treatment of children throughout the criminal justice system, creating a kind of calculus of criminalisation. In chapter one, an attempt was made to identify a framework of criminalisation; markers which could be used to evaluate criminalisation as applied to children as a group. The aim has been to track the course of criminalisation by looking at formal criminalisation such as legislation and judicial decisions and also the practical outcomes of criminalisation in terms of substantive practices. This means the impact of practices of policing, procedure and sentencing, the very issues which preoccupied Watson. By examining developments in these areas, the book set out to explore the route by which children came to be seen as raising distinct issues in relation to criminalisation. Chapter one concluded with the recognition of the importance of Lacey's and Ashworth's ideas on the centrality of criminal justice actors, of appreciating that while formal legislation may be the first stage, the practical impact of formal criminalisation is felt in its enforcement by criminal justice agencies.[75]

For children the first point of contact with the criminal justice system was usually a policeman. Taking Aberdeen in the 1840s as an example, the increased police presence and activity was crucial in ushering children into the criminal justice process. But changing police practices were critical too. Following the changes implemented by Watson, police co-operated with the new diversionary system by bringing vagrant and offending children directly to the Child's Asylum Committee for consideration; and the police assisted in a very direct way by providing two teachers for one of the industrial schools. However, it is important to recognise that the means by which children came to the attention of criminal justice authorities were not limited to official policing: as we have seen from the cases discussed in the book, organisations such as the RSSPCC in nineteenth-century Scottish cities, as well as individuals, ranging from church missionaries to parents accusing their children of some minor offence or of being beyond control, also took it upon themselves to initiate the process.

In terms of procedure, one of the most striking changes which affected children was, of course, the impact of summary jurisdiction. From 1828 onwards, summary procedure was widely used to allow lower courts to deal quickly and simply with offences. As discussed in chapter one, this had both positive and negative aspects for children. The main benefit was that the availability of summary procedure enabled their cases to be dealt with quickly, avoiding long periods in prison awaiting trial where they could be contaminated by contact with adult prisoners. On the one hand this was in line with the new modern ideas of childhood which cherished the notion of the child as vulnerable and in need of protection. On the other hand the use of summary procedure in the police and burgh courts had an adverse impact on children. In Scotland there is clear evidence to show that under summary procedure children appeared before the courts much more frequently than before. Effectively there was a system in place where the availability of fast procedure encouraged prosecution of trivial offences and children were repeatedly ushered quickly through the courts and subjected to a conveyer belt of short-term sentences of imprisonment, greatly increasing the volume of young offenders. Tracking the issue of procedure over time has revealed that under the statutory system the burgh and police courts sometimes neglected to follow basic procedural requirements, again to the detriment of children whose liberty was at stake.[76] By the end of the period studied, the juvenile courts were operational, offering a new conceptualisation of special procedure for children, although as we have seen in practice they adhered to much that was well established in the Victorian tradition and the break with the past was less radical than has been supposed.

Next the role played by the judiciary. This had two dimensions, one on a political level and the other the more traditional sentencing role. On the level of political action, it is noteworthy that in the early days of reform some of those most effective in bringing about change in ways of dealing with juvenile offenders in Scotland were the judges before whom young offenders appeared, especially Sheriffs. Foremost among the innovators in this area were, of course, Sheriff Watson in Aberdeen and, to a lesser degree, the Sheriff of Lanark, Sir Archibald Alison. Faced daily with the large numbers of children repeatedly appearing before local courts for minor offences such as begging, breach of the peace or trivial thefts,[77] Watson and Alison, in common with many other judges,[78] felt disillusioned. Not only did imprisonment of children expose them to adverse influences, it was seen as a hopeless deterrent and a spell in prison branded a child for life, making it difficult to secure employment in the future. As we have seen, in Aberdeen and Glasgow in particular it was Sheriffs who led the way in introducing new diversionary schemes to respond to juvenile offending. As noted in chapter one, in the early nineteenth century the recognisably modern role of the Sheriff was relatively new,[79] and Sheriffs held considerable sway. They were charged with overseeing the professionalised administration of justice in their Sheriffdoms, and occupied a privileged role at the centre of legal and political power. Their prominent position in society gave them an important political platform, enabling those with a zeal for reform to effect change within their local jurisdiction, and to influence change on a wider front.

Of course, the success of these diversionary schemes depended upon the willingness of judges to co-operate with them, and under both the pre-statutory and statutory systems the decisions made by judges were the ultimate determinant of children's fates. While most cases involving children were finally decided by judges in the burgh and police courts, the book has discussed the important role of the High Court of Justiciary in reviewing decisions made in the lower courts. From the earliest days of the statutory system and the case of *Hay and others* v. *Linton*[80] in 1855, recourse to the High Court of Justiciary was available, even if rarely resorted to, to challenge orders committing children to institutions. Though not all such challenges were successful, the High Court proved more than willing to quash decisions and order the release of children where it was satisfied that the lower court had acted oppressively in abusing procedural requirements by adopting irregular or unfair practices.

As well as considering the role played by criminal justice actors such as the police and judges, and the effect of procedural changes, it has also been vital to examine the impact of legislative changes on the criminalisation of children. Examining the detail and impact of legislation has been a crucial part of this study. Particular attention has been paid to the body of statutes governing the regulation of the reformatory and industrial schools, to the changes made over time as the system developed into a uniform regime across the UK, and to the criminalising impact of the net-widening effect of statutory diversionary approaches. Throughout the study it has been very clear that carrying out historical analysis of this kind has uncovered much that resonates strongly with issues that are topics of current discussion.

In chapter two, reference was made to the parliamentary furore over the criminalising capacity of the English statute, the Industrial Schools Act 1857, with one MP objecting to the 'multiplication of offences'. Concern about the unjustifiable creation of new criminal offences was also something which greatly agitated William Watson: he vehemently complained about the absurdity of the new criminal prohibitions under the Aberdeen Police Act, which created offences of a kind 'hitherto unnoticed'. As we have seen, the vigorous prosecution of offences intended to prevent nuisance behaviour in public spaces impacted particularly unfairly upon children. All of this has very obvious relevance for the contemporary debate on responses to antisocial behaviour by young people.[81] It also indicates that disquiet about over-criminalisation is far from being a new phenomenon.[82]

Similarly, Watson's comments on the injustice involved in 'raising harmless acts to penal offences punishable by fine and imprisonment',[83] a process of criminalisation then being replicated by local Police Acts across the country,[84] went right to the heart of many issues involved in criminalisation, demonstrating that Scottish lawyers in the early nineteenth century were perplexed by difficult philosophical questions about justifications for criminalisation, although perhaps this was not a frame of reference they would have recognised. Here Watson was grappling with issues of the kind being tackled by his contemporary, John Stuart Mill, whose notion of the 'harm principle' addressed the limits on the state's justification for imposing criminal punishment on its citizens.[85]

Watson was very concerned about this expansion of the criminal law. He considered it a deep injustice that the prisons were being filled with adults and children convicted for breaching new offences under Police Acts, especially when the stigma associated with imprisonment made employment almost impossible to find. According to Watson, this over-criminalisation had potentially drastic consequences: nothing could be more calculated to 'pauperise and demoralize the poor and increase the number of delinquents'.[86] For him it was an issue of the legitimacy of the law: in effect he was saying that people could accept *mala in se* offences such as assault but could not see the justice in being punished for *mala prohibita* offences they did not even know existed which criminalised 'harmless' activities. This of course was a period when the demands of increasing industrialisation and the chaotic clamour and disorder of overpopulated cities added to the pressure for regulation emanating both from government at a national level and from local urban centres. And the weight of this new mass of regulation undermined the traditional conception of criminal law as concerned with public wrongs[87] that were also moral wrongs. For Watson, and doubtless many of his contemporaries, it was difficult to see the moral transgression involved in breaching trivial regulations, and it is clear that he considered the moral basis of the criminal law as a foundational *sine qua non*.

While not using the expression the 'core' of the criminal law, this is obviously what was suggested when he indicated that offences such as assault or theft were properly described as crimes, while regulatory breaches were simply 'magnified into crimes'. According to Watson, to qualify as criminal an act had to be 'wilfully injurious to person or property', qualities which were conspicuously absent in the newly created offences criminalising children's activities such as flying a kite, throwing a snowball or sliding on ice. Here he grappled with central principles about the nature of the criminal law – issues of intention, what counts as harm, and justifications for the creation of criminal offences and imposition of punishment. Most noteworthy here is the idea that the criminal law had to be seen to be linked to common-sense notions of morality. To be just, in his view, criminal law had to concern itself with matters which ordinary people had an innate sense were in violation of commonly accepted standards of behaviour: matters such as theft, wife-beating or assault. Entirely absent from this discussion was any concept of a moral requirement to obey criminal law of the regulatory kind because it was moral to submit to such ordinances for the sake of the common good.[88] It is safe to say that Watson would have been baffled by such a notion. At this period the regulatory state was still in its infancy, and Watson's writing indicated his resistance to aspects of modernisation, and the growing burden of regulation which accompanied increasing industrialisation. The main impression given by Watson's comments is one of anger and frustration at what was perceived as a new, unjust and oppressive form of the criminal law. All of this emphasises the point that ideas about the relationship between criminal law and morality, and about justifiable criminalisation, are deeply anchored in their historical context.

TRANSJURISDICTIONAL INFLUENCES

Although the focus of the book has been on developments in Scotland and England, a wider dimension has also been recognised. We have seen that the need to address the profound consequences of rapid economic change was the catalyst for juvenile justice reform not only in the UK but in other European countries and the US too. The rapid population growth, the displacement of the poor and the brutal demands made on children in the labour market by the expansion of capitalism were all features which affected western economies. One very striking theme running through the book is the extent to which in the nineteenth century there were channels of communication and influence flowing to and from Europe and the US, spreading new ideas about juvenile justice reform. There was an active philanthropic network of reformers who eagerly exchanged new ideas and approaches. This was very evident from the way in which the reformatory movement in England was inspired by the Mettray model. Schools similar to Mettray appeared in many European countries, including, as we have seen, a Scottish version.[89] In turn, the founder of Mettray was influenced by visits to new types of schools for young offenders run by religious philanthropists in the US.[90] Similarly, Mary Carpenter was deeply influenced by developments being tried out by her Unitarian friends in New England.[91] There was undoubtedly a high level of interaction and awareness about international developments. Impressively, the section of the French criminal code, the *Code Pénal*, on children under sixteen being deemed to act *sans discernement* featured in the book written by Watson's co-reformer in Aberdeen, Alexander Thomson, in 1852.[92] This section of the French criminal code was also referred to as significant by Sydney Turner in one of his reports.[93] The spread of ideas from one jurisdiction to another continued throughout the century, as its closing decades witnessed the introduction of juvenile courts. All of this has relevance for contemporary theories about criminal justice policy convergence in the UK and the US, suggesting that this is a phenomenon which has well-established historical antecedents; it is not simply a feature of existence in today's western economies linked up by super-sophisticated instant global communication.[94]

Finally, the book has something to say which is of relevance to contemporary understanding of convergence/divergence within devolved jurisdictions in the UK. In particular, it has the power to shed light on the controversial question of the potential dangers associated with policy standardisation. This is a topic which has modern parallels in the recent concern about the effect on the Scottish welfare-based children's hearings system of an emergent punitive discourse.[95] One of the main contentions of the book is that in the nineteenth century the combined impact of standardising UK-wide legislation and centralising influences impacted negatively on the Scottish welfare-based system in such a way as to subvert its whole ethos. The historical perspective shows that this is not the first time that the distinctively Scottish, holistic approach to juvenile justice has been presented with challenges which have the capacity to undermine welfarist principles.

CONCLUSION

What has emerged strongly from the book is that Scotland's contribution in the field of nineteenth-century juvenile justice was far more extensive and complex than might be supposed on reading the conventional accounts of historians with a focus on the English situation. In common with other countries, much of the impetus for reform in Scotland was driven by philanthropic initiatives, but the Scottish experience in the 1840s and '50s differed from elsewhere in that Scottish reformers achieved a remarkable degree of success in setting up a unique pre-statutory national experiment to deal with juvenile offending. This innovative diversionary system was the first major attempt in Britain to set up an organised and widely implemented diversionary system for juvenile offenders. This provided a model forming the basis for the statutory system throughout the UK, underpinning a legislative framework which, thanks to British imperialism, was even emulated as far away as Australia.[96] From 1854 onwards, the original humane project underwent a transformation as it adapted to pressures to create a uniform system. The creation of a body of statutorily certified, largely residential institutions of a penal character subverted the original benign ideals of Scottish reformers, presenting a marked contrast to the pre-statutory system of Scottish day industrial schools which in many ways had been a genuinely crime-preventive, social welfare initiative. By the end of the nineteenth century, diversionary systems for juveniles within the criminal justice system had evolved into a mechanism for diverting large numbers of children into prolonged detention in penal residential establishments. These diversionary practices impacted excessively on Scottish children, entailing criminalisation on an immense scale. However, despite this gulf between the idealistic aspirations of the original Scottish reformers and the outcome as it developed in practice, it is important to recognise that the distinguishing feature of the pre-statutory system, humanitarianism of a radical kind, left its hallmark on the Scottish approach, which continued in some respects to reflect its legacy.

Table 5.1 Statistics on reformatory and industrial schools

	Children under detention in UK reformatory schools	Children under detention in UK industrial schools
1864	4,286	1,668
1866	4,798	2,462
1868	5,320	5,562
1870	5,433	8,280
1872	5,575	10,185
1874	5,688	11,409
1876	5,634	12,555
1878	5,963	14,106
1880	5,927	15,136
1882	6,601	17,614
1883	6,657	18,780

Source: 1884 Inspector's Report, p. 8 and 9.

Table 5.2 Statistics in reformatory and industrial schools

	England	Scotland
Population in 1896	30,731,092	4,186,849
Number of Reformatories	41	9
Average Inmates	3,999	765
Number of Industrial Schools	107	34
Average Inmates	13,527	4,711

Source: 1896 Report, p. 132.

Notes

INTRODUCTION

1. Hannay (1851).
2. For ease of analysis, the book adopts the terms 'pre-statutory system' to refer to the years prior to 1854, before the introduction of legislation on reformatory and industrial schools, and 'statutory system' to refer to the post-legislative situation in 1854 and thereafter.
3. Ritter (2001).
4. Watson, W., *My Life, Volume I*, p. 119 (unpublished handwritten manuscript).
5. Watson (1851).
6. Follett (2001); Checkland (1980); Prochaska (1980); Prochaska (2006).
7. Garland (1985).
8. Ibid., p. 5.
9. Ibid., p. 28. This included knowledge of the 'psychological problems of adolescence'.
10. Ibid., p. 18.
11. Foucault (1977).
12. Garland (1985), p. 3.
13. Ibid., ch. 1.
14. Foucault (1977).
15. Wiener (1990).
16. Bailey (1997).
17. Mair and Burke (2012); Vanstone (2004).
18. Hendrick (1994); Bradley (2009); Bradley (2008); Logan (2005); Logan (2009).
19. Behlmer (1998); Children Act 1908, 8 Edw 7, c. 67.
20. Garland (1985).
21. Garland (1985).
22. Clarke (1975); Mahood (1995).
23. Donzelot (1979); Mahood (1995); Lasch (1979); Behlmer (1998), p. 231.

24. Cale (1992); Cale (1993); Mahood (1995); Moore (2008).
25. Garland (1985), p. 8.
26. Nineteenth Report of the Inspector of Reformatory and Industrial Schools, 1876, p. 11.
27. Garland (1985).
28. Gillis (1975); Garland (1985); Wiener (1990); Behlmer (1998); Bradley (2009).
29. Kelly (2017a); Kelly (2016a); Rose (1985); *The Scotsman* (1935); *The Scotsman* (1936); *The Scotsman* (1939); *The Scotsman* (1941).
30. Behlmer (1998). On twentieth century: Finlayson (1990) and Berthezene (2016).
31. Radzinowicz and Hood (1990); Shore (1999); Cox (2013); Hurt (1984); Godfrey et al. (2017); Mahood (1995); Ralston (1988); Barrie and Broomhall (2014).
32. Kelly (2017a): McNeill (2005); McNeill (2009); McNeill (2010).
33. Farmer (1997); Carson and Idzikowska (1989); Barrie (2008); Barrie and Broomhall (2014).
34. Foucault (1977); Donzelot (1979); Mahood (1995); Mahood and Littlewood (1994); Cale (1993).
35. Rothman (1971); Rothman (1980).
36. Moore (2008).
37. Cox (2013); Mahood (1995); Donzelot (1979).
38. For example: Emsley (2005); Gillis (1974); Hendrick (1990); King (1998); Manton (1976); Margarey (1978); May (1973); Pinchbeck and Hewitt (1973); Radzinowicz and Hood (1990); Shore (1999); Wiener (1990).
39. Sargent (2013).
40. Cox and Shore (2002); Nilan (1997); Schlossman (1995).
41. Cale (1992); Cale (1993); Eade (1976); Stack (1979); Stack (1994); Hurt (1984).
42. Mahood (1995); Mahood and Littlewood (1994); Cox (2013).
43. Driver (1990); Dekker (2001).
44. Godfrey et al. (2017).
45. For modern Scottish examples: McAra and McVie (2010); McAra and McVie (2012).
46. Shore (1999).
47. Mahood (1995).
48. Cox (2013).
49. Humphries (2010).
50. Ibid., p. 121.
51. Thirteenth Report, 1870, p. 76.
52. Case of James Fall, 15 August 1874, Edinburgh Industrial School Complaints Book, 1871–7.
53. *McKenzie* v. *McPhee* 1889 2 White 188, 193; *Glasgow Evening Citizen* (1888).

54. Farmer (1997); Barrie (2008); Carson and Idzikowska (1989); Barrie and Broomhall (2014); Kilday (2015); McNeill (2009); McNeill (2010); McNeill and Whyte (2007); Jackson with Bartie (2014); Kelly (2016a); Kelly (2016b); Kelly (2017a); Kelly (2017b).
55. See *Hay and others* v. *Linton* 1855 2 Irv.57.
56. Clark (1977).
57. Ralston (1988); Moore (2008); Kaye (2009).
58. Godfrey et al. (2017).
59. Mahood (1995).
60. Report of the Departmental Committee on Reformatory and Industrial Schools, 1896 [C.8204], p. 138; *Taylor* v. *Tarras* 1901 3F. 39.
61. See also Young (1976); Garland (1985).
62. Kelly (2017a).
63. McNeill (2009); McNeill (2010); McNeill and Whyte (2007); Kelly (2017a).
64. Barrie and Broomhall (2014).
65. For example, case of James Eagle, Chapter 3.
66. Report of the Kilbrandon Committee on Children and Young Persons, Scotland, Cmnd 2306 (1964).
67. Farmer (1997).
68. Barrie (2008); Barrie and Broomhall (2014); McNeill (2005); McNeill (2009); McNeill (2010); Kelly (2017a).
69. Watson (1877).
70. Duff et al. (2010); Duff et al. (2011); Duff et al. (2013); Farmer (2016); Lacey (2016).
71. Kilbrandon Report (1964).
72. Husak (2007).
73. See Garland (2001) on a convergence of criminal justice policy in the US and UK recently in the context of a late-modern 'punitive turn'; Jones and Newburn (2007).
74. Muncie (2011).

CHAPTER 1

1. Radzinowicz and Hood (1990), p. 133.
2. In Scots Law, infants under seven were, according to Alison (1832), 'held to be incapable of crime', a view supported by Hume; in English law, a similar lack of criminal capacity in under sevens was recognised, and there was a rebuttable presumption (*doli incapax*) that children between the ages of seven and fourteen were unable to 'discern between good and evil, unless the prosecution proved otherwise', according to Blackstone (1857).
3. Hendrick (2003).
4. Elias (1984).
5. Note the raft of recent innovations, including anti-social behaviour orders, powers to disperse groups of children in public, measures to tackle teenage

binge-drinking and knife-carrying, parenting orders, acceptable behaviour contracts, curfews, tagging orders and intense measures of supervision; Scottish Executive Report (2007).

6. McAra (2004); McAra (2006); McAra (2008).
7. *Independent on Sunday* (2011).
8. *The Guardian* (2011a); *The Guardian* (2011b).
9. Pearson (1983); Cohen (2004); Garland (2008); Hall et al. (1978); Young (2009).
10. Ashworth and Zedner (2008); on symbolic point, see Chalmers (2010), p. 12.
11. Husak (2007); Ashworth and Zedner (2010).
12. Kilbrandon Report (1964).
13. McAra (2004); McAra (2006); McDiarmid (2011).
14. Farmer (1997).
15. Dubber (2010), p. 191.
16. Lacey (2009), p. 942.
17. Ashworth and Horder (2013), p. 22.
18. Ibid., p. 23.
19. Grovier (2008); Hendrick (2006). By the early 1850s, transportation was virtually abandoned: Emsley (2009); and judicial execution of juveniles did not occur in practice beyond 1831: Wilson (1973).
20. Watson (1851); Guthrie (1847).
21. See also Chapter 2 on Glasgow Houses of Refuge supported by household levy.
22. Schlossman (1995).
23. Manton (1976).
24. (17 & 18 Vict., c.86).
25. Manton (1976).
26. Ibid.
27. Stack (1979).
28. Manton (1976); Davenport Hill (1878).
29. Bartrip (2004).
30. King (2006).
31. Barclay (1848).
32. Farmer (1997).
33. Wiener (1990), p. 7, with reference to Foucauldian influence on Garland (1985) and Ignatieff (1978).
34. Rothman (1971); Rothman (1980).
35. Margarey (1978).
36. Hendrick (1997).
37. This right to consultation has been enacted in s.11(7)(b) of the Children (Scotland) Act 1995. Although the Convention rights cannot be directly enforced in domestic courts, the UK is committed to adhering to the

minimum standards contained in the Convention, and is expected to provide Reports to the UN on its degree of compliance with Convention rights.

38. Children's Hearings (Scotland) Act 2011. In terms of family law proceedings, s.12(3) of the Children (Scotland) Act 1995 provides that a child is a person under the age of sixteen. See also, Age of Legal Capacity (Scotland) Act 1991, s.1(1)(b), which provides that sixteen is the age at which a young person has legal capacity to enter into transactions.
39. Aries (1962); Elias (1984).
40. Bauman (1989); Elias (1994); Fletcher (1997); Garland (1990); Mennell (1992); Pratt (2005); Spierenburg (1984); Watson (2007).
41. Cee Cunningham (1995).
42. Aries (1962), p. 31.
43. Ibid., p. 128.
44. Aries (1962), p. 413.
45. Ibid., p. 413
46. See Chapter 2.
47. Cunningham (1995), p. 5.
48. Elias (1994), p. 141.
49. Ibid., p. 121.
50. Garland (1990), p. 217.
51. Elias (1994), p. xii.
52. Garland (1990), p. 224.
53. Spierenburg (1984).
54. Spierenburg (1996), p. 64.
55. *Violence-au-vol* (from violence to theft) refers to a decline in personal violence from feudal times continuing until the late nineteenth century, a pattern for which Elias's theory seems to offer an explanation. Spierenburg (1996), p. 64; and also Weinberger (1996), p. 200.
56. In 1939; Mennell (1992).
57. Nash (2007),
58. Mennell (1992).
59. Bauman (1989); Elias quote on regression cited in Fletcher (1997), p. 180.
60. Pratt (2005).
61. See McGowen (2007).
62. Hendrick (1997).
63. See Mennell (1992).
64. Wiener (1990).
65. Dunning and Mennell (1996); Pratt (2005); Garland (2001).
66. Margarey (1978); Gillis (1975).
67. Watson (1874), p. 29.
68. Ibid.
69. Hendrick (1997), p. 23.

70. Locke (1999), p. 38 and p. 265; Locke (1975), pp. 85, 95. Quoted in Cunningham (1995).
71. Rousseau (1993), p. 1 (quoted in Cunningham (1995), p. 66).
72. Ibid., p. i; Cunningham (1995).
73. Ibid., p. 43; Cunningham (1995).
74. Cunningham (1995), p. 69.
75. Quoted in Cunningham (1995), p. 73.
76. Pattinson (1978), p. 105.
77. Cunningham (1995), p. 143.
78. Hendrick (1997).
79. Pattison (1978), p. 73.
80. Cunningham (1995), p. 142.
81. Quoted in May (1973) and Hendrick (1997).
82. Pattison (1978).
83. Heasman (1962); Checkland (1980); Mahood (1995).
84. Quoted in Hendrick (1997), p. 25.
85. Radzinowicz and Hood (1990), p. 165.
86. Cunningham (1995) p. 74.
87. Quoted in Manton (1976), p. 109; Hendrick (1997), p. 29.
88. Carpenter (1853), p. 298; Pinchbeck and Hewitt (1973), p. 474.
89. Ibid.
90. Ibid.
91. Ibid.
92. Carpenter (1851), pp. 73–4.
93. Ibid.
94. Ibid.
95. Carpenter, Mary (1851), Chapter IV, praises Watson's Aberdeen. In her 1853 book (p. 42), she quotes from a work by Scottish reformer and judge, Sheriff Barclay (Barclay (1848)).
96. Watson's evidence to 1884 Report of the Commissioners on Reformatories and Industrial Schools [C.3876] [C.3876-I], p. 413, discussed in Chapter 3.
97. Watson (1851); Guthrie (1847).
98. Manton (1976).
99. Radzinowicz and Hood (1990), p. 156.
100. Thomson (1852), p. 112, referring to the French Code Penal, lib.ii c.1. s.66, on offenders under sixteen acting 'without discernment' being educated and detained at houses of correction such as the *Colonie Agricole* at Mettray. He recommended the adoption of a similar method in Britain (p. 113).
101. Demetz was influenced by agricultural colonies in France and Belgium such as the Rauhe Haus, as well as US establishments: *Reformatory and Refuge Journal*, January 1874, p. 145; Schlossman (1995).
102. Dekker (2001).

103. Foucault (1977), p. 293.
104. Ibid., p. 294.
105. Driver (1990); Dekker (2001).
106. Hornby (1897), p. iii.
107. Dekker (2001).
108. Radzinowicz and Hood (1990), p. 161.
109. Chapter 3.
110. Foucault uses the phrase 'coercive technologies of behaviour' to describe oppressive, interventionist systems using excessive, rigid regimes of surveillance and order to impose control and discipline. Such systems are found within the 'carceral continuum' encompassing institutional forms such as schools, hospitals, clinics, military organisations and penal institutions. Foucault (1977), 293.
111. Follett (2001).
112. Dekker (2001), p. 62.
113. Althusser (1971).
114. Ignatieff (1978); Emsley (2005).
115. Follett (2001).
116. Ibid.
117. Ignatieff (1983).
118. Follett (2001), p. viii.
119. Thompson (1991), p. 366.
120. Humphries (2010).
121. Elementary Education Act (1870), 33 & 34 Vict., c.75; Education (Scotland) Act 1872, 35 & 36 Vict., c.62.
122. Hendrick (1997), p. 31; Simon (1965); Hendrick (2003).
123. Simon (1965), p. 139.
124. Aries (1962).
125. Cunningham (1995).
126. Pinchbeck and Hewitt (1973), p. 434.
127. King (1998); Margarey (1987); May (1973); Gillis (1975).
128. See Chapter 4.
129. King (1998), p. 165.
130. Ibid.
131. Follett (2001).
132. Tallack, W. (1865), *Peter Bedford, the Spitalfields Philanthropist,* quoted in Pinchbeck and Hewitt (1973), p. 434.
133. *Report of the Committee of the Society for Investigating the Causes of the Alarming Increase of Juvenile Delinquency in the Metropolis* (1816); Pinchbeck and Hewitt (1973).
134. Pinchbeck and Hewitt (1973).
135. Shore (2002).
136. May (1973), p. 104.
137. Margarey (1978).

138. See Platt (2002); Platt (1977).
139. Margarey (1978).
140. Ibid.
141. Ibid.
142. Ibid.
143. Ibid.
144. Ibid.
145. Ibid., p. 118.
146. Cox, Shore (2002).
147. Shore (1999), p. 14.
148. King (2006).
149. Cox, Shore (2002).
150. Nilan (1997).
151. Wiener (1990).
152. Gillis (1975), p. 96; Gillis (1974), p. 95; Blanch (2007); The Gladstone Report described offenders under twenty-one as 'plastic' and amenable to external influences: Wiener (1990), p. 359.
153. Hendrick (2003), p. 23; Hendrick (1994); Garland (1985); Gillis (1974).
154. See Children Act 1908.
155. Shore (2002).
156. Fletcher (1997), p. 180.
157. Margarey (1978).
158. Shore (2002).
159. Gillis (1975).
160. 'Government "criminalising young"', www.bbc.co.uk/1/hi/uk/7580285. stm; Morgan (2008); The Times (June 2008); UK Children's Commissioners' Report to UN (2008).

CHAPTER 2

1. The Reformatory Schools (Scotland) Act 1854 (17 & 18 Vict. c.72-74), also known as Dunlop's Act; The Youthful Offenders Act 1854 (17 & 18 Vict. c.86).
2. 1852 Report from the Select Committee on Criminal and Destitute Juveniles (Paper 515, Vol. V11), hereafter 1852 Report; 1852–3 Report from the Select Committee on Criminal and Destitute Children (Paper 674, Vol. XX111), hereafter 1852–3 Report.
3. On policing, see Watson, My Life, Vol. II, Chapter entitled '1830–40'.
4. Rothman (1971); Rothman (1980); Fletcher (1852).
5. Mahood (1990) identifies a similar expansion in the nineteenth-century female penitentiary movement, noting parallels with the analysis in Cohen (1985); Cohen and Scull (1983).
6. On the gulf between idealism and practical outcomes, see Rothman (1971); Rothman (1980).

7. Emsley (2005).
8. Wilson (1973). However, it was not until s.101 of The Children Act 1908 that penal servitude and the death sentence in relation to children and young people were finally abolished by statute.
9. *HMA* v. *Beattie & Kelly* (1868) 1 Coup 1. In the 1840s, children who committed this offence were sometimes transported: *HMA* v. *Mary Ann O'Brien, Agnes Wallace and Janet McNaught*, Brown's Justiciary Reports 2 1844–5, p. 499.
10. See records relating to Wellington Reformatory Farm School from 1860 (Edinburgh City Archives).
11. Rowbotham (2003); McDiarmid (2007), p. 37; Wilson (1973).
12. Ralston (1988); Clark (1977); Mahood (1995).
13. Barrie and Broomhall (2014).
14. The Reformatory Schools (Scotland) Act 1854, Dunlop's Act.
15. The Youthful Offenders Act 1854.
16. The 1856 statute, 'An Act to amend the mode of committing Criminal and Vagrant Children to Reformatory and Industrial Schools' (19 & 20 Vict. c.109).
17. The Industrial Schools Act 1857 (20 & 21 Vict. c.48).
18. Smout (1997), p. 31.
19. 'Juvenile Criminal' (1848), p. 6.
20. Guthrie (1847).
21. 1852–3 Report, p. 31.
22. Watson (1872), p. 8.
23. Parliamentary Papers (Paper 447, Vol. V11).
24. Responses given by judges refer to both genders.
25. 1847 Select Committee Report (Lord Moncrieff), p. 104, citing as an example of aggravated offences those involving stabbing.
26. 1847 Select Committee Report, p. 66.
27. Ibid.
28. The separate system of imprisonment involved keeping prisoners apart in individual cells: Cameron (1983); Morris and Rothman (1995).
29. 1847 Select Committee Report, p. 65.
30. Ibid.
31. 9 Geo. IV c.29. The Act also applied to lower courts such as burgh and JP courts, and after 1833 became applicable to some police courts. Farmer (1997), p. 76.
32. 1847 Select Committee Report, p. 64. Similarly, the Lord Justice General referred to summary process in police courts (p. 57). Farmer (1997) discusses the development of summary process under a number of Police Acts; the various forms of summary process were similar, and under an Act of 1833 (3 & 4 Wm. IV c.46 ss.134, 136) police courts could use the forms of the 1828 Act. By later general Police Acts of 1850 (13 & 14

Vict. c.33) and 1862 (25 & 26 Vict. c.101), all cases before police courts were to use summary process, with cases presented on complaint without written pleadings and with procedure approved by senior judges (p. 77).

33. King (1998), p. 165.

34. Emsley (2005), p. 29. The legislation referred to here is the Juvenile Offenders Act 1847, Juvenile Offenders Act 1855 and the Criminal Justice Act 1855.

35. Watson (1877), p. 37.

36. 1847 Select Committee Report, p. 94.

37. Ibid., p. 75. Emphasis in original text. Hard labour involved soul-destroying practices such as the crank or treadmill. McConville (1995), p. 132. Some sources indicate that hard labour was practised in Scottish prisons: Watson (1872), p. 40.

38. Farmer (1997).

39. See Michie (1997).

40. Farmer (1997).

41. There was some dissent on this point.

42. 1847 Select Committee Report, p. 94.

43. Ibid., p. 66.

44. 10 & 11 Vict. c.82; Farmer (1997); Ralston (1988). The English Act of 1847 was part of a wider process of reform of already existing complex, irregular arrangements regarding summary process. In 1848 three Acts (named after their sponsor Sir John Jervis) were introduced, (1848) 11 & 12 Vict. c.42, 43, 44. Farmer (1997), p. 78 for details of this reform; Emsley (2005).

45. This statute represented an extension of summary jurisdiction: summary procedure had been commonly used in the prosecution of juvenile offenders in London charged with offences under the Metropolitan Police Acts: Shore (2002). Under the 1847 Act, two magistrates could try summarily children up to fourteen years of age charged with 'simple larceny'. In 1850 summary procedure was further extended to apply to those under sixteen, and under The Criminal Justice Act of 1855 all 'simple larcenies' involving sums of up to five shillings became subject to summary procedure. Godfrey and Lawrence note the 1847 Act resulted in 'a huge rise in prosecutions of juveniles – a phenomenon often mistaken for evidence of a rise in juvenile crime', and suggest the 1850 Act exacerbated matters so that there appeared to be a 'youth crime wave'. Godfrey and Lawrence, (2005) p. 130.

46. See also Archibald Alison, referred to shortly, with reference to 1832, and the later account given by the Governor of Aberdeen prison. The difficulty in obtaining statistics showing the exact numbers of children convicted before and after the 1828 Act is demonstrated by examining records of prison returns in Scotland in 1830. No distinction was made between juvenile and adult offenders; and many Reports did not include convictions under summary process. For example, Prison Returns for Scotland, 1830 (Paper 459, Vol. XX1V, p. 25).

47. Brebner (1829), p. 4; Mahood (1995).
48. Michie (1997).
49. Alison (1832), p. 663.
50. For example, 1847 Report, p. 57.
51. Radzinowicz and Hood (1990).
52. 1847 Report, p. 21.
53. 1847 Report, p. 382.
54. The letter contained an appendix of letters from supporters, including William Watson.
55. Brebner (1829), p. 4.
56. Ibid. Letter by James Mackenzie in Appendix, p. 38.
57. Ralston (1988); Mahood (1995).
58. Act of 1841 for repressing juvenile delinquency in the City of Glasgow, 4 & 5 Vict. c.36.
59. *The Glasgow Girls' Reformatory* (1860); *House of Refuge for females* (1840); *Glasgow Boys' House of Refuge Reports, 1854–60.*
60. Section 19, dealing with voluntary requests for admission by a child, did not specify any age requirement. This applied where a young person released from the Glasgow prison or Bridewell sought admission to the House of Refuge. Section 20 referred to children under twelve in a pre-trial situation.
61. Select Committee Report, p. 67.
62. Act of 1841 for repressing juvenile delinquency in the City of Glasgow, 4 & 5 Vict. c.36.
63. Report, p. 85. Also Lord Medwyn, p. 99.
64. Emphasis in original text. Report at p. 105.
65. Brown's Justiciary Reports 2 1844–5, p. 499.
66. Report, p. 103.
67. In this period, three Advocate Deputes dealt with prosecutions in the High Court. Michie (1997) re: the 1820s.
68. Thomson (1852), p. 111.
69. Guthrie (1847).
70. Watson's *My Life*, Vol. II, '1830–40' (unnumbered page of manuscript); Angus (1913).
71. 1852 Committee on Criminal and Destitute Juveniles. Carpenter quoted from Watson, demonstrating his 'incredible' achievement: "'In 1841 there were 328 vagrants and 61 juvenile delinquents in the county of Aberdeen; in 1844 there were 345 vagrants, a larger number although the feeding school had been in operation. The compulsory action began in May 1845; in that year the number of vagrants fell from 345 to 105 and in the next year the number of vagrants fell from 105 to 14; in the year 1850 only two could be found throughout the country." Now that is proof which cannot be disputed' (1852 Report, p. 99). See also evidence of Alexander Thomson, p. 292.
72. 'is born, not made': Davenport Hill (1878).

73. Angus (1913), biography of Watson by his granddaughter.

74. *Chamber's Journal* (1845).

75. Hannay (1851), p. 544.

76. Thomson (1847); Thomson (1852).

77. See Watson (1872), p. 6, quoting from Thomson (1857).

78. Watson (1872), p. 6.

79. In evidence to the 1852 Committee, Thomson stated that the schools did not distinguish between the convicted and the destitute, seeing them as members of the same class with the same types of problems: 'There is no condition whatever but poverty and destitution, and neglect on the part of the parent. Criminality is no bar to admission . . .' (p. 289).

80. Himmelfarb (1995); Himmelfarb (1984).

81. See Watson (1872), p. 7.

82. Thomson's evidence to the 1852 Committee, p. 289.

83. In a Letter to day industrial school campaigners in Glasgow (Watson (1874b)), he advised: 'The utmost care must be taken to make all the children come scrupulously clean to school'(p. 4).

84. Watson (1872), p. 17. In evidence to the 1852 Committee, Thomson (p. 292) stated that as a matter of principle children were not lodged at the schools, although in exceptional circumstances children were lodged out with respectable local people.

85. Letter to Thomson. Angus (1913), p. 59.

86. Watson (1877), p. 37.

87. On legislation in other Scottish cities: Barrie (2008), p. 197.

88. Margarey (1978).

89. Watson's *My Life*, Vol. II, '1830–40' (unnumbered page).

90. Angus (1913), p. 23.

91. Watson (1872), p. 8.

92. Watson (1877), p. 40.

93. Watson (1877), p. 40.

94. Ibid.

95. Sentences for similar offences could vary from fines of half a crown or five days' imprisonment to fines of twenty shillings or twenty days with or without hard labour. Watson proposed appointment of legally trained judges to remedy this. Watson (1872), p. 40.

96. Watson (1877).

97. Watson (1872); Hannay (1851), p. 544.

98. Smout (1997).

99. 1867 [3845] (xxv–xxvi), pp. 26–7. Quoted in Cruickshank (1967); McDermid (2006).

100. Devine (1999).

101. Watson (1872), p. 8.

102. Watson (1877), p. 43.

103. Thomson (1852), p. 111.

104. The sources do not provide a specific reference for this Act. Thomson's evidence to the 1852 Committee refers to a 'local Police Act' for 'the town of Aberdeen' which criminalised begging.
105. Thomson recorded that local judges supported Watson's ideas, sharing his disquiet about the plight of young children appearing in court.
106. Watson, *My Life*, Vol. III; Ralston (1988); Mahood (1995).
107. Watson, *My Life*, Vol. III, p. 13.
108. Watson, *My Life*, Vol. III, p. 13.
109. Ibid.
110. Chambers (1845).
111. Thomson's evidence to the 1852 Committee, p. 288.
112. Thomson (1847). Also his evidence to the 1852 Committee, p. 305.
113. Parochial boards administered the poor law.
114. Watson, *My Life*, Vol. III, p. 13.
115. Ibid.
116. 1852 Report, p. 288.
117. Watson (1851); Watson (1850); Watson (1872); Watson (1874a and 1874b); Watson (1877); Watson, *My Life*.
118. Watson, *My Life*, Vol. III (unnumbered page).
119. Some English towns adopted elements of the system in the mid- to late 1840s and very early 1850s, including Newcastle, York, Manchester, Bristol, Birmingham and London; Thomson (1852). However, provision of schools designed to help the most destitute of children in England was patchy. Most did not feed children and were 'evening teaching schools . . . though distinguished by the name *Ragged*' (emphasis in original text):Thomson, p. 140. These often concentrated on biblical rather than general education. Thomson recorded that of the 102 schools operating in London under the auspices of the Ragged School Union in 1852, only a small number were industrial feeding schools (p. 145).
120. 1852 Report, p. 295.
121. Angus (1913); Thomson (1852), p. 139, also mentions Stirling and Perth. See also Clark (1977).
122. Angus (1913).
123. Guthrie (1847); Mathieson (1997); *Short account* (1897).
124. Ritchie (2014–15).
125. 740 under fourteen in the previous three years, of whom 245 were under the age of ten: Guthrie (1847).
126. Ibid., p. 93.
127. Ibid., p. 30.
128. 1852 Report on Criminal and Destitute Juveniles.
129. Mary Carpenter's evidence to the 1852 Select Committee, p. 97.
130. 1852–3 Report, Minutes of Evidence.
131. As noted, 'Ragged' was a term associated with the very different ragged schools common in England, which were often simply evening schools not

providing food or industrial training. See Ralston (1988), p. 54, quoting a letter from 1861 in which Watson expressed disapproval of the term. Despite his distaste for the term, Watson discussed in *Chapters* (1872) the various understandings of the term 'ragged school', ranging from the evening school providing very basic education run by unpaid teachers, to the Aberdeen model inspired by him.

132. 1852–3 Report, Minutes of Evidence, p. 35.

133. The schools kept a check on the progress of former pupils, the girls usually becoming servants and the boys apprentices, some of whom returned to school for evening meals. He reported that out of fifty-two children leaving in one year, only five had relapsed into crime: 1852–3 Report, p. 36.

134. On arrival at school, children had to shower or bathe before changing from their ragged clothing into school dress, which had to remain at school for fear parents would sell it for whisky:1852–3 Report, p. 32.

135. Guthrie's evidence, p. 33. Dormitory accommodation was provided only for girls and young boys of eight and under. Boys requiring accommodation were lodged with respectable local families. Accommodation was only given for cases of 'indispensable necessity' (p. 34). Lodging out also happened in Aberdeen in cases of exceptional need.

136. 1852–3 Report, p. 40.

137. Ibid. In Edinburgh the proportion of prison admissions relating to children under fourteen was given as 5 per cent in 1847, the first year of operation, and less than 1 per cent by 1852; similarly, in Dundee since the introduction of the schools the proportion of juveniles in prison was said to have halved to 4.5 per cent by 1852.

138. 1852–3 Report, p. 42. At p. 41, Guthrie noted that fifty-two out of 297 presently in his school had been sent by the magistrates. He stated that prior to the existence of the schools, children committing petty offences were not necessarily imprisoned but instead punished by fines or whipping.

139. 1852–3 Report, p. 41.

140. Ibid.

141. See Chapter 3.

142. 1852–3 Report, p. 53. Guthrie's evidence contained a draft of the proposed Bill, as did Alexander Thomson's evidence to the 1852 Committee.

143. Under the draft Bill, magistrates could send to an industrial school children appearing for criminal offences and also children brought before them for being 'idle or vagrant' though not charged with any offence.

144. The legislation which came into effect differed from the draft in some respects.

145. 1852–3 Report, p. 31. He complained about Glasgow industrial schools admitting children entitled to go to the charity workhouse, thus diverting resources from those without claim to any relief. In Aberdeen, schools arranged with parochial boards to recover some contribution for pauper children attending the schools, although all cases of true destitution were admitted: Carpenter (1851), p. 240.

146. 1852–3 Report, p. 31.
147. 1852–3 Report, p. 41.
148. Ibid., p. 53. See Thomson's evidence to the 1852 Committee.
149. Watson (1851), p. 15.
150. Thomson (1852) has an appendix with a draft of the Bill.
151. Guthrie's evidence to the 1852–3 Committee on Criminal and Destitute Children, p. 34. He referred to arrangements between the schools and employers to recover a portion of the parent's earnings; this happened in Dundee too.
152. Thomson (1852); also Guthrie's evidence, p. 50.
153. Thomson was present as chairman of Aberdeen county prisons board. Other Scots included John More, Professor of Scots Law from Edinburgh University as well as a director of prisons, the Governor of Edinburgh gaol and the honorary secretary of Glasgow industrial schools. Watson did not attend in person but his name was on the list of those supporting the event. *Ragged School Union Magazine* (1852), p. 15. The Conference on Juvenile Delinquency became an annual event. Manton (1976).
154. Manton (1976).
155. Himmelfarb (1984).
156. The Scottish model was much admired by Mary Carpenter: Carpenter (1851).
157. 1852 Committee.
158. Carpenter complained to the 1852 Committee that English ragged schools did not qualify for adequate government aid, as they were excluded from the more generous capitation grants (allowances per head) given to other voluntary schools in 1856, and in 1862 a Revised Code on education linked the payment of an annual grant to satisfactory attainment. Carpenter argued the educational standards the schools required under the Code were impossible for children from this background. Manton (1976), p. 162.
159. 1852 Report.
160. Parliamentary debate on 8 July 1857 (p. 1148) on Industrial Schools Act 1857.
161. Himmelfarb (1984).
162. (17 & 18 Vict. c.72-74), sponsored by Alexander Murray Dunlop.
163. The parliamentary debates on the parallel English measure on industrial schools in 1857 aroused controversy too, not on religious issues but because of the criminalising capacity of the Bill, lack of procedural protections, and ancillary offences relating to parental financial obligations. Stapelton MP criticised 'the multiplication of offences' (Parliamentary debate on 8 July 1857, p. 1148).
164. Under s.5, where no payment was forthcoming from the parents the cost was to be met by the Parochial Board of the Parish on which the child would have been chargeable if a pauper.
165. The criticisms of English MPs led the English Industrial Schools Act 1857 to require a conviction for vagrancy before a child could be admitted to

an industrial school under court order (s.6), which was not the case under the Scottish legislation. By amending the legislation in 1861, the condition of conviction was dispensed with, putting the legislation in this respect on the same footing as that in Scotland (Industrial Schools Act 1861 (24 & 25 Vict. c.113)).

166. *Edinburgh Evening Courant* (1856). Quoted in Ralston (1988), p. 48.

167. This was to change in the 1860s, when the schools began to accept only those sent under court order and the schools became residential in character. See Chapter 3.

168. Under s.2.

169. s.3 and s.5.

170. Manton (1976), p. 106.

171. Watson (1877), p. 37.

172. The *Act to amend the mode of committing Criminal and Vagrant Children to Reformatory and Industrial Schools*. This Act applied across the UK. The statute also provided that the schools to which young offenders were committed need not be named in the sentence.

173. Wellington reformatory records show many boys being sent to there from courts in Edinburgh, Glasgow and the Borders from the early 1860s, nearly all for trifling thefts. The standard sentence imposed on them was fourteen days' imprisonment followed by five years in the reformatory.

174. 2 Irv.57, where the statute is described as The Reformatory Schools Act and also The Reformatory and Industrial Schools Act.

175. *The Edinburgh Courant* (1855).

176. First Report of the Inspector of Reformatory Schools, 1857–8, p. 17.

177. (24 & 25 Vict. c.132). Hornby (1897), p. vi.

178. At this point the statute applying throughout the UK was The Youthful Offenders Act 1854.

179. Further evidence of the way that children admitted to industrial schools were in practice treated as criminals is provided by records from Edinburgh burgh and police courts in the 1870s showing that in many cases the term 'guilty' was used although no criminal charge was involved: for example, the case on 13 August 1874 of twelve-year-old James Robertson found 'wandering and not having any home or settled place of abode or proper guardianship or visible means of subsistence'. Under s.14 of the 1866 Act, James was sent to the industrial school training ship *Mars* at Dundee until the age of sixteen.

180. Thirteenth Report of Inspector of Reformatory Schools 1870, p. 16.

181. Report of the Departmental Committee on Reformatory and Industrial Schools, Vol. I. Report and Appendices, 1896.

182. Watson (1872).

183. Ibid., p. 20.

184. Ibid., p. 17.

185. On English poor law: Charlesworth (2010).

186. In 1857 the first inspectorate Report noted difficulties in recovering contributions from parents, stating some had been imprisoned for ten days for failure to pay. The inspector complained about lax attitudes towards recovering contributions in Scotland, repeating this in the second Report.
187. Turner's second Inspector's Report, 1859.
188. Watson (1877).
189. Watson (1872).
190. See Wellington reformatory.
191. Carlebach notes the failure to meet the hopes of early reformers envisaging reformatories under voluntary management free to develop individual 'systems of reformation' under government inspection: in reality, the primary task of inspectors was often protecting children from 'the worst hardships' (Carlebach, p. 70).
192. 1857 Report at p. 7. Turner's comments are on reformatory schools just set up in England under the Youthful Offenders Act 1854.
193. He notes there are forty certified reformatory schools in England in 1857, p. 17.
194. By the end of the decade the Wellington Reformatory Farm School was operational too.
195. First Report of Inspector of Reformatory Schools, 1857, p. 17.
196. Report, p. 18.
197. See 'London Police Courts' (1875), p. 382; *McKenzie* v. *McPhee*, High Court of Justiciary, 1889, Vol. 2, p. 189.
198. 1852 Report, p. 98.
199. Ibid.
200. Barrie (2008).
201. Margarey (1978).
202. Watson (1872), p. 8.

CHAPTER 3

1. Reformatory Schools Act 1866 (29 & 30 Vict. c.117); Industrial Schools Act 1866 (29 & 30 Vict. c.19).
2. 1884 Report of the Commissioners on Reformatories and Industrial Schools.
3. *Reformatory and Refuge Journal* (1861), p. 55. Report of address by Guthrie on Edinburgh schools in London. See also a paper by Mary Carpenter on day industrial schools in 1872, Vol. LV, p. 269.
4. *Reformatory and Refuge Journal* (1862), p. 87.
5. For example, 'The Industrial School at Signa, Tuscany', *Reformatory and Refuge Journal* (1870), p. 305.
6. William Watson wrote that he had 'long corresponded' with Carpenter, praising her 'energy' and adding she was 'held in great respect by all philanthropists' (*My Life*, '1850–60', unnumbered pages).

7. The journal reported on emigration schemes. See 1861, Vol. 1. p. 102. By the 1870s the failures of child emigration, especially exploitation of child labour, were apparent: Turner's Eighteenth Report, 1875; *Reformatory and Refuge Journal* (1875), Vol. LXVI, p. 363.
8. Reports to the Secretary of State for the Home Department on the state of the law relating to the treatment and punishment of juvenile offenders: 1881 [C.2808].
9. Norton (1887), p. 119, arguing that the schools should prioritise education and not be viewed as prisons.
10. 1884 Report of Commissioners.
11. Ibid., p. 412.
12. See Chapter 4.
13. *Maguire* v. *Fairbairn* 1881 4 Couper, 536; *Wilson* v. *Stirling* 1884 2 Couper, 518.
14. Each admission record has an extract of conviction giving details of offence, place of conviction, previous record and sentence, with detailed information about the child, including assessment of parental 'character'.
15. Nineteenth Report, 1876, pp. 5 and 14, where Turner describes the adaptation of Mettray principles at Red Hill, emphasising the French principle of young offenders acting 'sans discernement'. See Chapter 1.
16. Foucault (1977). The principle of small units was adopted fully in Wellington and at reformatories at Calder Farm (Yorkshire) and North-Eastern, Netherton (Northumberland): 1876 Report, p. 14.
17. See Chapter 3 on Glasgow House of Refuge's failure to create 'smaller family divisions'.
18. Edinburgh City Archives.
19. Cale (2014–15).
20. Turner was scathing about schools ignorant of post-discharge destinations; Twelfth Report, p. 21.
21. Briggs (1924), pp. 85–6. Quoted in Carlebach (1970), 123.
22. See Thirteenth Report, 1870, p. 76. The Report is critical of the reformatory for admitting very young boys, neglecting them and housing them in unsatisfactory dormitories. Of the brick-making the Report says that it might be profitable but it is very dirty and 'has a lowering rather than an elevating effect upon the mind'.
23. Tenth Report, 1867, p. 7.
24. Ibid.
25. Twelfth Report, p. 7.
26. Carlebach (1970), p. 127.
27. Ibid.
28. Nineteenth Report, 1876, p. 36. There were also regional officers in some cities, including Glasgow, to recover parental contributions.
29. Sydney Turner's final Report, 1876.

30. Under s.12 of the Reformatory Schools Act 1866, the Home Secretary was required to produce rules regulating reformatories.
31. Stephen Cave MP, HC, 27 July 1866, Hansard Vol. 184 cc 1606–13.
32. In 1874 (37 & 38 Vict. c.74, s.2) prison authorities were authorised to borrow to meet capital expenses of reformatories, and the Prison Act 1877 (40 & 41 Vict. c.53, s.67) transferring local prisons to the state reserved the power of prison authorities to contribute to reformatories. Hornby (1897).
33. Cale (1992); Cale (1993); Mahood (1995); Moore (2008).
34. Garland (1985), p. 8.
35. Ibid., p. 8. Garland is alluding to wider changes in attitudes towards reformation of criminals in the early twentieth century.
36. Sydney Turner, Nineteenth Report, 1876, p. 11.
37. Garland (1985), p. 14.
38. Ralston (1988), p. 49. In 1857 grants announced the previous year were removed for uncertified industrial schools, leaving them reliant on charitable donations, and in both certified and uncertified schools allowances of fifty shillings a year for every child were replaced by allowances of five shillings for voluntary cases while committed cases received five pounds.
39. Ibid., p. 50. Not all schools opted for certified status, as discussed shortly.
40. *Reformatory and Refuge Journal* (1861), p. 55. Guthrie pointed to the reduction in juvenile crime in Edinburgh, protesting that despite this the government gave only five shillings a year for children in industrial schools (as voluntary admissions) while they lavished six shillings a week on every child convicted of an offence and taken into a reformatory.
41. 1861 Report, pp. 144, 136.
42. 1861 Report, p. 136. Charles Ferguson of Edinburgh United Industrial School made the same point.
43. However, advocates for English ragged schools, especially Mary Carpenter, argued vigorously for proper public funding, contrasting the resources of provincial schools and London schools with financial support from Lord Shaftesbury: Carpenter to 1861 Committee, p. 98.
44. The Committee stressed the desirability of self-reliance but Watson argued his schools simply sought help with educational expenses which the government already gave to other types of schools. 1861 Report, p. 140.
45. Ibid.
46. Twelfth Report, 1868, p. 18.
47. Ibid. Also Ralston (1988), p. 51.
48. Report of 1861 Committee, p. 132. Neither of the two girls' schools was certified, while the school for boys and the mixed school for boys and girls were both certified.
49. Under section eleven of the Industrial Schools (Scotland) Act 1861 (24 & 25 Vict. c.132), not in force at the time of the Committee hearings, power was given to school managers to permit a child committed under

the Act to lodge with its parent or any respectable person, but Watson had adopted this policy anyway: 1861 Report, p. 135.

50. The *Reformatory and Refuge Journal* (1861–3), p. 82: the manager of an English institution explained that seeking statutory certification might result in losing both private support and freedom.

51. 1861 Report, p. 139. This was also Turner's view: Fifth Inspector's Report, 1862, p. 22.

52. Ibid., p. 142. Watson referred to the Industrial Schools (Scotland) Act 1861, arguing that children associating with thieves were in moral danger and required a substitute family.

53. See case of James Eagle, Chapter 3.

54. But generally the Board did not pursue impoverished parents: 1861 Report, pp. 134–5.

55. *Hay and Others* v. *Linton* 1855 2 Irv.57.

56. 1861 Committee, p. 150.

57. Watson: 1861 Report, pp. 136, 141.

58. 1861 Report, p. 146.

59. Hornby (1897), p. vi.

60. 1861 Report, p. 142.

61. 1861 Report p. 141.

62. 1870 Inspector's Report, p. 16.

63. Ibid.

64. Ibid.

65. Aberdeen Industrial School for Roman Catholic girls.

66. Inspector's Report for 1870, referring to 1869.

67. Inspector's Report for 1878.

68. Inspector's Report for 1870, referring to 1869.

69. See Inspector's Report for 1878, although there were a small number of voluntary cases recorded.

70. 1856 'Act to amend the mode of committing Criminal and Vagrant Children to Reformatory and Industrial Schools'.

71. In 1861 an English Act on industrial schools in similar terms was passed (24 & 25 Vict. c.113). This provided a clearer definition of vagrancy than existed in the English Act of 1857. Turner described this as the 'first effective Industrial Schools Act' for England (Eighteenth Report, 1875, p. 4). Ralston (1988) argues that at this point industrial schools became more widespread in England. On this point, also see Clark (1977).

72. He commented that parents were encouraged to send their children voluntarily by the 'indirect compulsion' effected by the existence of the legislation. Fifth Report, 1862, p. 22.

73. Tenth Inspector's Report, 1867, p. 24.

74. s.14. As in the earlier legislation, magistrate included 'sheriff, sheriff substitute, justice of the peace of a county, judge in a police court, and provost or baillie of a city or burgh' (s.4).

75. See cases referred to in Edinburgh Industrial School Complaints Book.
76. s.14 of the Act.
77. s.26.
78. The licence could permit the child to live with any 'trustworthy and respectable person'.
79. Under s.15: 'Where a child apparently under the age of twelve years is charged before two justices or a magistrate with an offence punishable by imprisonment, or a less punishment, but has not been in England convicted of felony, or Scotland of theft, and the child ought in the opinion of the justices or magistrate (regard being had to his age and to the circumstances of the case), to be dealt with under this Act, the justices or magistrate may order him to be sent to a certified industrial school.'
80. s.16. See cases in Chapter 4.
81. s.17. In England this applied to children in a workhouse. The categories of children admissible to industrial schools was further extended in 1871 by section fourteen of The Prevention of Crime Act (34 & 35 Vict. c.112) to include children under fourteen of a woman twice convicted of 'crime'; and again in 1880 by the Industrial Schools Amendment Act (43 & 44 Vict. c.15) under section one, of which children found lodging, living or residing in a house with common or reputed prostitutes could be sent to an industrial school.
82. Nineteenth Report, 1876, p. 13.
83. For court battles between inspectors of the poor and the Inspector of Industrial Schools (on behalf of the Treasury), see *Lord Advocate* v. *Brown* 1875 3 Rettie 188 and *Deas* v. *Stewart* 1885 5 Couper 638.
84. 1896 Report, p. 143.
85. Chapter 3, p. 95.
86. Under s.14.
87. Tenth Inspector's Report, 1867, p. 19.
88. See Guthrie in *Reformatory and Refuge Journal* (1861), p. 55, on the importance of prevention. Also Guthrie's comment (quoted in Ralston, p. 50) comparing giving more money to reformatories to giving a man money to buy a wooden leg having refused him money to save his leg.
89. Discussing the primary importance of the industrial school, Watson stated that reformatories were 'auxiliary' to industrial schools and did not 'supercede' them. *My Life*, Vol. 3 (unnumbered page).
90. Case of James Eagle, Chapter 3.
91. 1861 Report, p. 138.
92. See Chapter 2, where Watson refers to the practice as useless.
93. Watson may have been discounting those cases where children were sentenced to short periods in prison, perhaps a day or two.
94. Wellington's admission records indicate it was not their policy to admit first offenders under the age of twelve, 'as such can be committed to an industrial school' (see Industrial Schools Act of 1861).

95. *Reformatory and Refuge Journal* (1861–3), p. 87.

96. Ibid.

97. Ibid.

98. See *HMA* v. *Beattie and Kelly* Couper's Reports, 1868–70, Vol. I, 1. Although Wellington did not admit first offenders, other reformatories were not so scrupulous: Thirteenth Report, 1870, p. 76. See also 1862 Inspector's Report, p. 10, on the overuse of Scottish reformatories and the tendency to admit first offenders for trivial offences.

99. See the cases of eleven-year-old Thomas Mitchell and Alex Walsh, convicted at the Police Court in Edinburgh on 28 February 1874 for stealing sheets from the dormitory of the Original Ragged School in Edinburgh. Both boys had been detained in the ragged school under court order for five years after a previous act of theft. They were sentenced to a period of ten days in prison followed by five years in Wellington.

100. Edinburgh City Archives. James Eagle's case was heard at Edinburgh Police Court on 18 March 1861.

101. Like James Eagle, Thomas had a previous conviction. Case heard 8 June 1867.

102. Couper's Reports, 1868–70, Vol. I, 1. This case was dealt with under the Reformatory Schools Act 1866.

103. Ibid., p. 3.

104. Similar language is used in sentencing in the 1861 English case of *Barratt and Bradley*, see Chapter 2.

105. Twelfth Report, 1868, p. 18; Ralston (1988), p. 51.

106. In many cases, petitions were presented by parents alleging that children were beyond control, keeping bad company and likely to fall into crime. A typical case is that of John McQueen Cameron on 28 July 1874, whose mother said he was unruly and not attending school. Under section sixteen of the Industrial Schools Act 1866, John was sent to *Mars* until the age of sixteen.

107. Thirteenth Report, 1870, p. 121.

108. See *Reformatory and Refuge Journal* Report criticising *Cumberland*'s policy of having 'agents at the law courts ready to seize on every boy they can get' (1872–5), p. 383.

109. Eighteenth Report, 1875, p. 4.

110. Ibid., p. 4.

111. Ibid., p. 4.

112. By this he meant that children should be able to remain at home with their parents rather than being sent to residential establishments.

113. Watson, *My Life*, Vol. 4.

114. In England this campaign resulted in an amendment to the Elementary Education Act 1876 (39 & 40 Vict. c.79) to make provision for day industrial schools, a final triumph for Mary Carpenter.

115. Glasgow Juvenile Delinquency Prevention and Repression Act 1878 (41 & 42 Vict. c.cxxi). Under s.30 of the Act of 1878, certified day feeding schools were introduced in Glasgow.
116. Day Industrial Schools (Scotland) Act 1893 (56 Vict. c.12).
117. Carlebach (1970), p. 75; Norton (1887).
118. Reports to the Secretary of State for the Home Department on the state of the law relating to the treatment and punishment of juvenile offenders, 1881, p. 210.
119. Ibid.
120. Ibid., p. 212. A Glasgow Sheriff questioned whether s.14 of the Reformatory Act 1866 on prior imprisonment to a reformatory was intended to apply to offences under local statutes.
121. *Maguire* v. *Fairbairn* 1881 4 Couper 536. For an example of the High Court of Justiciary limiting the operation of the Industrial Schools Act 1866, see *Wilson* v. *Stirling* 1884 2 Couper 518.
122. In evidence to the Royal Commission in 1884, p. 432.
123. See *Maguire* v. *Fairbairn* 1881 4 Couper 536, p. 541.
124. 1884 Report of Commissioners.
125. See ibid., p. lxiv for a summary of recommendations.
126. Other recommendations included proposals to limit punishment in reformatories and to establish new institutions to cater for 'refractory cases'. Carlebach (1970), p. 77.
127. 1884 Report of Commissioners, p. 412.
128. Ibid., p. 413.
129. Ibid., p. 413.
130. s.15. Ibid., p. 413.
131. Ibid.
132. Ibid., p. 413.

CHAPTER 4

1. 1884 Report of Commissioners.
2. See Chapter 3.
3. See *Wilson* v. *Stirling* 1884 2 Couper 518.
4. Garland (1985).
5. Kilbrandon Report, p. 16.
6. Garland (1985); Wiener (1990).
7. Garland (1985), p. 8; Cale (1992); Cale (1993); Mahood (1995); Moore (2008).
8. Nineteenth Inspector's Report, 1876, p. 11.
9. See Introduction; Wiener (1990); Hendrick (1994); Bradley (2008); Bradley (2009); Mair and Burke (2012); Vansone (2004).
10. Garland (1985), p. 222.

11. See Report from the Departmental Committee on Prisons, 1895, C.7702, under Herbert Gladstone: though sceptical about continental ideas of criminal anthropology, this was peppered with allusions to individual reformation, paving the way for novel ideas about ways of treating different types of offenders. See also Departmental committee on habitual offenders, vagrants, beggars, inebriates, and juvenile delinquents (Scotland). 1895 [C.7753] [C.7753-I].
12. Bailey (1997), p. 293.
13. Ibid.
14. See Chapter 1.
15. See the Elementary Education Act 1876, authorising certified day industrial schools in England. But the idea of day industrial schools never really caught on: according to the 1908 Inspector's Report, there were only sixteen in England.
16. The Day Industrial Schools (Scotland) Act 1893, 56 Vict. c.12.
17. Glasgow Juvenile Delinquency Prevention and Repression Act 1878.
18. See *Calendar* (1910).
19. The average daily prison population in England and Wales in 1893–4 was 18,233 (Gladstone Report from the Departmental Committee on Prisons, 1895 p. 3). The average number of children who were inmates in English reformatory and ordinary residential industrial schools that year was 17,526: Report of the Departmental Committee on Reformatory and Industrial Schools, 1896, p. 132.

    For Scotland the average daily prison population in 1893–4 – a figure of 2,686 – appears in the Sixteenth Annual Report of the Prison Commissioners for Scotland 1894 [C.7470], p. 5. The average number of children who were inmates in Scottish reformatories and residential industrial schools in the same year was 5,476. See Report of the Departmental Committee on Reformatory and Industrial Schools, 1896, p. 132.

    Note that the figures of child inmates did not include all of those under order of detention, as there were always a number of children out on licence. These figures also do not include children in truant industrial schools (in England) or those in day industrial schools.
20. Report of the Departmental Committee on Reformatory and Industrial Schools, 1896, pp. 8, 132.
21. From an English perspective, see Radzinowicz and Hood (1990); Carlebach (1970).
22. Memorandum A, p. 155 of the Report. With reference to the 'prison tradition', the Memorandum drew attention to Turner's 1870 Report, in which he called reformatories 'juvenile houses of correction'. For his comment on industrial schools, see Chapter 4.
23. Memorandum B at p. 158.

24. 1896 Report on Reformatory and Industrial Schools (hereafter 1896 Report), p. 15. (Partly quoted in Radzinowicz and Hood (1990), p. 209.)
25. 1896 Report, p. 84.
26. Ibid.
27. Ibid.
28. Ibid.
29. Ibid.
30. 1896 Report, p. 95.
31. Fifty-fourth Inspector's Report, 1911.
32. Reformatory Schools Act 1899 (62 & 63 Vict. c.12); see Radzinowicz and Hood (1990).
33. 1896 Report, p. 138.
34. 1896 Report, p. 131.
35. s.15 of Industrial Schools Act 1866. Under s.58(2) of the Children Act 1908, the requirement that there should be no previous conviction was removed.
36. See Chapter 3.
37. 1896 Report, p. 131: the industrial schools were described as 'various in quality', mainly 'treasury maintained schools' receiving less support from local authorities than English schools, and having lower income.
38. *Wilson v. Stirling* 1884 2 Couper 518.
39. Departmental committee on habitual offenders, etc. (1895).
40. The general section of the Report discussed the UK-wide system.
41. 1896 Report, p. 131.
42. 1896 Report, p. 138.
43. Turner's final Report, 1876 Inspector's Report, p. 10.
44. 1896 Report, p. 138. Scottish 'repugnance' towards child imprisonment was given as the reason for the reformatory system having failed to develop there to the same extent as the industrial school network (an argument also, to a lesser degree, applicable to England: Radzinowicz and Hood (1990), p. 205). For the UK, the 1896 Report gives the 1894 figures under detention in the fifty reformatories nationwide as 5,587 (generally between thirteen and eighteen years old) while the number under detention in 141 industrial schools was between 17,000 and 18,000 children aged six to sixteen (p. 8). In Scotland the same year there were 765 children who were inmates in nine reformatories, and 4,711 children who were inmates in thirty-four industrial schools. 979 children were admitted to Scottish industrial schools in 1894 (p. 132). It should be noted the Scottish figures giving the number of inmates did not include those out on licence. Later in the Report one of the dissenting memoranda (A) refers to the 'rapid' expansion of the numbers in industrial schools over the years from the relatively low figure of 2,500 in 1866 (p. 157). The 1906 Inspector's

Report states that the numbers in industrial schools (including truant schools in England) doubled from 8,788 in 1870 to 16,446 in 1880. In 1906 there were 20,534 in industrial schools in the UK (pp. 6–7).

45. Reformatory Schools Act 1893 (56 & 57 Vict. c.48), also known as Lord Leigh's Act. Under this the period of detention was to be not less than three and not more than five years, and not beyond the age of nineteen.

46. 1896 Report, p. 100. All the quotes in this paragraph are from this page of the Report.

47. Reformatory Schools Act 1899.

48. 1896 Report, p. 20.

49. 1896 Report, p. 23. By 'juvenile houses of correction' Turner meant reformatories, while his reference to 'houses of detention for young vagabond and petty misdemeanant' applied to industrial schools.

50. Ibid., quoting from Turner's final Report in 1876.

51. Ibid., p. 23.

52. Ibid., p. 21.

53. Ibid.

54. Garland (1985); Wiener (1990); Gillis (1974); Blanch (2007).

55. Garland (1985).

56. Ibid., p. 26.

57. Ibid.

58. Ibid.

59. 1896 Report, p. 22. The Report referred to the 17,000 children in industrial schools.

60. Ibid.

61. Ibid.

62. Report from the Departmental Committee on Prisons, 1895, p. 8.

63. Ibid.

64. In 1924 prison administrator Ruggles-Brise wrote in withering terms about the 'dogmas of Lombroso', dismissing the influence of American and European interest in criminological theory on the English criminal justice system. Ruggles-Brise (1924), p. 15.

65. Bailey (1997), p. 304.

66. Dr Warner and Mr Legge reported results of individual physical and psychological examinations of more than 100,000 children in different kinds of schools, including certified industrial schools, poor law schools, orphanages and day schools: 1896 Report, p. 22.

67. Ibid.

68. 1896 Report, p. 145.

69. Ibid.

70. Ibid.

71. Ibid.

72. 1896 Report, p. 144, para. 267.

73. Ibid.

74. 1896 Report, p. 142.
75. Ibid.
76. 1896 Report, p. 146.
77. Ibid.
78. Ibid., pp. 140–1.
79. The Elementary Education Act 1876.
80. Report, p. 146. The full treasury allowance depended on the date the school was established and could be either three shillings and sixpence or five shillings (although the Report also mentions English school boards making the allowance up to six or seven shillings).
81. Day Industrial Schools (Scotland) Act 1893, s.3(b). Under local legislation in 1878, Glasgow already had day industrial schools. See Chapter 3.
The fact that the powers granted to English school boards in relation to industrial schools were not available to school boards in Scotland until much later – the 1893 Act – was said to be the reason that by 1896 there were no school board industrial schools or truant schools in Scotland. The only example of a 'public authority' being managers of either a Scottish reformatory or industrial school was the Glasgow Delinquency Board.
82. Ibid., p. 140. In fairness to the Glasgow school board, it was also noted that there had been no representation made on the board's behalf.
83. Glasgow Juvenile Delinquency Prevention and Repression Act 1878 established day industrial schools in Glasgow.
84. 1896 Report, p. 141. Even for fining parents the old Act of 1872 was used.
85. The previous practice of presenting dubious evidence of wandering under section fourteen (supplemented by evidence of truancy) and having children admitted under this more lucrative section was halted by the Crown Agent. But under the 1893 Act, Scottish school boards could now contribute to maintenance so they could persuade schools to accept children for the lower fee available under s.16 by making up the difference themselves.
86. Ibid., p. 141.
87. Early truant schools were described in the 1908 Inspector's Report as more interested in imposing solitary confinement than instructing pupils: 'they smacked of prison rather than of the school' (p. 23).
88. Ibid., p. 27. In December 1906 the number of children in the school was 139, with 189 on licence.
89. Ibid., p. 26.
90. Ibid., p. 28.
91. (56 & 57 Vict. c.48).
92. Industrial Schools Act 1866, s.38.
93. 1896 Report, p. 143.
94. Ibid.
95. Ibid., p. 145.

218 JUVENILE JUSTICE IN VICTORIAN SCOTLAND

96. Hall and Pretty (1909), p. 2.
97. Hendrick (1994).
98. The Act also granted courts increased capacity to enforce parental contributions by parents of children in institutions. Radzinowicz and Hood (1990), p. 211.
99. Kilbrandon Report (1964), pp. 11 and 12.
100. The Reformatory Schools (Scotland) Act 1854 (Dunlop's Act); *Hay and Others v. Linton* 1855 2 Irv.57.
101. In Scotland under the Reformatory Schools Act 1866, s.25 and the Industrial Schools Act 1866, s.40, wages of parents failing to pay contributions could be arrested.
102. Under s.22 of the Reformatory Schools Act 1866, parents could be fined up to £20 or given two months in prison with or without hard labour; s.34 of the Industrial Schools Act 1866 applied the same penalties.
103. s.94 unless the alleged crime was serious or in pressing circumstances, like the need to remove the child from 'any reputed criminal or prostitute'. Under s.131 a child was defined as someone under the age of fourteen, while a young person was someone aged between fourteen and sixteen.
104. s.108.
105. Penal servitude was imprisonment and hard labour. Morris and Rothman (1995).
106. s.102.
107. s.102. Under s.103 the Act also abolished capital punishment for children and young people.
108. Manton (1976); Stack (1979). For Turner's views, see his 1876 Report, p. 10.
109. Reformatory Schools Act 1899.
110. Radzinowicz and Hood (1990): little used in practice, this enabled children to be referred to places such as orphanages or the care of a police sergeant. Note that it had been possible for the courts to avoid committing children to prison on remand since the Industrial Schools Act 1866, which had given power to magistrates to have children sent to the workhouse (poorhouse in Scotland) while awaiting trial.
111. 1881 Reports to the Secretary of State for the Home Department on the state of the law relating to the treatment and punishment of juvenile offenders, p. 210.
112. In 1880 Home Secretary William Harcourt responded to public reaction over one egregious case by discouraging child imprisonment, instructing magistrates to inform him of any sentence of imprisonment on a child under fifteen: Radzinowicz and Hood (1990), p. 626.
113. Ibid.
114. Ibid., p. 627. For remand cases and where there was a conviction for serious offences and no reformatory was available.
115. Ibid.; Holland and Hart-Davis (2000) p. 847.

116. Wilde (1995).
117. Radzinowicz and Hood (1990), p. 627.
118. s.111(1).
119. s.111(4). However, journalists were not excluded.
120. Kilbrandon Report, p. 16.
121. Ibid.
122. Platt (1977); Tanenhaus (2001); Tanenhaus (2004); Willrich (2003). For Australian juvenile courts, see Ritter (2001). Under the State Children's Act 1886, South Australia introduced juvenile courts in 1890.
123. Platt (1977); Tanenhaus (2004).
124. Manton (1976).
125. See Chapter 1; Stack (1979).
126. Willrich (2003).
127. Ibid.
128. Tanenhaus (2004); Willrich (2003).
129. The US Supreme Court decision *In Re Gault* 387 U.S.1 (1967) marked a change of approach, declaring that children appearing in juvenile courts were entitled to due process protections.
130. Tanenhaus (2001), p. 555; Willrich (2003), p. 79.
131. Tanenhaus (2001).
132. See Radzinowicz and Hood (1990), p. 631, noting early examples of juvenile courts in England after one was established in Birmingham in 1905.
133. Garland (1985).
134. Radzinowicz and Hood (1990), p. 633.
135. Departmental Committee on Reformatory and Industrial Schools in Scotland 1914–16 [Cd. 7887].
136. Ibid., p. 809.
137. Ibid., p. 291.
138. Ibid., p. 290.
139. Morton Report (1928), *Committee on Protection and Training.* Edinburgh: HMSO. On English Molony Report (1927): Kelly (2017a).
140. Report of the Morton Committee, p. 51.
141. The Children and Young Persons (Scotland) Act 1932 was consolidated in the Children and Young Persons (Scotland) Act 1937.
142. Logan (2005); Logan (2009); Bradley (2008); Bradley (2009).
143. For more on Scottish juvenile courts, see Kelly (2017a).
144. 1908 Act, s.58(1)(e).
145. (48 & 49 Vict. c.69).
146. s.58(d). As Garland notes, a child was liable to be removed where a parent was a thief or a prostitute. These situations could have been covered by s.58(d). The subsection dealing with a situation where a child was associating with thieves does not refer specifically to a parent, although it could include a parent. According to subsection (f), a child could be removed where found in a house with prostitutes, in line with previous

legislation, the Industrial Schools Amendment Act 1880, s.1. However, the 1908 Act added the qualification that a child living with a mother who was a prostitute was not liable to be sent to an industrial school where the mother had taken 'due care to protect the child from contamination'.

147. s.58(2).
148. s.58(3).
149. s.57. Under the Reformatory Schools Act 1893, 56 & 57 Vict., c.48, commitment to reformatories was allowed for convicted offenders between twelve and sixteen, but younger children were admissible if they had previous offences.
150. s.14.
151. s.17. Under this section, children could be sent to the industrial school where the court accepted the recommendation of managers of the workhouse or poorhouse school (also applicable to children considered troublesome or 'refractory' in pauper schools).
152. Donzelot (1979); Lasch (1979).
153. Garland (1985), p. 222.
154. Ibid. Garland quotes Lord Advocate Shaw's use of the term 'revolutionary principle'.
155. Ibid., p. 223.
156. Garland (1985), p. 223.
157. Quoted in Garland (1985), p. 223: Clarke (1975).
158. Donzelot (1979); Lasch (1979).
159. Introduction.
160. s.58(4).
161. Probation of First Offenders Act 1887; Probation of Offenders Act 1907. See Kelly (2017a) for Probation of Offenders (Scotland) Act 1931.
162. Platt (1977), p. 135.
163. See Chapter 3.
164. Garland (1985), p. 14.
165. Turner's Nineteenth Report, 1876, p. 11.
166. Edinburgh City Archives. Records available from 1871 up to 1935.
167. If sent to a day industrial school, the child would be ordered to attend until the age of fourteen.
168. s.14. This refers to children found begging 'or receiving alms (whether actually or under the pretext of selling or offering for sale any thing)'; wandering with no home or 'visible means of subsistence' or destitute.
169. RSSPCC circular of 1909. See Clapton (2009).
170. Ibid.; noting that the Social Work (Scotland) Act 1968 'signalled the end of the RSSPCC's dominance in the field of the prevention of child cruelty'.
171. Under s.1 of the Industrial Schools Amendment Act 1880, a child was eligible to be sent to an industrial school if 'lodging, living or residing with common or reputed prostitutes, or in a house resided in or frequented by prostitutes for the purposes of prostitution'.

172. This was before the Children Act 1908 came into effect.
173. Fifty-fourth inspector's Report, 1911, p. 38. The Report for 1908 (Fiftieth Report for 1906) notes that 'reformatories have ever aroused much interest in Scotland'. The high point in reformatory numbers was 1880, with fifty-two reformatories in England and twelve in Scotland. By 1908 there were seven reformatories in Scotland, p. 10.
174. Ibid., p. 12.
175. Ibid., p. 6.
176. Ibid., p. 5. Additionally, there were children living in auxiliary homes for working children who had left institutions.
177. See Chapter 4.
178. See Chapter 3.
179. Reformatory Schools Act 1893.
180. The reference to stripes was to whipping.
181. Dekker (2001).
182. Ibid.
183. Ibid.
184. 1881 4 Couper 536.
185. Ibid., p. 541.
186. Ibid.
187. 1884 2 Couper 518.
188. Ibid., p. 528.
189. 1889 2 White 188.
190. Ibid., p. 219.
191. Ibid., p. 220.
192. Ibid., p. 219.
193. *Hunter* v. *Waddell* 1905 7F. 61.
194. In cases where young children appeared before the courts on offence grounds, judges might decide not to convict but to order detention in an industrial school instead. This could be done if children were under the age of twelve and had no previous convictions. Under s.58(2) of the Children Act 1908, the requirement that there should be no previous conviction was removed.
195. *Taylor* v. *Tarras* 1901 3F. 39.
196. 1884 2 Couper 518.

CHAPTER 5

1. Report of the Departmental Committee on Reformatory and Industrial Schools, 1896, pp. 8, 132.
2. The total number of committed cases in the schools on 31 December 1914 was 25,357. Fifty-eighth Report of the Chief Inspector of Reformatory and Industrial Schools 1914–16 [Cd. 8091].
3. Bailey (1987), p. 11; Smith (2007).

4. See *In Re the Clyde Industrial Training Ship Association* (1925) 22 Ll. L. Rep. 272: this was a petition to wind up and dispose of the assets of the industrial school training ship *Empress*. The petitioners stated: 'From 1908 onwards the number of boys in the ship had steadily declined, chiefly . . . owing to the Courts having departed from the practice of sending juvenile delinquents to industrial schools. By 1923 there were only 149 boys on board, the full complement being 400' (p. 272). The numbers of admissions to Scottish industrial schools in 1925 was 521 (368 boys and 153 girls), compared to 955 in 1894. Admissions to Scottish reformatories in 1925 reflected a similar trend, standing at 126 new admissions (115 boys and eleven girls), compared to 207 in 1894. Judicial statistics, Scotland, 1925. 1928 [Cmd. 3007], pp. 62, 63. See Chapter 4.

5. Rose (1967), p. 11; On various forms of institutionalisation as the instinctive nineteenth- century response to social problems in the US, see Rothman (1971); Rothman (1980).

6. As Home Secretary in 1910, Winston Churchill ordered an inquiry into revelations about an English reformatory published in *John Bull* under the title of 'Reformatory School Horrors – How boys at the Akbar School are Tortured – Several Deaths'. The findings of the inquiry rejecting the claims of brutality led to accusations of a cover-up and 7,000 people attended a public protest on the matter, which was debated in Parliament: see Carlebach (1970), p. 85. Lobbying against the system also came from the Howard League for Penal Reform, which in 1919 revealed the contents of an unpublished Departmental Committee Report on the schools, accusing them of reducing the children in their care to 'little factory hands in inefficient factories': Carlebach (1970), p. 89. In similar vein, there was an outcry in Scotland in 1918 about children at Kibble reformatory being sent to work in a munitions factory in Paisley: Smith (2007).

7. Hendrick (2003).

8. The Judicial Statistics, Scotland, 1925 (Cmd. 3007), published by HMSO in 1928, record the figure of 826 probation orders made in cases before the juvenile courts in that year. This was out of 9,950 cases of children coming before the juvenile courts charged with a criminal offence. Of the 7,726 convicted, more than half (4,182) were admonished, while 3,182 received a fine. A sizeable number, 255, were ordered to be whipped – this was over twice the number ordered to a reformatory school. For discussion of the prevalence of whipping and the controversy surrounding the continuation of this practice (which was frowned upon in England by this stage), see Mahood (2002). On Scottish probation history: McNeill (2005); McNeill and Whyte (2007); McNeill (2009); McNeill (2010); Kelly (2017a). On probation in England, see Mair and Burke (2012); Vanstone (2004); Young (1976); Rose (1967), p. 11; Rose (1985); Carlebach (1970) p. 89.

9. The Children and Young Persons (Scotland) Act 1932 was consolidated in the Children and Young Persons (Scotland) Act 1937.

10. The Committee reported in 1928, see Chapter 4; Smith (2007); Kelly (2017a). On the issue of raising the age of criminal responsibility, see the 2002 Scottish Law Commission 'Report on Age of Criminal Responsibility', discussing section fourteen of the 1932 Act at p. 5. The Report notes that this provision placed the age of criminal responsibility on a statutory basis, bringing the law in both Scotland and England into line, and 'moved Scots Law away from its earlier emphasis on not punishing children accused of crime rather than deeming them incapable of guilt'.

11. 1934–5 [Cmd. 4757] Judicial statistics, Scotland, 1933. Of the 9,179 children proceeded against, 547 were acquitted or had the charge withdrawn. Where the charge was proved and an order was made without conviction, 824 were dismissed, 1,225 received a probation order, sixty-three were sent to an industrial school and fifty-three were subject to a bond with or without securities. 6,465 children were convicted by the juvenile courts. Of these, 4,058 were admonished, 2,000 fined, 207 were sentenced to whipping (birching), 124 were ordered to a reformatory, seventy-three were subject to caution with or without securities and three were committed to places of detention, to be known as Remand Homes when the 1932 Act came into effect on 1 November 1933. This date marked the end of industrial and reformatory schools. Thereafter the schools were designated approved schools and the figures relating to them appeared in Scottish Education Department returns. The school committals in the 1933 judicial statistics included those sent to approved schools in November and December that year. Under the 1932 Act, the age limit for young persons was raised to seventeen, and juvenile courts dealt with children up to seventeen, rather than sixteen: pp. 9, 64. The number of young offenders sentenced to borstal detention in Scotland in 1933 was 135 – 130 boys and 5 girls (aged between sixteen and twenty-one): p. 9.

12. The Departmental Committee on Corporal Punishment 1937 (Cadogen Committee) reported that unlike the other jurisdictions within the UK where probation had replaced corporal punishment, Scottish courts continued to order whipping 'more freely' than elsewhere. Mahood (2002), p. 446.

13. Ibid. This article discusses the impact of the vocal and politicised anti-birching lobby in Scotland.

14. Mahood (2002) discussed the protests made by the Scottish Women's Co-operative Guild and the Scottish Women's Labour Party.

15. Cadogen Comittee; Mahood (2002).

16. Kilbrandon Report (1964).

17. Ibid., p. 6.

18. Ibid., pp. 79, 80.

19. Children's Hearings (Scotland) Act 2011.

20. Children's Hearings (Scotland) Act 2011, s.154.

21. Kilbrandon Report, pp. 9, 77.

22. Ibid., pp. 9, 80.

23. Ibid., pp. 14, 77.
24. Ibid., p. 16.
25. Ibid., p. 16.
26. Ibid., p. 6. 'Juvenile delinquents and juveniles in need of care or protection or beyond parental control, we take to mean broadly those juveniles who may in certain specified situations or circumstances be brought before a juvenile court. The law recognises four such groups – juveniles alleged to have committed crimes or offences, children in need of care or protection, children who are refractory or beyond parental control, and children who are persistent truants.' These were grounds under the 1937 Children and Young Persons (Scotland) Act.
27. Kilbrandon Report, p. 11.
28. Ibid., pp. 11, 12. The Report states: 'so far as fines are concerned, it therefore appears that in Scotland the present position in relation to juveniles is of fairly recent statutory origin, and that, in so far as it imports the idea of applying, subject to certain qualifications, penalties on the parents for the misdeeds of their children, it represents a concept not otherwise found in the criminal law, or to any appreciable extent in the civil law.' The statutory provisions created a rebuttable presumption, with the onus on the parent to show no failure to exercise due care of the child, so 'it is not necessary for the court to be satisfied affirmatively that the parent has conduced to the commission of the offence; and in practice courts are no doubt guided, in the absence of any positive attempt at rebuttal by the parents, by the background Report and other information before them, and by the parents' general demeanour on appearance before them.'
29. Ibid., p. 1; Kilbrandon and Mack (1968).
30. Kelly (2016a); Kelly (2017b).
31. Kilbrandon (1968), p. 239.
32. Kilbrandon Report, pp. 8, 43.
33. Kilbrandon and Mack (1968), p. 236: Lord Kilbrandon speaking at the University of Glasgow on 13 February 1968. This reference relates to juvenile offenders. The Kilbrandon Report noted, 'By law juvenile offenders comprise offenders aged 8 or over and under 17' (p. 6). However, the children's hearings also consider cases of children in need of 'compulsory measures of care' from infancy up to the age of seventeen (ibid., p. x).
34. McK. Norrie (2013), p. 1; McAra (2006).
35. See Chapter 4.
36. Report of the Departmental Committee on Reformatory and Industrial Schools, 1896, pp. 8, 132.
37. 1896 Report, p. 138.
38. See Lord Justice Clerk in *Taylor* v. *Tarras*, Chapter 4.
39. See reference by Lord Neaves to the 'penal element' of industrial schools in the case of *Wilson* v. *Stirling* 1884 2 Coupar 518.
40. See *Taylor* v. *Tarras* (supra).

41. Report of the Departmental Committee on Reformatory and Industrial Schools, 1896, pp. 131, 132, 137.
42. Abrams (1998).
43. See Chapter 4.
44. See Chapter 2.
45. Hannay (1851), p. 544.
46. Watson described the role of children in their 'family circle' as being that of 'home missionary in homes so wretched the self-regarding missionary would have feared to enter': Watson (1851), p. 25.
47. Spierenburg (1996).
48. See Chapter 1 with reference to knife-carrying.
49. See Chapter 1.
50. Mary Carpenter's term. See Chapter 2.
51. Mary Carpenter's expression: 1852 Select Committee on Criminal and Destitute Juveniles, p. 98.
52. See Nineteenth Inspector's Report on Industrial and Reformatory Schools, 1876, p. 5, where Sydney Turner describes the adaptation of Mettray principles at Red Hill reformatory in Surrey; also Driver (1990).
53. Manton (1976).
54. See Sydney Turner's comments at p. 10 of Nineteenth Inspector's Report.
55. Stack (1979).
56. Platt (1977).
57. See Chapter 3.
58. Garland (1985), p. 8.
59. Chapter 3 for parliamentary quote on the schools in 1866 as 'public' or 'state institutions'.
60. Nineteenth Report, 1876, p. 11. See Chapter 3.
61. Garland (1985), p. 14.
62. s.58(1)(d).
63. s.17, Industrial Schools Act 1866.
64. s.14.
65. Garland (1985); Wiener (1990); Gillis (1974); Blanch (2007).
66. Garland (1985).
67. Ibid., p. 26.
68. Ibid.
69. Ibid.
70. See Bailey (1997) argument that judges in the early twentieth century adhered to classical notions of proportionate rather than indeterminate sentencing of the positivist-inspired variety (p. 304). Bailey's scepticism about the influence of criminological discourse is supported by the comment from the Gladstone Report quoted in Chapter 4.
71. 1896 Report, p. 20.
72. 1896 Report, p. 22.
73. See Chapter 1.

74. Margarey (1978).
75. See Chapter 1.
76. *McKenzie* v. *McPhee*.
77. Letter by Watson to Thomson, Angus (1913) p. 59.
78. For example, Sheriff Barclay of Perth. See Chapter 1.
79. Farmer (1997).
80. 2 Irv.57.
81. Scottish Executive Report (2007); Ashworth and Zedner (2010).
82. See Ashworth and Zedner (2008); Husak (2007).
83. Watson (1877), p. 40.
84. Barrie (2008).
85. Mill (1859).
86. Watson (1877), p. 40.
87. Farmer (1997); Farmer (2010); Lacey (2013).
88. Tadros (2010).
89. See Chapter 3.
90. See Chapter 1.
91. Manton (1976).
92. Thomson (1852), p. 112. See Chapter 1.
93. See Chapter 3.
94. See Garland (2001); Jones and Newburn (2007).
95. See Chapter 1.
96. Ritter (2001).

References

RECORDS FROM EDINBURGH CITY ARCHIVES

Edinburgh Industrial Schools Complaints Books.
Records relating to admissions to Wellington Reformatory Farm School, Edinburgh.
Log book of St John's Hill Day Industrial School, Edinburgh.

BOOKS AND ARTICLES

Abrams, L. (1998), *The Orphan Country: children of Scotland's broken homes from 1845 to the present day*, Edinburgh: John Donald.

Alison, A. (1832), *Principles of the Criminal Law of Scotland*, Edinburgh: Blackwood.

Althusser, L. (1971),'Ideology and Ideological State Apparatuses', in L. Althusser (ed.), *Lenin and philosophy and other essays*, London: NLB, pp. 127–86.

Angus, M. (1913), *Sheriff Watson of Aberdeen: the story of his life and work for the young*, Aberdeen: D. Wyllie & Son.

Aries, P. (1962), *Centuries of Childhood*, London: Pimlico.

Ashworth, A. and J. Horder (2013), *Principles of Criminal Law* (7th edn), Oxford: Oxford University Press.

Ashworth, A. and L. Zedner (2008), 'Defending the Criminal Law: Reflections on the Changing Character of Crime, Procedure and Sanctions', *Criminal Law and Philosophy* 2:1, 21–51.

Ashworth, A. and L. Zedner (2010), 'Preventive orders: A Problem of Undercriminalisation', in A. Duff, L. Farmer, S. Marshall, M. Renzo and V. Tadros (eds) (2010), *The Boundaries of the Criminal Law*, Oxford: Oxford University Press, pp. 59–87.

Ashworth, A. and L. Zedner (2014), *Preventive Justice*, Oxford: Oxford University Press.

Bailey, V. (1987), *Delinquency and Citizenship: Reclaiming the Young Offender, 1914–1948*, Oxford: Clarendon Press.

Bailey, V. (1997), 'English Prisons, Penal Culture and the Abatement of Imprisonment, 1895–1922', *The Journal of British Studies* 36:3, 285–324.

Barclay, H. Sheriff (1848), *Juvenile Delinquency; its Causes and Cure by a Country Magistrate*, Edinburgh and London: Blackwood & Sons.

Barrie, D. (2008), *Police in the Age of Improvement*, Devon: Willan.

Barrie, D. and S. Broomhall (2014), *Police Courts in Nineteenth-Century Scotland*, Farnham: Ashgate.

Bartrip, P. W. J. (2004), 'Hill, Matthew (1792–1872)', *Oxford Dictionary of National Biography*, Oxford: Oxford University Press.

Bauman, Z. (1989), *Modernity and the Holocaust*, Cambridge: Polity.

Behlmer, G. (1998), *Friends of the Family: the English Home and its Guardians, 1850–1940*, Stanford, CA: Stanford University Press.

Behlmer, G. (1982), *Child Abuse and Moral Reform*, Stanford, CA: Stanford University Press.

Blackstone, W. (1765–9), *Commentaries on the Laws of England*, Oxford: Clarendon Press.

Berthezene, C. (2016), 'A voluntary organisation financed by the state' or 'a state service furnished by volunteers'? Women's voluntary services, local government and the debate around the role of voluntary social service in the British welfare state 1945–47. In: European Social Science History Conference, University of Valencia, 30 March–2 April 2016.

Blackwood's Edinburgh Magazine (1875), 'London Police Courts' 118: (October 1875), 379–89: (unattributed).

Blanch, M. (2007), 'Imperialism, Nationalism and Organised Youth', in J. Clarke, C. Critcher and R. Johnson (eds), *Working Class Culture; Studies in History and Theory*, London: Routledge, pp. 103–12.

Bradley, K. (2008), 'Juvenile Delinquency, the Juvenile Courts and the Settlement Movement 1908–1950: Basil Henriques and Toynbee Hall', *Twentieth Century British History* 19:2, 133–55.

Bradley, K. (2009), 'Inside the Inner London Juvenile Court, c. 1909–1953', *Crimes and Misdemeanours* 3:2, 37–59.

Brebner, W. (1829), 'Letter to Lord Provost of Glasgow', Glasgow: John Smith & Son.

Briggs, I. (1924), *Reformatory Reform*, London: Longmans.

Cale, M. (1992), 'Working for God? Staffing the Victorian reformatory and industrial school system', *History of Education* 21:2, 113–27.

Cale, M. (1993), 'Girls and the Perception of Sexual Danger in the Victorian Reformatory System', *History* 78:253, 201–17.

Cale, M. (2014–15), 'Turner, Sydney (1814–1879) Church of England clergyman and school inspector', in *Oxford Dictionary of National Biography*, Oxford: Oxford University Press.

Calendar, 1910, of Institutions under the Glasgow Juvenile Delinquency Prevention and Repression Acts, Glasgow: David Clark.

Cameron, J. (1983), *Prisons and Punishment in Scotland*, Canongate: Edinburgh.

Carlebach, J. (1970), *Caring for children in trouble*, London: Routledge & Kegan Paul.

Carpenter, M. (1851), *Reformatory Schools: For the Children of the Perishing and Dangerous Classes and for Juvenile Offenders*, London: Gilpin.

Carpenter, M. (1853), *Juvenile Delinquents – their Conditions and Treatment*, London: W. & F. G. Cash.

Carson, K. and H. Idzikowska (1989), 'The Social Production of Scottish Policing, 1795–1900', in D. Hay and F. Snyder (eds), *Policing and Prosecution in Britain, 1750–1850*, Oxford: Oxford University Press, pp. 267–97.

Chalmers, J. (2010), *The New Law of Sexual Offences in Scotland*, Edinburgh: W. Green.

Chambers, W. (1845), 'Visit to the Aberdeen Schools of Industry', *Chamber's Journal* 38: 15 November 1845, 305–8.

Charlesworth, L. (2010), *Welfare's Forgotten Past: A Socio-Legal History of the Poor Law*, Abingdon: Routledge.

Checkland, O. (1980), *Philanthropy in Victorian Scotland*, Edinburgh: Donald.

Children's Commissioner for Scotland website: www.sccyp.org.uk.

Clapton, G. (2009), 'Yesterday's Men: The Inspectors of the Royal Scottish Society for the Prevention of Cruelty to Children, 1888–1968', *British Journal of Social Work* 39:6, 1043–62.

Clark, E. A. G. (1977), 'The Superiority of the "Scotch System": Scottish Ragged Schools and their Influence', *Scottish Educational Studies* 9:1, 29–39.

Clarke, J. (1975), 'The three Rs – repression, rescue and rehabilitation; ideologies of control for working class youth', CCCS stencilled occasional paper, 41.

Clarke Hall, W. and A. H. F. Pretty (1909), *The Children Act 1908 (3rd edition) of The Law Relating to Children*, London: Stevens & Sons Ltd.

Cohen, S. (1985), *Visions of Social Control*, Cambridge: Polity.

Cohen, S. and A. T. Scull (eds) (1983), *Social Control and the State*, Oxford: Blackwell.

Cohen, S. (2004), *Folk Devils and Moral Panics*, 3rd edn, London: Routledge.

Cox, P. (2013), *Bad Girls in Britain: Gender, Justice and Welfare, 1900–1950*, Basingstoke: Palgrave Macmillan.

Cox, P. and H. Shore (eds) (2002), *Becoming delinquent: British and European Youth, 1650–1950*, Aldershot: Ashgate.

Cunningham, H. (1995), *Children and Childhood in Western Society Since 1500*, Harlow: Longman.

Cruickshank, M. (1967), 'The Argyll Commission Report 1865–8: A Landmark in Scottish Education', *British Journal of Educational Studies* 15:2, 133–47.

Davenport Hill, R. & F. (1878), *The Recorder of Birmingham: a memoir of Matthew Davenport Hill*, London: Macmillan.

Dekker, J. (2001), *The Will to Change the Child: Re-education Homes for Children at Risk in Nineteenth Century Western Europe*, Frankfurt: Lang.

Devine, T. (1999), *The Scottish Nation 1700–2000*, London: Penguin.

Dickens, C. (2000), *Oliver Twist*, Ware: Wordsworth.

Dickens, C. (1992), *David Copperfield*, Ware: Wordsworth.

Donzelot, J. (1979), *The Policing of Families*, London: Hutchinson.

Driver, F. (1990), 'Discipline without Frontiers? Representations of the Mettray Reformatory Colony in Britain, 1840–1880', *Journal of Historical Sociology* 3:3, 272–93.

Dubber, M. (2010), 'Criminal Law between Public and Private Law', in A. Duff, L. Farmer, S. Marshall, M. Renzo and V. Tadros (eds), *The Boundaries of the Criminal Law*, Oxford: Oxford University Press, pp. 191–213.

Duff, A., L. Farmer, S. Marshall., M. Renzo and V. Tadros (eds) (2010), *The Boundaries of the Criminal Law*, Oxford: Oxford University Press.

Duff, A., L. Farmer, S. Marshall., M. Renzo and V. Tadros (eds) (2011), *The Structures of the Criminal Law*, Oxford: Oxford University Press.

Duff, A., L. Farmer, S. Marshall., M. Renzo and V. Tadros (eds) (2013), *The Constitution of the Criminal Law*, Oxford: Oxford University Press.

Dunning, E. and S. Mennell (1996), 'Introduction', in N. Elias, *The Germans*, Cambridge: Polity, pp. 1–20.

Eade, S. (1976), 'The Reclaimers: A Study of the Reformatory Movement in England and Wales, 1846–1893', unpublished PhD, Australian National University.

Elias, N. (1984), *The Civilising Process*, Oxford: Blackwell (original edition 1939).

Elias, N. (1994), *Reflections on a Life*, Cambridge: Polity Press.

Elias, N. (1996), *The Germans*, Oxford: Blackwell.

Eliot, G. (1993), *Silas Marner*, Ware, Wordsworth.

Eliot, G. (1999), *Mill on the Floss*, Ware, Wordsworth.

Emsley, C. (2005), *Crime and Society in England, 1750–1900,* London: Longman.

Farmer, L. (1997), *Criminal Law, Tradition and Legal Order: Crime and the Genius of Scots Law, 1747 to the Present*, Cambridge: Cambridge University Press.

Farmer, L. (2016), *Making the modern criminal law: criminalization and civil order*, Oxford: Oxford University Press.

Farmer, L. (2010), 'Criminal Wrongs in Historical Perspective', in A. Duff, L. Farmer, S. Marshall, M. Renzo and V. Tadros (eds) (2010), *The Boundaries of the Criminal Law*, Oxford: Oxford University Press, pp. 214–37.

Finlayson, G. (1990), 'A moving frontier: Voluntarism and the state in British social welfare 1911–1949', *Twentieth Century British History* 1:2, 183–206.

Fletcher, J. (1852), 'Statistics of the Farm School System of the Continent, and of Its Applicability to the Preventive and Reformatory Education of Pauper and Criminal Children in England', *Journal of the Statistical Society of London*, Vol. 15:1, 1–49.

Fletcher, J. (1997), *Violence and Civilization*, Cambridge: Polity Press.

Follett, R. R. (2001), *Evangelicalism, Penal Theory and the Politics of Criminal Law Reform in England, 1808–30*, Basingstoke: Palgrave Macmillan.

Foucault, M. (1977), *Discipline and Punish: The Birth of the Prison*, London: Allen Lane.

Garland, D. (1981), 'The Birth of the Welfare Sanction', *British Journal of Law and Society* 8:1, 29–45.

Garland, D. (1985), *Punishment and Welfare*, Aldershot: Gower.

Garland, D. (1990), *Punishment and Modern Society: A Study in Social Theory*, Oxford: Oxford University Press.

Garland, D. (2001), *The Culture of Control*, Oxford: Oxford University Press.

Garland, D. (2008), 'On the Concept of Moral Panic', *Crime, Media, Culture* 4:1, 9–30.

Gillis, J. R. (1974a), 'Discovery of Adolescence, 1870–1900', in J. R. Gillis, *Youth and History*, London: Academic Press, pp. 95–131.

Gillis, J. R. (1974b), *Youth and history: tradition and change in European age relations 1770–present*, London: Academic Press.

Gillis, J. R. (1975), 'The Evolution of Juvenile Delinquency in England 1890–1914, *Past and Present* 67:May 1975, 96–126.

Glasgow Evening Citizen (1888), 21 November.

Glasgow Boys' House of Refuge Reports, 1854–60, Glasgow: Reformatory Institution.

Glasgow Girls' Reformatory or Juvenile Department of the Females' House of Refuge from 1840–1860 (1860), Glasgow: Reformatory Institution, Duke Street.

Godfrey, B. and P. Lawrence (2005), *Crime and Justice 1750–1950*, Devon: Willan Publishing.

Godfrey, B., P. Cox, H. Shore and Z. Alker (2017), *Young criminal lives: Life courses and life chances after 1850*, Oxford: Clarendon Series in Criminology, Oxford University Press.

Griffiths., A., J. Fotheringham and F. McCarthy (2015), *Family Law*, Edinburgh: W. Green.

'Government "criminalising young"', www.bbc.co.uk/1/hi/uk/7580285.stm

Grovier, K. (2008), *The Gaol: The Story of Newgate, London's Most Notorious Prison*, London: Murray.

Guthrie, T. (1847), *Plea for ragged schools, or, prevention better than cure*, Edinburgh: John Elder.

Hall. S., C. Critcher, T. Jefferson, J. Clarke and B. Roberts (1978), *Policing the Crisis*, London: Macmillan.

Hannay, J. (1851), 'Lambs to be Fed', in C. Dickens (ed.), *Household Words*, 3:75, 544–9.

Heasman, K. (1962), *Evangelicals in Action*, London: Bles Ltd.

Hendrick, H. (1994), *Child Welfare: England 1872–1989*, London: Routledge.

Hendrick, H. (1997), 'Constructions and Reconstructions of British Childhood: an Interpretive Survey, 1880 to the Present', in A. James and A. Prout (eds), *Constructing and Reconstructing Childhood* (2nd edn), Basingstoke: Falmer, pp. 34–62.

Hendrick, H. (1990), *Images of Youth: Age, Class and the Male Youth Problem 1880–1920*, Oxford: Clarendon Press.

Hendrick, H. (1997), *Children, Childhood and English Society*, Cambridge: Cambridge University Press.

Hendrick, H. (2003), *Child Welfare: historical dimensions, contemporary debate*, Bristol: Policy Press.

Hendrick, H. (2006), 'Histories of Youth Crime and Justice', in B. Goldson and J. Muncie (eds), *Youth Crime and Justice*, London: Sage, pp. 3–18.

Himmelfarb, G. (1984), *The Idea of Poverty, England in the Early industrial Age*, London: Faber.

Himmelfarb, G. (1995), *The De-moralization of Society: from Victorian Virtues to Modern Values*, London: IEA Health and Welfare Unit.

Holland, M. and R. Hart-Davis (eds) (2000), *Complete letters of Oscar Wilde*, London: Fourth Estate.

Hornby, F. V. (1897), *The Reformatory and Industrial Schools Acts*, London: Eyre & Spottiswoode.

House of Refuge for females, Parliamentary Road, Glasgow (1840), Glasgow: John Graham.

Humphries, J. (2010), *Childhood and Child Labour in the British Industrial Revolution*, Cambridge: Cambridge University Press.

Hurt, J. (1984), 'Reformatory and industrial schools before 1933', in *History of Education* 13:1, 45–58.

Husak, D. (2007), *Overcriminalization: the Limits of the Criminal Law*, Oxford: Oxford University Press.

Ignatieff, M. (1978), *A Just Measure of Pain: The Penitentiary in the Industrial Revolution, 1750–1850*, London: Penguin.

Ignatieff, M. (1983), 'State, Civil Society and Total Institutions: A Critique of Recent Social Histories of Punishment', in Cohen and Scull (eds), *Social Control and the State*, Oxford: Blackwell.

Jackson, L., with A. Bartie (2014), *Policing Youth: Britain, 1945–70*, Manchester: Manchester University Press.

Jones, T. and T. Newburn (2007), *Policy Transfer and Criminal Justice: Exploring US influence over British Crime Control Policy*, Maidenhead: Open University Press.

'Juvenile Criminals' (1848–49), *The North British Review* 10:November 1848, 2–38 (unattributed).

Kaye, R. (2009), *The spirit of a real Home: Lucy Greenwood and the Halstead Industrial School*, Chellow Dean Press.

Kelly, C. (2016a), 'Continuity and change in the history of Scottish juvenile justice', *Law Crime and History* 6:1, 59–82.

Kelly, C. (2016b), 'Reforming juvenile justice in nineteenth-century Scotland: the subversion of the Scottish day industrial school movement', *Crime, History and Societies* (online), 20:2. Available at: http://chs.revues.org/1670 (accessed 19 July 2017).

Kelly, C. (2017a), 'Probation Officers for Young Offenders in 1920s Scotland', *European Journal of Probation*, 9:2, 169–91.

Kelly, C. (2017b), 'Juvenile crime and justice in Scotland', in J. Turner, P. Taylor, K. Corteen and S. Morley (eds), *A Companion to the History of Crime and Criminal Justice*, Bristol: Policy Press, pp. 117–19.

Kilbrandon, Lord and J. Mack (1968), 'The Scottish Reforms: the impact on the public', *The British Journal of Criminology* 8:3, 235–46.

Kilday, A. M. (2015), *Women and Violent Crime in Enlightenment Scotland*, Woodbridge: Boydell & Brewer.

King, P. (1998), 'The rise of juvenile delinquency in England 1780–1840: changing patterns of perception and prosecution', *Past and Present* 160:1, 116–66.

King, P. (2006), *Crime and law in England, 1750–1840: remaking justice from the margins*, Cambridge: Cambridge University Press.

Lacey, N. (2009), 'Historicising Criminalisation: Conceptual and Empirical Issues', *Modern Law Review* 72:6, 936–60.

Lacey, N. (2013), 'What Constitutes Criminal Law?', in A. Duff, L. Farmer, S. Marshall, M. Renzo and V. Tadros (eds), *The Constitution of the Criminal Law*, Oxford: Oxford University Press, pp. 12–29.

Lacey, N. (2016), *In Search of Criminal Responsibility: Ideas, Interests and Institutions*, Oxford: Oxford University Press.

Lasch, C. (1979), *Haven in a Heartless World; the Family Besieged*, New York: Basic Books.

Locke, J. (1975), *An Essay Concerning Human Understanding*, P. H. Nidditch (ed.), Oxford: Oxford University Press.

Locke, J. (1999), *Some Thoughts Concerning Education,* in J. W. and J. S. Yolton (eds), *The Clarendon Edition of the Works of John Locke*, Oxford: Oxford University Press, pp. 83–265.

Logan, A. (2005), 'A Suitable Person for Suitable Cases: The Gendering of Juvenile Courts in England, c. 1910–39', *Twentieth Century British History* 16:2, 129–45.

Logan, A. (2009), 'Policy Networks and the Juvenile Court: The Reform of Youth Justice, c.1905–1950', *Crimes and Misdemeanours* 3:2, 18–36.

'London Police Courts', *Blackwood's Edinburgh Magazine* (October 1875), Vol. CXV111, p. 382.

McDiarmid, C. (2007), *Childhood and Crime*, Dundee: Dundee University Press.

Mackenzie, J. (1829), 'Letter' in Appendix to William Brebner's 'Letter to Lord Provost of Glasgow', Glasgow: John Smith & Son.

Mahood, L. (1990), *The Magdalenes*, London: Routledge.

Mahood, L. and B. Littlewood (1994), 'The "vicious" girl and the "street-corner" boy: sexuality and the gendered delinquent in the Scottish child-saving movement, 1850–1940', *Journal of History of Sexuality*, 4:4, 549–78.

Mahood, L. (1995), *Policing gender, class and family, 1850–1940*, London: UCL.

Mahood, L. (2002), '"Give him a doing": the Birching of Young Offenders in Scotland', *Canadian Journal of History* 37:3, 439–58.

Mair, G. and L. Burke (2012), *Redemption, Rehabilitation and Risk Management: A History of Probation*, Abingdon: Routledge.

Manton, J. (1976), *Mary Carpenter and the Children of the Streets*, London: Heinemann.

Margarey, S. (1978), 'The invention of juvenile justice in early nineteenth century England', *Labour History* 34:May 1978, 11–27.

Mathieson, P. (1997), *Thomas Guthrie and the Ragged Schools*, Edinburgh: Friends of the Kirk of the Greyfriars.

May, M. (1973), 'Innocence and experience: the evolution of the concept of juvenile delinquency in the mid-nineteenth century', *Victorian Studies* 17:1, 7–29.

McAra, L. (2004), 'The Cultural and Institutional Dynamics of Transformation: Youth Justice in Scotland, England and Wales', *Cambrian Law Review* 35, 23–54.

McAra, L. (2006), 'Welfare in Crisis? Key Developments in Scottish Youth Justice', in B. Goldson and J. Muncie (eds), *Comparative Youth Justice*, London: Sage, pp. 127–45.

McAra, L. (2008), 'Crime, Criminology and Criminal Justice in Scotland', *European Journal of Criminology*, 5:4, 481–504.

McAra, L. and S. McVie (2010), 'Youth crime and justice: key messages from the Edinburgh study of youth transitions and crime', 10:2, 179–209.

McAra, L. and S. McVie (2012), 'Negotiated Order: the groundwork for a theory of offending pathways', *Criminology and Criminal Justice* 12:4, 347–75.

McConville, S. (1995), 'The Victorian Prison', in N. Morris and D. Rothman, *The Oxford History of the Prison*, Oxford: Oxford University Press, pp. 117–50.

McDermid, J. (2006), 'Gender, National Identity and the Royal (Argyll) Commission of Inquiry into Scottish Education (1864-1867)', *Journal of Educational Administration and History* 38:3, 249–62.

McDiarmid, C. (2007), *Childhood and Crime*, Dundee: Dundee University Press.

McDiarmid, C. (2011), '"Juvenile offending: welfare or toughness"', in E. Sutherland, K. Goodall, G. Little and F. Davidson (eds), *Law Making and the Scottish Parliament: The Early Years*, pp. 225–49.

McGowen, R. (2007), 'Cruel Inflictions and the Claims of Humanity in Early Nineteenth Century England', in K. Watson (ed.), *Assaulting the Past: Violence and Civilisation in Historical Context*, Cambridge: Cambridge Scholars Publishing, pp. 38–57.

McNeill, F. (2005), 'Remembering probation in Scotland', *Probation Journal* 52:1, 23–38.

McNeill, F. (2009), 'Helping, holding, hurting: recalling and reforming punishment', in: The 6th Annual Apex Lecture. Signet Library, Parliament Square, Edinburgh, 8 September, pp. 1–9.

McNeill, F. (2010), 'Supervision in historical context: Learning the lessons of (oral) history', in F. McNeill, P. Raynor and C. Trotter (eds), *Offender Supervision: New Directions in Theory, Research and Practice*, Cullompton: Willan, pp. 492–508.

McNeill, F. and B. Whyte (2007), *Reducing Reoffending: Social Work and Community Justice in Scotland*, Cullompton: Willan.

Mennell, S. (1992), *Norbert Elias: an introduction*, Oxford: Blackwell.

Michie, M. (1997), *An enlightenment Tory in Victorian Scotland: the career of Sir Archibald Alison*, East Linton: Tuckwell Press.

Mill, J. S. (1859), *On Liberty*, London: Parker.

Moore, M. (2008), 'Social control or protection of the Child? On the industrial schools Acts 1857–94', *Journal of Family History* 33:4, 359–87.

Morgan, R. (2008), 'Summary Justice: Fast – but Fair?', London: Centre for Crime and Justice Studies, King's College.

Morris, N. and D. Rothman (eds) (1995), *The Oxford History of the Prison*, Oxford: Oxford University Press.

Muncie, J. (2004), *Youth and Crime*, London: Sage.

Muncie, J. (2011), 'Illusions of Difference: Comparative Youth Justice in the Devolved United Kingdom', *British Journal of Criminology* 51:1, 40–57.

Nash, D. (2007), 'Blasphemy and the anti-civilising process', in K. Watson (ed.), *Assaulting the Past; Violence and Civilisation In Historical Context*, Cambridge: Cambridge Scholars Publishing, pp. 58–76.

Nilan, C. (1997), 'Hapless innocence and precocious perversity in the courtroom melodrama: representations of the child criminal in a Paris legal journal 1830–1848', *Journal of Family History* 22:3, 251–85.

Norrie, K. McK. (2013), *Children's Hearings in Scotland*, Edinburgh: W. Green.

Norton, C. (1887), 'Schools as prisons and prisons as schools', *Nineteenth Century* 21, 119.

Pattinson, R. (1978), *The Child Figure in English Literature*, Athens: University of Georgia Press.

Pearson, G. (1983), *Hooligan; a history of respectable fears*, London: Macmillan.

Pinchbeck, I. and M. Hewitt (1973), *Children in English Society*, Vol. 2, London: Routledge.

Platt, A. (1977), *The Child Savers: The Invention of Delinquency*, Chicago: Chicago University Press.

Platt, A. (2002), 'The triumph of benevolence: the origins of the juvenile justice system in the United States', in J. Muncie, G. Hughes and E. McLaughlin (eds), *Youth Justice; Critical Readings* (originally published in R. Quinney (ed.), *Criminal Justice in America*, Boston: Little, Brown, 1974), pp. 177–96.

Pratt, J., D. Brown, M. Brown, S. Hallsworth and W. Morrison (eds) (2005), *The New Punitiveness: Trends, Theories, Perspectives*, Cullompton: Willan Publishing.

Pratt, J. (2005), 'Elias, punishment and civilisation', in J. Pratt, D. Brown, M.Brown, S. Hallsworth and W. Morrison (eds), *The New Punitiveness: Trends, Theories, Perspectives*, Cullompton: Willan Publishing, pp. 256–71.

Procacci, G. (1978), 'Social Economy and the Government of Poverty', in G. Burchill et al. (eds), *The Foucault Effect; Studies in Governmentality*, 1991, London: Harvester Wheatsheaf, pp. 151–68.

Prochaska, F. (1980), *Women and Philanthropy in nineteenth century England*, Oxford: Clarendon Press.

Prochaska, F. (2006), *Christianity and Social Service in modern Britain: the disinherited spirit*, Oxford: Oxford University Press.

Radzinowicz, L. and R. Hood (1990), *The Emergence of Penal Policy in Victorian and Edwardian England (A History of English Criminal Law, Vol 5)*, London: Steven & Sons.

Ragged School Union Magazine (1852), January, pp. 4, 37.

Ralston, A. G. (1980), 'The Tron Riot of 1812', *History Today* 30, pp. 41–5.

Ralston, A. G. (1988), 'The Development of Reformatory and Industrial Schools in Scotland, 1832–1872', *Scottish and Economic Social History* 8, 40–55.

Reformatory and Refuge Journal 1861, Vol. 1: Article on address by Thomas Guthrie, pp. 55–62.

Reformatory and Refuge Journal 1861, Vol. 1.

Reformatory and Refuge Journal 1861–3.

Reformatory and Refuge Journal 1870, Vol. XLVI, 'The Industrial School at Signa, Tuscany', p.305.

Reformatory and Refuge Journal 1872–5.

Reformatory and Refuge Journal January 1874, Obituary of Demetz, pp. 145–6.

Report of the Kilbrandon Committee on Children and Young Persons, Scotland, Cmnd. 2306 (1964).

Reports: see Index.

Ritchie, L. A. (2014–15), 'Guthrie, Thomas (1803–1873), Free Church of Scotland minister and philanthropist', *Dictionary of National Biography*, Oxford: Oxford University Press.

Ritter, L. (2001), 'Inventing juvenile delinquency and determining its cure or, how many discourses can you disguise as one construct?', in M. Enders and B. Dupont (eds), *Policing the Lucky Country*, Sydney: Hawkins Press, pp. 108–30.

Rose, G. (1967), *Schools for Young Offenders*, London: Tavistock.

Rose, N. (1985), *The Psychological Complex: Psychology, Politics and Society in England, 1869–1939*, London: Routledge.

Rothman, D. (1971), *The Discovery of the Asylum: Social Order and Disorder in the New Republic*, Boston: Little, Brown.

Rothman, D. (1980), *Conscience and Convenience: The Asylum and its Alternatives in Progressive America*, Boston: Little, Brown.

Rousseau, J.-J. (1993), *Émile*, London: Everyman.

Rowbotham, J., K. Stevenson and S. Pegg (2003), 'Children of Misfortune: Parallels in the Cases of Child Murderers Thompson and Venables, Barratt and Bradley', *The Howard Journal* 42:2, 107–22.

Ruggles-Brise, E. (1924), *Prison Reform*, London: Macmillan & Co.

Sargent, P. (2013), *Wild Arabs and Savages: A History of Juvenile Justice in Ireland*, Manchester: Manchester University Press.

Schlossman, S. (1995), 'Delinquent children: the juvenile reform school', in N. Morris and D. Rothman (eds), *The Oxford History of the Prison*, Oxford: Oxford University Press, pp. 325–49.

Scottish Executive Report (2007), 'Use of Antisocial Behaviour Orders in Scotland', available at www.scotland.gov/Resource/Doc/198276/0053019.pdf

Shore, H. (1999), *Artful Dodgers: Youth and crime in early nineteenth century London*, Woodbridge: Boydell Press.

Shore, H. (2002), 'Reforming the juvenile: gender, justice and the child criminal in nineteenth century England', in J. Muncie, G. Hughes and E. McLaughlin (eds), *Youth Justice; Critical readings*, pp. 159–72.

Short account of the work done in the Edinburgh Original Ragged Industrial Schools founded in 1847 by Rev Dr Guthrie (1897), Edinburgh: Supplement to the 50th annual Report of Edinburgh Original Ragged Industrial Schools, Liberton and Brunswick Rd, Leith Walk.

Simon, B. (1965), *Education and the Labour Movement*, London: Lawrence & Wishart.

Smith, D. (2007), 'Official Responses to Juvenile Delinquency in Scotland During the Second World War', *Twentieth Century British History* 18:1, 78–105.

Smout, T. C. (1997), *A Century of the Scottish People 1830–1950*, London: Fontana Press.

Spierenburg, P. (1984), *The Spectacle of Suffering: Executions and the evolution of repression*, Cambridge: Cambridge University Press.

Spierenburg, P. (1996), 'Long-term trends in homicide; theoretical reflections and Dutch evidence, fifteenth to twentieth centuries', in E. Johnson and E. Monkkonen (eds), *The Civilization of Crime*, Illinois: University of Illinois, pp. 63–105.

Stack, J. A. (1979), 'The Provision of Reformatory Schools, the Landed Class, and the Myth of the Superiority of Rural Life in Mid-Victorian England', *History of Education* 8:1, 33–43.

Stack, J. A. (1994), 'Reformatory and industrial schools and the decline of child imprisonment in mid-Victorian England and Wales', *History of Education* 23:1, 59–73.

Tadros, V. (2010), 'Criminalisation and Regulation', in A. Duff, L. Farmer, S. Marshall, M. Renzo and V. Tadros (eds), *The Boundaries of the Criminal Law*, Oxford: Oxford University Press, pp. 163–90.

Tallack, W. (1865), *Peter Bedford, the Spitalfields Philanthropist*, London: Partridge.

Tanenhaus, D. (2001), 'Growing up Dependent: Family Preservation in Early Twentieth Century Chicago', *Law and History Review* 19:3, 547–82.

Tanenhaus, D. (2004), *Juvenile Justice in the Making*, New York: Oxford University Press.

The Glasgow Girls' Reformatory or Juvenile Department of the Females' House of Refuge from 1840–1860, Duke Street, Glasgow: Reformatory Institution.

The Daily Chronicle (1897), Letter by Oscar Wilde, 28 May.

The Edinburgh Courant (1855), Article on *Hay and others* v. *Linton* 1855 2 Irv.57, 17 December.

The Edinburgh Evening Courant (1856), 16 January.

The Glasgow Herald (1874), Letter by W. Watson, 3 October.

The Guardian (2011a), 'Senior legal figures attack riot sentences', 18 August.

The Guardian (2011b), 'Revealed: the full picture of riot sentences – Guardian data confirms courts opt for tougher punishments', 19 August.

Independent on Sunday (2011), 'Scotland and the riots' by D. J. Taylor, 14 August.

The Times (2008), 'Law Creates underclass of child criminals', 9 June.

The Scotsman (1935), 'Juvenile Delinquency: Child Guidance Clinics', 28 February.

The Scotsman (1936), 'Child Guidance: Scotland's Social Service Need', 28 February.

The Scotsman (1939), 'Child Guidance Clinic: Work of Dundee Organisation', 21 December.

The Scotsman (1941), 'Child Guidance: Proposed Clinic in Fife', *The Scotsman*, 5 September.

Thompson, E. P. (1991), *Making of the English Working Class*, London: Penguin.

Thomson, A. (1847), *Industrial Schools: their origin, rise and progress in Aberdeen*, Aberdeen.

Thomson, A. (1852), *Social Evils, Their causes and Cure*, London: J. Nisbet & Co.

Thomson, A. (1857), *Punishment and Prevention*, London: J. Nisbet & Co.

UK Children's Commissioners Report to UN (2008): www.sccyp.org.uk.

Vanstone, M. (2004), *Supervising Offenders in the Community: A History of Probation Theory and Practice*, Aldershot: Ashgate Publishing Ltd.

Watson, K. (2007), *Assaulting the Past, Violence and Civilisation in Historical Context*, Cambridge: Cambridge Scholars Publishing.

Watson, W., *My Life* (unpublished handwritten manuscript).

Watson, W. (1850), *Can juvenile vagrancy be prevented? or, A day's experience among the ragged of Liverpool*, Liverpool: Deighton & Laughton.

Watson, W. (1851), *The Juvenile Vagrant and the Industrial School, or, Prevention better than Cure*, Aberdeen and London: George Davidson; Nisbet & Co.

Watson, W. (1872), *Chapters on Ragged and Industrial Schools*, Edinburgh and London: Blackwood & Sons.

Watson, W. (1874), Letter to day industrial school campaigners in Glasgow, dated 16 October 1874.

Watson, W. (1877), *Pauperism, vagrancy, crime and industrial education in Aberdeenshire 1840–75*, Edinburgh and London: Blackwood & Sons. Aberdeen: John Smith.

Weinberger, B. (1996), 'Urban and rural crime rates and their genesis in late nineteenth and early twentieth century Britain', in E. Johnson and E. Monkkonen (eds), *The Civilization of Crime*, Chicago: University of Illinois Press, pp. 198–216.

Wiener, M. J. (1990), *Reconstructing the Criminal: Culture, Law and Policy in England, 1830–1914*, Cambridge: Cambridge University Press.

Wilde, O. (1995), *Ballad of Reading Gaol*, Poole: Woodstock Books.

Willrich, M. (2003), *City of Courts: Socializing Justice in Progressive Era Chicago*, New York: Cambridge University Press.

Wilson, P. (1973), *Children who Kill*, London: Michael Joseph.

Young, J. (2009), 'Moral Panic: its origins in resistance, resentment and the translation of fantasy into reality', *British Journal of Criminology* 49:1, 4–16.

Young, P. (1976), 'A sociological analysis of the early history of probation', *British Journal of Law and Society* 3:1, 44–58.

Index

EU representative:
Easy Access System Europe
Mustamäe tee 50, 10621 Tallinn, Estonia
Gpsr.requests@easproject.com

www.ingramcontent.com/pod-product-compliance
Lightning Source LLC
Chambersburg PA
CBHW052000270326
41929CB00015B/2728